HOW TO USE
HUMOUR IN
BUSINESS AND LIFE

PETE CROFTS

Ordering Information:

Prime Seven Media
518 Landmann St.
Tomah City, WI 54660

Printed in the United States of America

START WITH A LAUGH

K nowledge is the essence of the globalised economy. A sense of humour is a specialised knowledge and is at the heart of Australia's national identity. When we fully understand the power of our specialised humour knowledge, we will be better able to use it - just like any other specialised skill. The following joke illustrates my point:

A $500,000 computer that was running a business suddenly conked out. We all know that feeling, don't we? No one in the business could fix it, so reluctantly, they called a consultant from the manufacturer. On arriving, he took a tiny hammer from his extensive tool case and tapped a specific spot on the side of the computer... *tapppp* ... and bingo, it started immediately. He gave the manager his bill for $1000 and the manager went berserk, saying: 'A thousand dollars, all you did was tap the thing with a hammer, I want you itemize the bill.' The consultant wrote on the bottom of the bill: 'Tapping computer with hammer $1: knowing where to tap, $999.'

My hope is that after reading this book, your knowledge in using 'Ha Ha Skills' will get you the results you desire.

Have fun and make profits; laugh mates!

Pete Crofts

THIS BOOK IS DEDICATED TO:

The pioneering Australians and my European and Australian ancestors, who recognized the powers oh humour and laughter. These hardworking survivors made laughter such a large part of our national subconscious culture making the phrase 'You've got to laugh, mate' our national philosophy.

My great grandparents and grandparents, my Mum, Iris Crofts, and my Dad, Sid Crofts, my brothers Michael and Chris Crofts, my sister, Margaret Strode, my children, Charly and Damien, and my grandchildren, Mia and Zion. I love you all very much.

TABLE OF CONTENTS

Chapter 2

How Humour Can Work For You In Business And Life

Chapter 4

Chapter 5

Chapter 6

Chapter 7

Chapter 8

ACKNOWLEDGMENTS

Lots of luck and love and laughs to anyone who has loved, supported or assisted me.

Gordon Piggott, David Bull, Paddy Spruce, Brother Majelia, Alf Goring, Tom Moore, Bill Green, Steve Williams, Charlie Seal, Paul Mutimer, Rudolf Matess, Lorraine Benham, Bruce Way, Jeff Favaloro, Freddie Fox, Simon Barnett, Jim Morris, Lee Ramsay, John Harris, Dave Pincombe, Jan Hall, Karen Wescombe, Nifty Nichols, Greg Costaras, Leon Nacson, Maurie Rayner, Charles Kovess, Steve Ehrenreich, Ian Stephens, Maurice Whitta, Hyram Davies, Annette Gabrielson, Mike Lally, Max Dumais, Murray Jones, Ray Crawford, Dave Grant, Lovis Stomm, Mel Meikie, Ruth Ostrow, Barry Kotze, Vane Lindesay, Adrian Kebbie, Martin Ralph, Reg Gorman, Jon Doust, Bronwyn McAkersy, Robert Elmore, Roger Anthony, Tony Strode and Don Burnard

To Claire, my promise to you is: 'We will sing in the sunshine, we will laugh every day' A special thank-you to my first wife, Edie Reiber, who shared laughter with me for 23 years. Deep gratitude to comedian, Johnny 'Rubberface' Craig and his wife Joan, who believed in me and helped me fulfil my dream to become a comedian. I wish to honour four American comedians who inspired me with their truth comedy: Lenny Bruce, Jackie Mason, Bill Hicks and Bill Cosby. I have been blessed by the creativity and wisdom of some of the leading humour scholars and practitioners in the world, either through personal meetings or their books, or both. Joel Goodman, Art Gliner, Don Nilsen, Joseph W. Meeker, William E. Fry Jnr., Harvey Min-dess, Robert Orben, Conrad Hyers, Branko Bokun, Edward DeBono, Evan Esar,

Annette Goodheart, Norman Cousins, Allen Klein, Patch Adams, Avner Ziv, Gene Perret, Jessica Milner Davis, Dotty Walters, Christie Davies, Virginia Tooper, Melvin Helitzer, Paul Herzich, Christine Davies and D.H. Monroe.

Joyous thanks to my cherished partner, Denise Thamrin, who inspires me to be a better person and who deeply touches my life with her love, creative spirit and sense of fun. A host of thanks to my brother, Michael Crofts, his wonderful wife, Heather and their son David Crofts, for their much-needed support and belief in my work over the years.

Many special thanks to the generous hearts and friendships and constant encouragement of Jim Bridges and Jack Levi. My dream to write a book would never have been possible without the amazing typing support of Noel Ballantine; the brilliant editing and constant encouragement of Sheridan Morris; special thanks to a man who has consistently promoted Australian humour and was kind enough to write the forward for this book, the man who linguistically is beyond words, Phillip Adams; the motivation of the man who first suggested I write the book, Robert Coco; the enthusiasm and talent of illustrator and cartoonist Angelo Madrid; the 'Man of Abundance' Jon Michail from Image Group International; the 'Guru with the Camera' Paul Velissaris; and the total belief and influential guidance of the publisher, Michael Wilkinson. My dream is now fulfilled, thanks to you all. An extra special thank-you to all those who have lightened my life, whom I have neglected to mention; you are not forgotten.

A big thank-you to the thousands of people who have been to my talks, workshops and program, studied at the Pete Crofts *Humourversity* or bought my products, I hope you were enriched by the experience.

PS One last thank-you to anyone who has ever laughed at one of my jokes was kind enough to give me a lift when I was hitchhiking around our magnificent country, Australia.

ABOUT THE AUTHOR – PETE CROFTS

Pete was born a natural tragic little fellow, coming from a Catholic, Protestant, Communist, capitalistic family background. As a young man, he understood politics and religion in the way Custer understood Indians, and he still does. At 18, he packed his swag of Aussie jokes and began a 15-year career touring Australia as a stand-up comedian. In those years, Pete was known to have brought a smile to the face of at least one person. Others claim that person had indigestion!

In 1972, he founded the world's first *Humourversity*, dedicating his lite to researching, understanding and teaching the dynamics and psychology of humour, comedy and laughter. Backed by years of his own research and support by studies from around the world, Pete firmly believes that the development and use of good Humour Attitude and Humour Action can dramatically increase corporate profits and make profound changes in our individual lives.

Pete also developed his revolutionary theory of Business Show. Every person and every business is 'on show' and people like doing business with people who are fun. Pete claims that we live in a time of recognition economics. Being seen or not being seen makes the difference between whether you win or lose.

Graduates from the Pete Crofts *Humourversity* include some of Australians leading business professionals, salespeople, trainers, speakers, health professionals, mothers and fathers, lawyers, psychologists, media personalities, comedians, educationalists and small business people.

Pete says: 'We must first learn to laugh at ourselves. Humour is not about jokes; it's like grace: when it shines from within, it automatically liberates you and those around you.'

He believes humour is of intrinsic value for most Australians, which works to our national competitive advantage, and is one of Australia's biggest and most misunderstood selling points. He would like to see us become a nation of 'egalitarian tall poppies'. Pete Crofts is Australia's foremost authority on humour comedy and laughter, has authored two books on the subject, and is known as Australia's humour pioneer and corporate humour consultant and speaker.

FOREWORD BY
PHILLIP ADAMS

Human beings are defined, even dignified, by the fact that they seem alone of all God's creatures in their painful awareness of their own mortality. This awareness considerably intensifies man's response to existence, acting as a sort of all-purpose aphrodisiac for living. The knowledge that we kick the bucket adds urgency and intensity to all our activities.

But, of course, it also fills us with dread. And we cope with this in a number of interesting ways. First of all, we invent religions that, in turn, invent an after-life - so that death is no longer an end but a beginning to a happy everafter that lasts for, yes, ever after.

And, as well, we laugh. Even if we don't believe in a hereafter, we believe in humour. Evolutionary theory has never come up with a fully satisfactory reason for laughter. If the species is not advantaged by this or that anatomical detail or behaviour pattern, the detail or pattern will disappear. Or else the creature itself. But how does laughter aid our survival?

Whilst I'm no palaeontologist, I can't help but suspect that the dinosaurs would still be around, had they developed a sense of humour. For surely this has been one of evolution's greatest gifts. Apart from ameliorating the dread of death, it helps us deal with a host of minor demons.

Having collected countless thousands of jokes for various Penguin books, I've learnt that jokes (just one aspect of humour) are little acts of exorcism, that allow us to deal with all sorts of things we suspect, fear or dislike. This is why jokes about politicians and lawyers come at the top of the list, along with jokes about medical problems, sexual difficulties, old age, mothers-in- law and other irritants.

If we can laugh at it, we can cope with it. We can bear it. This is why jokes abound in unbearable circumstances. It is no accident that the Jews, persecuted for millennia, have made such an overwhelming and disproportionate contribution to the history of humour. And you'll find carapacing other victims of bigotry, whether they're homosexuals, blondes or recent waves of immigrants.

Nonetheless, humour is conspicuous by its absence in a number of important realms. Take religion. Whilst I find religions immensely amusing – if you want a good laugh you'll find more in theology than you will in a Penguin book of jokes – the hierarchies of the major faiths are exceedingly grim. You won't find a lot of laughs in the Old Testament, the New Testament or the Koran. You might recall Umberto Ecco *The Name of the Rose,* an immensely important novel about the search sor a joke – a very subversive joke – in the great library of a monastery. The mere thought of its existence was enough to prompt a series of murders.

Equally murderous is the sad lack of jokes in big business – although, as I write these words, many of us are convulsed by the hilarities of the HIH collapse, and the way the Packer and Murdoch dynasties have burnt a billion dollars in One.Tel. But by and large, the religion of money is as humourless as the religion of religion, and personal ambitions and corporate arrogance seem inimical to the idea of humour, let alone out and out mirth.

This is why I'm happy to acknowledge the existence, and the virtues, of this book.

Pete Crofts, who has laboured mightily in the vineyard of humour, has decided to apply his skills to the world of business, using humour as a technique, a tool, a therapy, a driving force. There is little doubt that, it you follow Crofts advice, humour will considerably improve your professional prospects whilst adding to your company's bottom line. And once the author has conquered the corporate world, I expect him to apply his considerable skills, and comic sensibility, to Christianity, Judaism and Islam. Having revolutionised corporate life he will, I know, go on to sort out the Middle East crisis and bring peace to the Balkans.

Am I joking? You'll have to read this book to find out.

Phillip Adams

INTRODUCTION

'**G**et serious this is business!'

'You can't work and play at the same time!'

'Wipe that smile off your face'

'This is no laughing matter!'

'What's so funny about that?'

It's sayings like these that litter the laugh track back to the origins of humour history. The ancient Greeks Coined the word *komos*, which meant 'comedy' and comedy stood for 'rejoicing', festivity, merry-making and anyone in cheerful spirits up until the Renaissance. Then comedy became confused with the word 'humour', which derived from the term *humors*, meaning 'the fluids in the body that stimulated a pleasant attitude and healthy disposition'. Scholars, humorists, philosophers and psychologists, dating back as far as Plato, Socrates, and Aristotle, to Darwin and Freud, Eastman and Pittington, through to Koestler and Mindess. Plus scores of others have proposed more than 100 theories of humour and laughter, some of them brilliant investigations into the social and behavioral nature of humour and laughter.

Until recent times, very little research has examined the art or the science of humour. The art concerns the humorous persona, image, identity, metamessage, timing and delivery, and the science involves the study of the structural elements, the essential properties, the patterns, rules, forms and formulas of humour.

The history of mankind's polar-opposite attitudes could be summed up in the story of Humour and Serious, who decided to go into business together.

Humour thought about it and finally he said to Serious: 'While you can go on getting respect, admiration from lecaders, support from religion, you will achieve astounding success: while I'll be treated as frivolous, hounded as an outlaw. And Serious said: "That's all right; that's the way it is with joint ventures.'

The tide began turning on Serious is the early 1930s and Humour will definitely get the last laugh. The arrival on the market in 1972 of Goldstein and McGhee's breakthrough book, *The Psychology of Humour'*, showed the necessity for research into this area. The book's bibliography contained 1100 items. Today it would contain several thousand items under such subject heading as: anthropological, biological, sociological, ethological, psychological, and philosophical aspects of humour. In 1976, the humour community got together for the first of many successful international humour, laughter and comedy conferences. Finally, after two thousand years of recorded theories on humour and laughter, people were thinking there is some inner reason for the laughter to account for the laughter.

The first terminology of the science 'hunmourology' was published in 1978, called *The Comic Encyclopaedia*. The author was the supreme comedy explorer, Evan Esar. You can't have a study of a subject without a terminology. So the study of humour is actually a mere 23 years old. In 1979, the book that catapulted humour to world attention was written by

Norman Cousins, entitled *The Anatomy of an Illness*. This revolutionary book told the story of how he was cured from a crippling disease by a program of humour and laughter therapy.

The phenomena of the 80s and 90s has been linking the academic research to the humour elements, combining these with developing the appropriate persona, thern infiltrating the resulting humour expressions, through active use into mainstream social arenas, education, religion, politics, health and business. At present, there are humour classes and courses, workshops and seminars in universities, colleges, hospitals, factories, offices, and board rooms. Humour is being studied as a hobby, an art form, a selling aid, an academic achievement, a leadership skill and a business strategy. It 1s also being studied as a therapeutic training and communication tool, and abovc all, as an attitude and a lifestyle. It was reported that through a humour workshop held at the Digital Equipment Corporation, in Colorado, USA, sometime ago, productivity increased 15 per cent and sick days were halved. Their Ha Ha Skills brought fun and profit to the organisation!

Comedy clubs are springing up twice as fast as countries having coups. Two comedy chains are listed on the stock exchange in America. There are also two full-time cable television stations in America, running 24-hour-a-day comedy programs, and there is one comedy channel here in Australia. We now have 24-hour-a-day comedy radio stations as well. Comedy records, videos, training films, TV shows, radio shows and films have never been more popular. Comedy and humour books, magazines, postcards and comics are making great sales. Cities are having comedy festivals, shopping centres are having comedy weeks, and schools are having humour days. TV stations have a 'good news day'; hotels have 'happy hours'; comedy stickers and Garfield cats are stuck all over cars and company vehicles. Telephone companies are running joke lines. Airline companies have inflight comedy shows; traffic schools have comedians to teach the classes, and one undertaker is running funny funerals and wakes. Plus, every time you turn around you bump into a clown. Everyone is learning the benefits of developing their Business Show.

When we are exposed to such an unprecedented range of humour and comedy stimuli and expressions, we need to think about what functions they serve. Is it a release of the extra stress and strain of the space age, modern-day restraints, sexual, environmental and ethnic issues, staying healthy, and all those social pleasures that are becoming increasingly unfashionable? More importantly, what are the future effects of this whirlpool of humour? Will we become a senseless, irresponsible, sniggering society? dont think we will. When we understand the emotional, chemical, attitudinal, behavioral and changing components of humour - when humour awareness evolves -other dimensions of humour become visible. And the deeper dimensions of humour are reconciliation, accommodation, integration and equilibration. The fads, fashions and formats of what will be funny in the future will change because of consumer demands, media interest and social, political and economical developments. The circumstance and situations of where and when humour has, and will have, a licence to be used, are changing dramatically also. Another interesting thought is how humour is, and will be, cultivated and appreciated. There are already humour rooms in hospitals and Patch Adams is lightening up the world's medical fraternity.

I own and operate the world's first *Humourversity*, where people are trained to use and teach humour. There are humour museums, archives and libraries. I imagine that in the not-too-distant future, large Government bodies and corporations will have humour consultants on staff to advise, personalise, localise and advertise, the image, philosopy, and communications of humour, both internally and externally,

Humour is no longer just an escape from economic bad times but a resource capable of generating economic good times. With this massive demand for humour comedy and laughter, it is quite possible that in the future, humour and humorous products, services and expressions, will be key parts of our planet's economic base. Knowing what we know about humour tells us we need to know more about it; how it can be used efficiently and effectively, creatively and deliberately, personally and professionally, nationally and internationally, for social harmony and business energy.

PREFACE

Having a sense of humour and using humour both need to be seen in a new light. They are state-of-the-art, internal and external communication techniques. For 2000 years they have been seen as mystical gifts, given to some and withheld from others.

So what are you running off to be born for? Stand in that sense-of-humour queue and wait your turn or it won't be much fun when you are born!

The sense of humour is:

- An acquired attitude
- A practiced perception
- A trained tolerance
- A learned lifestyle
- The use of humour is:
- A studied skill
- A built ability
- An actioned art
- An exercised expertise

Humanity has been systematically trained to ignore three of its major resources-humour, comedy and laughter. We have been trained to disregard these precious gifts during our daily life and working week. Then we are encouraged to turn on the television set or pay to see a comedian in concert in our free time. What we should be doing for ourselves, we pay a fortune to comedians to do for us. This truthful paradox makes us readers, watchers and targets when we should be continuous creators, participants and beneficiaries of the releases, relationships and rewards that humour offers. This sort of defeats the purpose. Behaviour can happen to anybody.

There was the managing director of the multinational company who had become so unapproachable and so snobbish that he wouldn't get into the same car as his chauffeur!

The first sections of this book bring to life the creative elements and energies of humour, the types and styles, and the very nature of humour. As you progress through the pages, you will discover the benefits of developing your Ha Ha Skills and Business Show. The final chapter looks at the history and development of our own brand of Australian humour. The object of this book is to show how you can discover, develop and use positively your personal and professional humour.

You can enjoy using humour the way people everywhere do.

- For improving health
- Releasing stress
- Building self-image
- Motivating staff
- Increasing productivity
- Selling successfully
- Enhancing organisational dynamics
- Making business profitable and pleasurable.

Humour can provide your business with a creative tool which offers positive attitudes, friendliness, mateship, optimism, enthusiasm, hope and loads of fun. No matter what your humour awareness is, as you read this book, you will realise that learning to understand humour is no different than learning to understand any other business communication tool. 'This book will show you how to break your business out of the SERIOUS ZONE by employing humour and putting humour to work for yourself and your company, so you can develop your Ha Ha Skills for fun and profit.

You will Learn:

- Useful humour strategies
- Innovative techniques
- Major principles
- Key practices
- Practical exercises

You will also benefit from many other methods from the bucket-load of humour our history and experiences provide, so you can maximise the positive potential of humour and measure its effectiveness in your business. Many executives and managers take their job responsibilities very seriously They should, but they also take themselves too seriously, and while many think they have a sense of humour, the effect is just the opposite - it is negative humour.

There was the boss who called all his staff into his office to tell them his latest joke and they all laughed -all except one. The boss said: 'What's wrong With you; don't you have a sense of humour'. And the worker said: "Yes, but I don't have to laugh, I'm leaving tomorrow'.

In chapter two, we look at the positive uses of humour. Chapter one gives an excellent insight into how humour improves business communications in a wide range of areas, no matter what management style or corporate personality. The time has long gone where it is acceptable to have a passive approach to the use of humour in corporate life. Years ago, it was thoughtthat a business leader needed humour the way a fish needed a bicycle. Today, a business leader without humour is like a fish without water. The strong, silent type has been replaced by the sense-of humour type. I will show in chapter seven how to buiid a humour environment into a business setting. We look at the situations and circumstances in which humour blossoms, and the practical techniques and methods for generating and maintaining a humour mood in the workplace. I also propose an original theory on Australian humour, which, as a product, has tremendous export possibilities worthy of a survival and a financial handshake with a much-troubled world.

Humour is not just a buzz word used by trendies. It is a business advantage, a corporate edge, a zest for life, a natural high and a survival kit, which can be developed and exercised by all manner of organisational personnel. Humour can be used as a tool for creativity, change management, co-operation. co-existence, coping and communication in all aspects of life and work.

Some of the jokes and cartoons in this book are original; however, most are from my personal collection. I give credit to the writers and cartoonists if I know who they are. I thank the others for their creative content and apologise for not keeping better records. I have tried to expand some of the concepts of a few humour techniques by making their form visual in the way of cartoons, graphics and charts.

When I opened the Humour, Comedy and Laughter Centre in 1975, I was not aware of the humour revolution that had begun in the other parts of the planet. This book would not have been possible without some of the extraordinary material made available by humour pioneers from an infinite variety of disciplines and practices. Among them are, academics, psychologists, linguists, sociologists, humorologists, comedy writers, comedians, collectors, promoters and marketers. They all come under the banner of humour, comedy and laughter crusaders, futurists and visionaries. My deepest appreciation and heartfelt thanks goes to them one and all. Thanks to them, the laughs are with all of us for a long time.

CHAPTER 1

How Humour Improves Your Business Communication

'I know you believe you understand what you think I said, but I am not sure you realise that what you heard is not what I meant.'

In today's corporate world, you need the insight of a fortune-teller to make sense of a lot of corporate communication. In this book, we will explore humours potential for strengthening many facets of your business communication:

- Your leadership potential
- Your management style
- Your listening skills
- Your conversational capacity
- The ability to make your point effectively and powerfully

Corporate Communication Is Changing

When Robert Holmes a Court died on September 2, 1990, businessman Alex Mairs said.

'He had a keen sense of humour, a fine wit, a good turn of phrase, all attributes of what American humorist Russ Fisher would call a humour-cator.'

Humour-cators are people who use positive humour, are entertaining to listen to and easier to work with. They are never sarcastic, threatening or patronising. Their humour touches, enthuses, instructs and inspires by constantly surprising and arousing their listeners. They keep others interested, amused and motivated. By adjusting and changing their humour tactics, they can reach the emotions, minds and spirit of their listeners. They create an environment of greater co-operation, higher enthusiasm and increased productivity. Humour-cation means business. HA HA skills bring fun and profit!

You don't have to be a fortune-teller with a crystal ball to predict that business communication, the foundation of corporate society, will go through some significant changes in the decade ahead. However, to be truly effective, business humour must be positive humour communication. It needs to be:

- Relevant
- Appropriate
- Victimless
- Enjoyable
- Egalitarian

It involves HA HA skills-developing a *Humour Attitude* and implementing *Humour Action*. These principles of humour will become the corporate compass used to navigate the difficulties and challenges of the business environment. It's about learning the theories of humour and putting them to practical use...

Peter Costello, Australia's Treasurer, attended a lecture by an international expert on physics. At question time Costello asked: 'What you have been talking about is purely theory, isn't it? Does it have any practical value?'

The physicist looked puzzled. 'What do you mean, practical?'

To which Peter Costello replied: 'Can it be taxed?'

Positive Humour Communication Generates Good Feelings

Positive humour communication, in the corporate environment has practical value because it generates feelings of group trust, mutual respect, and enjoyment which places employer and employees in an environment of creative freedom and true purpose. That translates into money saved, money made and 'money's worth'.

The Five Areas of Communication

We spend about three-quarters of each day in five areas of communication.

1. Listening-43%
2. Talking-28%
3. Reading- 15%
4. Writing -9%
5. Self-communication, thinking - 5%

When you listen to someone with a sense of humour, you radiate a feeling of warmth, which encourages honest sharing of feelings. When you speak with humour, you provoke thought, pass on information, build rapport and open opportunities for you to express feelings and philosophies.

When you write with humour, you humanise the words, removing the wall of formality and adding your personality.

When you read with a *Humour Attitude*, you open yourself to new ideas. When you read humour your imagination soars, and you open your mind to unlimited creativity.

When you think with humour, you become more relaxed, amusing and assertive.

People with a Sense of Humour Are Hired First

There are definite benefits for people with a sense of humour. In 1980, a survey of 480 chief executives found the majority felt a sense of humour was pivotal to their work. Many of them agreed that they are more inclined to hire qualified job candidates who demonstrate a sense of humour, than more serious candidates who are equally qualified.

Positive And Negative Humour

At the Melbourne Sales Congress in 1990, Pete Johnson demonstrated the importance of accentuating a positive approach to business with these words:

> 'Keep your thoughts positive because it's those thoughts that become your words. Keep your words positive, because it's your words that become your actions.
>
> Keep your actions positive, because it's our actions that become our habits. Keep your habits positive, because it's your habits that become your destiny.'

Start with Yourself...

I don't advocate positive thinking. I advocate positive, positive thinking! That is positive thinking with a *Humour Attitude*. And if you use humour to communicate with yourself, before communicating with others, you can overcome some of the imperfections, contradictions and sensitivities of business communication.

My job demands I do a lot of filing, and sometimes I need something important immediately. But if I can't find it, I don't give myself a hard time, like so many people do, by saying things like: 'You're a bloody fool, Peter, what sort of an idiot are you not being able to find this?' Instead, I use positive communication to myself, *through self-realisation humour lines* like: 'I like to put things where I can never lose them... and then lose them,' or: 'My filing cabinet is a place where I can lose anything systemically.'

By giving yourself positive feedback with humour, you can feel good about yourself.

Ego Is Not a Dirty Word

Ego is important. Positive ego enables you to tackle your dreams and goals. However, take care not to lose yourself in ego, image and ambition. Don't be like the highly paid yuppie who drove his BMW off the road and wiped it out. When the paramedics arrived and discovered that the young executive had lost his left arm, they carefully broke the news to him. The high-flyer screamed: 'My BMW, my BMW, it's smashed to Again, the ambulance men pointed out his lost arm, but he couldn't hear them; his smashed car meant so much to him. At last they got him to look down to where his left arm used to be. The yuppie, semi-comatose exec simply shouted: 'Oh no, I've lost my Rolex too!'

Three Types of Humour-cators

There are three distinct types of humour-cators: the sarcastic wit, the nit wit and the clowning wit.

The Sarcastic Wit uses humour directed at others - it is <u>laughing at others.</u>

The Nit Wit uses humour indiscriminately - it is <u>laughing at the wrong time.</u>

The Clowning Wit jokes about himself/herself reality and life - it is <u>laughing with others.</u>

The secret to HA HA skills which create fun and profit to use humour that's:

- Amusing, not abusing
- Supportive, not sarcastic
- Brings people closer instead of dividing them
- Is based on caring, not contempt
- Goes for the jocular vain, not the jugular vein
- Is courteous, not contemptuous
- Excites feeling not violates emotions
- Has empathy, not lack of sensitivity
- Builds confidence, not destroys it

Effective humour-cators always use humour that is laughing with, not laughing at.

Positive Humour:

- Constructive
- Appropriate
- Relevant
- Safe
- Identify
- Builds
- Invites
- Therapeutic
- Acceptance
- Promotes
- Strengthens

Negative Humour:

- Destructive
- Inappropriate
- Irrelevant
- Unsafe
- Alienate
- Destroys
- Offends
- Harmful
- Rejection
- Prevents
- Weakens

Use this Positive and Negative Chart to Check Out Your Humour-cation Style:

Humour-cator type	Humour Targets	Humour Forms	Humour Effects
Sarcastic Wit	People's: – Beliefs – Colour – Intellect – Religion – Appearance – Work habits	Sarcasm Satire Practical jokes Insults Mockery Send-up Sick	Hostility Aggression Alienation Retaliation Offensiveness
Nit Wit	Wrong: – Time – Targets – Subject – Content – Place – People – Reason – Occassions	Corny Kidding Offbeat Back-handed Pointed ambiguity Puns Come-backs Freudian slip Irrelevant Irrevent	Confusion Not enjoyed Misunderstanding Not appreciated Feeling Bamboozled Dislike

| Clowning Wit | Pokes fun at user's:
– Mistakes
– Failings
– Weaknesses
– Aspirations
– Human folly

Is just for fun! | Self-putdown
Irony
Word play
Nonsense
Standing joke
Pathos
Farce
Fancy
Fantasy
Mirroring reality
Non-sequitur | Enjoyable
Integration
Inspiration
Attention-getting
Changes attitudes
Relaxes
Fosters trust
Created synergy |

Twelve Questions to Distinguish Positive and Negative Humour

To use humour effectively you must understand the effects of your humour. To get more insight into the difference between positive and negative humour, ask yourself these questions. Remember that the 'effect' of your humour not only depends on what you mean to do but how your hearer takes your words.

1. Does the humour relate to the topic, or are you using it just for the sake of being funny?
2. Does the humour implant a particular idea, suggest a compliment, or offer praise?
3. Does the humour dodge the issues or answer them creatively?
4. Does the humour you're considering make you feel comfortable and confident, or does something about the situation, occasion, content or target make you hesitate?
5. Does the humour consider the listener's situation, circumstances, Wants and needs?
6. Does the humour alienate some of the listeners or actively include all the listeners in the fun?

7. Does the humour target a particular group, attack a stereotype making it the butt of the joke?

8. Does the humour offer appreciation, recognition, a sense of belonging and encouragement?

9. Does the listener have a relationship with you built on trust and emotional honesty?

10. Does your listener give any clues that he or she uses humour as a way of survival?

11. Does the humour open an awareness and suggest alternative thinking?

12. Does the humour highlight your responsibility and maintain your credibility?

Positive Humour Rating

During the 1990 Australian elections, Prime Minister Bob Hawke was walking around a supermarket when he appeared to spontaneously pick up a large telescope.

Surrounded by media cameras he clowned, put it to his eye and said:

'I can't see our opponents' policies even with this!'

I rate this performance an 'A'. All the subtleties, elements and implications of the use of positive humour were present. My *Positive Humour Rating Scale* includes:

Absolute
Brilliant
Capable
Demeaning
Excruciating

Build into your *Humour Attitude*, the energies and elements of positive humour and omit negative humour. Planning and prepare with a positive attitude. You will feel happy and healthy, you will use humour more effectively and your audience will feel happy and healthy receiving it. Plus, you'll open opportunities to make your point and make a positive impression.

Domino Humour Effect List

When learning to distinguish between positive and negative humour, don't stop at noting the laughter, but go on to study the 'domino effect'.

- Was it effective?
- What needs did it serve?
- Was the mood improved?
- Was there a shared insight?
- Any negative stimulation?
- Did the sender betray him/herself?
- What positive/ negative interpretations could one make?
- Why was it used?
- Did it make an intellectual point and /or stir an emotion?
- What business benefit did it give?

Accentuate the Positive - Eliminate the Negative Humour

Prepare to put your *Humour Attitude* into *Action!* When you are working in such a pressurised environment, laughing at the pressure or what's causing it, immediately relieves the pressure and adds a feeling of shared experience.

Draw up your own 'accentuate the positive, eliminate the negative' humour list.

1. Write down events, situations, targets, people, behaviours, things and feelings, of your private and professional life.
2. Note the sensitive areas or experiences you have in common that can titillate and delight

Accentuate:	Eliminate:
Reasons for celebration	Workmates' sensitive feelings
Understanding change	Criticism, hopelessness
Human worth, goal-setting	Self-blame, guilt
Peak experiences	Negative news, sexist remarks, and
Meaningful communication	vulgarity
Titillating situations	Flippant remarks
Outstanding achievements	People's embarrassments
Workmates' successes and	Exploitation, scoffing
important work	Attacks on mistakes, jeering
Self-fulfilment, mood control	Highlighting failure
Things they want taken seriously	Sniggering
Warm fuzzies	Smirking
Happy memories	Distorted truth
Personal disclosure	Derogatory suggestions
Conflict resolution	Quibbling and squabbling
Celebration of diversity	Racist behaviour
Shared feelings and experiences	Power games and unsolicited advice
Job satisfaction	Unemployment

Taking Humour Seriously Makes Dollars and Sense

You and I cry and feel sad about the same situations and events, yet we laugh for different reasons. There are many personal variables environmental forces, and connections, which determine our use and enjoyment of humour. Yet the pressure of the corporate environment demands that we take part and remain contemporary and competitive. That means that taking humour seriously makes dollars and sense because it helps us deal with the pressure constructively and improves productivity and creativity.

Positive humour is about making yourself and others feel good, so we can work at peak performance. To do this well, you need to understand the methods, mechanisms, and the truths of humour. You don't achieve positive humour by chance. You need to program positive attitudes and humour into your work life.

Leadership through Humourship

How important is humour in developing strong leadership? This quote from Carmine M. Consalvo explains it well:

> 'Leadership involves the cultivation of an environment in which freedom and flexibility will flourish. According to the old German saying, humour gives freedom and freedom gives humour. Freedom and flexibility can be both encouraged and enhanced by the introduction of unconventional problem-solving process and personnel. Ultimately, a leader must commit to the survival of the organisation. Humour can be both the avenue tor resilience and the expression of adaptability necessary for organisational survival.'

Like humour, leadership is an art that needs to be practised, experienced and applied. In his book *Effective Leadership*, John Adairs list these leadership characteristics:

Task Initiative   – The aptitude for starting action.

Perseverance   – The ability to keep going tenaciously.

Team Integrity   – The attitude that creates a team climate of trust.

Individual Tact   – Showing sensitive perception of what is fit.

Compassion   – Show sympathetic awareness.

Humour   – Invaluable for relieving tension in a group, an individual or the leader themselves ,closely related to a sense of proportion, a useful asset in anything to do with people.

Former US President Ronald Reagan displayed this leadership humour when an assassin made an attempt on his life. With a bullet in him he was throwing one-liners all the way to the operating theatre. To the surgeons operating, his aside was: "I hope you're all Republicans.'

Find Humour Lines for Your Leadership Needs

Corporate leaders continually find themselves involved in certain repetitivetasks and situations including:

- Showing support
- Admitting mistakes
- Reprimanding
- Controlling conflict
- Expressing corporate values

With a little preparation, humour can be a powerful ally to a creative leader. Make a list of your personal needs. Research these to discover humor to serve different situations. From this observation and research, create *Leadership Support Lines* that are right for you.

'I am not going to make a big fuss over you, Mary. I am Just going to treat you like any other brilliant person.'

'I am impressed with what you are doing, Jack. I know more people believe in you than Santa Claus.'

Alleviate the hassles, which inevitably crop up in the working environment by using *Foresight Frustration Lines* such as:

'Some days you're the fly and some days you're the swatter.'

'Everybody makes mistakes, even Noah. He threw two cats off the ark. He thought they were fighting.'

Soften reprimanding remarks with lines such as:

'Jim, did you design that T-shirt, Make Friends Not Deadlines?'

'David, you heard about the executive who dreamt he was working in office and when he woke up he found that he was.'

With a wide variety of personalities within a team, there are often times when tempers flare or dissatisfaction can hamper team performance. Having a few *Conflict Control Lines* up your sleeve can help everyone laugh away the tension and see things from a different perspective:

'Nothing is so embarrassing as watching one of your employees doing something you told them couldn't be done.

'I don't like arguing and fighting. We should all love one another. I know there are people in the world who don't like each other, and I hate people like that.

Affirm loyalty to your organisation's philosophy with *Corporate Value Lines* like:

'Our credit is the only commodity that gets better the less we use it.'

'Service to others is the rent we pay for the privilege of living on this planet.'

Failure Isn't Fatal

Leadership is often hard, lonely and unappreciated, yet great leaders keep up their enthusiasm and balance. Developing a *Positive Humour Attitude* assists this process. Success cannot be achieved without some trial and error, which can leave you open to criticism. A strong leader understands that 'failure isn't fatal' and faces up to any setback, mistake or criticism immediately and directly.

Robert Orben explains the failure-isn't-fatal technique in an article from his comedy book, The Uses and Limits of Humour, Part Two.

'When a company, organisation, or individual has problems that are known and cannot be ignored, jokes will inevitably surface concerning them. Smart public relations is when you do the joke first. You have an embarrassment, a crisis or you make a terrible mistake. If you are the first to do the jokes about it, chances are it will diminish or diffuse the other slings, arrows and one-liners that may follow.'

No Subject Is Too Sensitive

As President, Ronald Reagan performed public relations miracles by not being afraid to mention his gaffes and vulnerabilities, and he countered all attacks with humour. He has been among the first, and certainly the foremost of those, doing jokes about Ronald Reagan.

His work habits, his age, his mis-speaking, his memory, his operations – all the areas many of us might try to hide or ignore – he covered with the spotlight of humour. Sometimes Reagan even put them all together in one joke.

In early 1987, Reagan was under an onggoing media attack for his role in the Iran Contra matter. At a prestigious Gridiron Washington dinner roast, he tactfully acknowledged the firestorm of criticism by saying: 'Remember the flap when I said we begin bombing in five minutes? Remember when I fell asleep during my audience with the Pope? Remember Pittsburgh? Boy, those were the good old days.'

George Bush, a less-than-great communicator, used failure-isn't-fatal humour in his acceptance speech at the Republican Convention. He said he would try to keep his charisma in check.

Robert Orben says.

> 'The bottom line is that when something is so big you
> can't ignore it, don't. When life hands you a lemon, make
> lemonade. When life hands you a mishap, make jokes and
> the mishaps don't have to be memorable ones.'

As a leadership communication tool, humour offers a multitude of stylistic touches. With humour you can propose, announce, instruct and suggest. Look at the following list and decide which ones best suit your style.

Advise	Announce	Approve	Arouse	Bamboozle
Blame	Boast	Bolster	Bombard	Boost
Bridge	Calm	Celebrate	Challenge	Charm
Cheer	Co-exist	Compliment	Confront	Congratulate
Connect	Consolidate	Consult	Control	Convert
Correct	Create	Criticise	Crystalise	Cushion
Cure	Dazzle	Deal	Declare	Decline
Deflate	Defuse	Delight	Deliver	Demand
Demonstrate	Denounce	Describe	Detour	Digest
Dilute	Disagree	Disarm	Distract	Ease
Elaborate	Elate	Embellish	Empower	Encourage
Endear	Endorse	Enforce	Enhance	Enlighten
Entertain	Enthral	Establish	Estimate	Evade
Exaggerate	Examine	Excite	Exhilarate	Expand
Explain	Exploit	Express	Facilitate	Familiarise
Feel	Fix	Flirt	Fluster	Focus
Force	Foresee	Forge	Forgive	Foster
Fraternise	Garnish	Generate	Give	Grace
Grant	Grow	Handle	Harmonise	Heal
Hear	Heckle	Hel	Herald	Hint
Host	Hypothesise	Identify	Illuminate	Illustrate
Implore	Improve	Incite	Increase	Infer
Influence	Inform	Initiate	Inquire	Inspire
Instruct	Introduce	Involve	Join	Jolt
Justify	Kindle	Knock	Lavish	Lead
Liken	Link	Lobby	Luxuriate	Magnify
Maintain	Manage	Match	Maximise	Mirror
Modify	Modernise	Mystify	Narrate	Negotiate
Notify	Nullify	Order	Oversimplify	Offer
Open-up	Oppose	Orate	Out-flank	Out-smart
Overcome	Patronise	Penalise	Perform	Permit
Persist	Personalise	Persuade	Philosophise	Play
Plead	Please	Point out	Pressure	Probe
Promise	Promote	Protest	Publicise	Purge
Puzzle	Qualify	Question	Quieten	React
Recite	Refine	Reflect	Refresh	Reinforce
Reject	Rejoice	Rejuvenate	Relate	Relieve
Remind	Renounce	Repeat	Report	Request
Resolve	Respond	Retaliate	Reveal	Reverse
Reward	Roast	Sanction	Satisfy	Sell
Serve	Solve	Specify	Speculate	Star
Startle	Submit	Suggest	Support	Surprise
Survive	Tame	Teach	Tempt	Thank
Titillate	Toast	Urge	Understand	Unite
Update	Voice	Warm	Warn	Wow

Management And Humour

My obligation as a manager is to manage in a way that enables the needs of the business to be met and the joint objectives of my colleagues and myself to be achieved. In bringing this about, I have the responsibility to see that the people responsible to me, who are fulfilling the task, have the opportunity to extract satisfaction and fun doing it.Yes I do mean fun. When the fun goes out of a job, one should seriously consider whether one is equipped to cope. Being a manager today certainly requires a sense of humour.'

Humour helps managers manage themselves. Successful managers use humour to create an atmosphere in which employees feel happy about their employer, their duties, their organisation, and its services and products. This positive environment leads to greater productivity. At the same time, managers have to be tough enough to 'step on the toes of the devil, look him in his face and laugh'.

Four Humour Devices For Self Management

Managing others begins with knowing how to manage yourself. Try these four humour devices:

Booster/Boaster Lines.
The fact is that the only way to push yourself ahead is by patting yourself on the back!

Say or think lines like this:

'You know, I have done a great job today. If T hear thunder this afternoon, I think I'll take a bow.'

Managerial Burial.

When you make a mistake, use some kind of ceremony to announce that it is dead, then bury it. Write all the dreaded details on a sheet of company letterhead, read it to your staff, fold it up ceremoniously and place it in a matchbox coffin. Choose a staff member as the gravedigger, equip them with a spoon, then lead the others with heads held low, through the building, to the plot. Cremate it, place a headstone and visit it from time to time.

Manager's Self-Congratulations.

When you celebrate a birthday, a company anniversary or promotion, send yourself a put-down telegram, or gorilla gram. The whole office will enjoy the laugh break and work better as a result

Formal Protest

James Krolle Jr says: 'True, our traditional attitudes towards work derive in large part from the dour puritan ethic that linked labour with earnestness and earnestness with lack of levity. But the reasons that the office remains such a tough room to play, lie not in the past attitudes but in the present organisation of work in this culture. Humour abounds in the American workplace but it is often covert and encoded. The Matisse prints cover the walls of the boardroom, but every other wall, every desktop, and every locker door is plastered with joked-up headlines, printed slogans, parody samples and cartoons clipped from magazines and newspapers. Most comment on work, and most of them imply a criticism of it. Read carefully however. Such messages constitute a collective critique of specific conditions and specific rules. They are a silent petition. Like graffiti, they provide a means of complaint to those of whom complaining is inopportune. The issue is not whether to laugh on the job, but who gets the laugh and at what.

Manage Others with Humour

Robert Hale International, the executive recruiting firm, and Bourke Marketing Research recently surveyed Personnel Directors and Vice Presidents of 100 large US corporations. Nearly one-third of the respondents said that top management had the best sense of humour, while slightly fewer thought that the middle management was so blessed. Relatively fewer (18 per cent) thought the lower-level staff had the best sense of humour.

The Holistic Approach

The HA HA skills of *Humour Attitude* and *Action* enable managers to take a holistic approach to the work environment. To help develop this, begin using a paradox box. Place your latest jokes, cartoons, humour quotes and truth experiences into a container. When you're faced with an important decision or problem, remove the humour from the box and replace it with notes of all your techniques and strategies along with all the company's policies and practices. Take a little time reading the humour. This will put you in a positive mood and open your right-brain qualities of intuition, subtle insights and creativity. Now look at your challenges again. You'll find you can interpret the situation more clearly and flesh out original ideas and actions.

Using your right-brain qualities covers many situations. I'm reminded of the executive who was filling out an application for a life insurance policy came to the line 'cause of father's death' and his father had been hung for murder. He pulled out a collection of Gary Larson cartoons, read them, then wrote: "Taking part in a public ceremony when the platform gave way'

A Powerful Profit-Making Tool

Stephen Juan wrote in a newspaper story:

'Evidence suggests that humour in the workplace is a powerful profit-making tool and some of the world's corporations such as IBM, Monsanto and General Foods are cashing in.'

Dr Alice Isen's studies show that people put in a good mood organise information better and are more creative in word association, categorisation, and tasks involving memory. Indeed, humour also improves decision-making and negotiating abilities. Dr Isen said that mild elation seems to lead to the kind of thinking that enables people to solve problems requiring ingenuity or innovation. She added: 'Someone who is happy can perceive subtle relationships between things because positive material is stimulated in his memory.'

A Sense of Accomplishment Is Fun.

At the Californian State University, Long Beach, Dr David Adramis surveyed 341 people and found they took fun at work very seriously and considered a sense of accomplishment to be fun. Interestingly, Dr Adramis discovered a clear relationship between intending to have fun and actually having some. Those who think fun belongs at work, enjoy themselves most. The buzz word for this is 'psychpay', meaning a psychological reward instead of money

Laurie Winter, from National Mutual Insurance, told me of his first manager, who made a habit of smiling at work first thing every morning Then he would say: 'Well, I've got that out of the way, let's get back to business.'

Managers who apply a positive sense of humour are trusting, as well as forceful and dynamic. They are not afraid to take risks and make mistakes. The added bonus is that people enjoy working with them.

But I'm Not a Funny Person!

Take the advice of Malcolm Kushner, who runs a humour consulting firm in California. 'Managers, dont dismiss your humour potential because you're not a spontaneous person. Sure we all know people who can say the right funny thing at just the right time, but humour does not have to be spontaneous. That's an unfunny myth.'

If you are a left-brain type who's cool and calculating, then take advantage of that ability. Go through your workplace and calculate humorous solutions to specific problems. Can you coldly calculate a humorous solution? Sure you can. For example, your office may contain a photocopying machine that often breaks down. Inevitably, such malfunctions occur when copies are needed in a hurry. Co-workers will get angry and frustrated. Anger and frustration lower their productivity. This is a problem worthy of your attention. So to help everyone overcome this frustration, why not put a sign over the photocopier that says: "Temporarily in working order. When the machine breaks down, your co-workers will be able to laugh about the situation and remain productive. That's well-calculated humour! How can you apply this to other problems and pressures?

Listening and Humour

> 'My boss is a firm believer in listening skills. If you don't
> listen to what he says, you're fired.'

More people have built a reputation for their sense of humour by listening to other people's humour than by using humour themselves. By becoming a Humour Listener, you get laughs and material. Plus, by listening to the humour your co-workers use, what they laugh at or don't laugh at, you get insights into their frustrations and passions.

Our brains can think eight to 10 times quicker than we can speak. So while they speak, you can enjoy watching their body language, listening to the way they speak and the words they use. This helps you get to know who they are and what they are really saying. You will be free of the trouble some teams have, where the staff talk in English and the boss listens in knucklehead!

What an Executive Does

As everybody knows, an executive has <u>practically nothing</u> to do except decide what has to be done. This is usually followed by telling somebody to do it, then having to listen to the reasons why it should not, or cannot be done that way. Then listening to why it should be done a different way or by someone else. Then, all that remains is to follow up to see if the thing has been done; finding out it has not and asking why; then listening to excuses from the person who should have done it. The final step is to follow up again to see if the thing has been done, only to find it has been done wrongly! There's nothing to it!

Humour Listening

Research shows that most of the time the average person uses only 25-30 per cent of therir listening ability. One hundred per cent listening is not just with your ears; you need to be sure you are listening with:

- An open mind
- Emphaty
- A positive *Humour Attitude*

You need to make sure you:

- Pay attention
- Show concern
- Nod (although not too much!)
- Maintain eye contact

Humour listening is not just listening for the jokes or the cue to tell jokes, but listening to build a harmonious relationship based on integrity, sensitivity, flexibility and a win-win philosophy. It's about creating a synergy between the listener and the sender.

Listen for the opportunity to express humour by using what I like to call *humour synergy lines*. Here are a few for you to try:

1. Emotional Bonding lines are based on the universal similar join sender and receiver in a fundamental human truth.

   'When I was young I was told to listen to my elders. Now I'm an elder, I'm told to listen to teenagers. Somehow I missed life along the way'

2. Emotional Security lines alert the receiver to the emotional impact of what the speaker is about to say, so the receiver can prepare for the feeling to come.

   'Times have changed. Years ago, collective bargaining was a system of determining wage increases in which management bargained, and labour collected. (pause) Today...'

3. Sales Self lines. Because we tend to put people into categories, we need to show sides of ourselves that are not in tune with stereotypes.

    'I love change because I get bored quickly. I have to take a yo-yo whenl go bungee jumping.'

4. Showing Emotional Self lines. Life has us changing from one mood to another. At times we need to share these feelings. For example, if you've been off work sick and you are still not feeling 100 per cent, you could say.

    'I've got the world's top doctor. If he can't cure you, he'll touch up your x-rays.'

5. Passing Intormation lines. Communication is about passing data, whether petty or important. From discussing weather, to the economic climate, humour makes your data digestible. Instead of saying, 'It's raining', say:

    'Struth, I reckon the angels were on the beer last night. Don't complain about too much tax; say: 'I'm trying to work out a deal with the government. I've asked them to let me keep the tax, and they can have the income.'

6. Issue Statement lines. During any talk or meeting, issues will be raised and sometimes you must show your feelings about them. With humour you can do this indirectly without starting an avalanche of opposition. Planning to put on a function for a client you're in two minds about, you could say:

    'Life's a laugh. You spend money you haven't impress clients you don't like.'

Eight Elements of Humour To Listen For

When nearly half your working day is spent listening, it makes sense to study the science of listening. And there Is a connection here with the science of humour. Listening this way IS an exciting, exhilarating art. Listen for:

Ambiguity
One word has many meanings. You can expect one meaning but receive another by listening carefully. A friend of mine who is a personnel manager told me he interviewed 10 of the best-dressed men he had ever seen for the position of public relations director, and chose the man best suited for the job.

Juxtapositions
Putting together unlike ideas is cousin to the non-sequitur, where two unrelated statements are linked to make fun. It brings into play the what if' of humour:

What if the chairman ran this corporation entirely by himself? Would he still be in business?

'Thank God this is a free country, where we can do what the Government pleases'

Paradox
Paradoxical thinking is one of the foundation stones of a *Humour Attitude*. A paradox is a statement that seems false but could be true, or a statement that seems to be true but could be false. In his book, *Thriving on Chaos*, Tom Peters says: 'Todays business leaders will be those who are most flexible of mind. An ability to embrace new ideas, routinely challenge old oncs, and live with paradox will be the effective leader's premier trait.

Further, the challeng is for a lifetime ... Leaders will have to guide the ship while simultaneously putting everything up for grabs, which is itself a fundamental paradox.'

Paradox can be a self-contradictory statement such as:

'I like to do the work I do, because it's not work.'

Unexpected honesty
Most humour comes from saying what is not expected. Therefore, when humour is expected, speaking the truth can become the unexpected element. Sometimes it is amusing to divulge.

'No wonder I was confused as a child. One of my parents was a man and the other was a woman.'

'There is only one thing wrong with the boardroom: it's full of bosses.'

'I was ruined by money ... I couldn't get anyway.'

When the bank robber, Willie Sutton, was asked why he robbed banks, he said: 'Because that's where the money is.'

Crossed purpose
This is where two people believe they are talking about the same thing, but each has a different purpose in mind. So each misunderstands the other.

> The new sales rep. walked into his boss's office and saw for the first time, his beautiful secretary. They chatted for a while before she said: 'I am going to make a rather unusual request of you, but first you will have to promise to keep it a strict secret. He agreed to this. Then she said:

Its embarrassing to talk about, but you see, my boss is really a nice bloke. Unfortunately, he has, let me put it this way, a certain physical weakness, a certain disability. Now I'm a woman, and you're a real man. That's right, That's right,' interrupted the rep. 'And since I have been wanting to do it for so long, will you please help me move this filing cabinet.'

Freudian slips

This term comes from Sigmund Freud's suggestion that slips of the tongue arise from suppressed ideas, which find the energy to burst out 'by mistake' in everyday talk.

> I overheard a financial adviser say: 'I am more interested in stocks than blondes.' A sales executive in an extremely competitive business greets her opposition from a competitive firm with the words: 'Pleased to beat you… what I mean is, meet you.' (Switched from Motley 1987, page 27)

As well as listening for slips of the tongue, listen for tongue-in-cheek, reverse of what they mean.

> 'That was really a great job you did, John.'

Alliteration

This rhetorical device begins each key word with the same letter.

> 'The three most important parts of life are labour, leisure and love.'

Antithesis

Aristotle called this one of the three greatest categories of comedy. This is another use of the reverse formula: presenting the direct opposite, the contrast of ideas.

> 'The more civil servants, the less service.'

> 'The rich have better food, the poor man a better appetite.'

Listening is an important part of knowing what kind of humour will work best and when to use it. Try to be a *creative listener*. Take note of their:

- Body language
- Facial and verbal expressions
- Voice pitch, force, volume, rhythm and rate

These cues help you understand what the other person is feeling. At the same time, listen to yourself and focus on what you are feeling. Consider how you can convey your feelings to them using *Humour Attitude* and *Action*.

Conversation and humour

> 'Laughter is not a bad beginning for a friendship and it is
> the best ending for one.'
> Oscar Wilde

When you stand in line at the bank, sit next to somebody at a seminar, or mingle at a product launch, you will benefit if you know how to use humour in conversation. It makes you confident and creative, plus there are other bonuses.

Humour makes you memorable.

In the business world a brief chat is like a television commercial. If you're going to be remembered and accepted, your personal advertising must fit you, get attention and amuse others.

Who said that relevision killed the art of conversation?

All I hear is talk complaining about how bad the shows are!

Humour:

- Destroys reason for rejection
- Shatters resistance
- Invites receptiveness
- Opens relationships
- Shares experiences
- Shows friendliness
- Builds trust
- Increase intimacy
- Makes your image pleasant

You become a breath of fresh air, a supplier of surprises. An invaluable remedy for life's ills. When you tickle people's funny bones they feel good and when you make them feel good, they are more inclined to agree with you. They will also listen to you, buy from you and open themselves to your vision, reality and truth. Talk is cheap, but humour conversation is an exception to the rule.

Laughter contributes to coversation.

Laughter not only encourages more conversation, it makes everyone feel better. There is a real physical benefit. In his book *The Laughter Prescription*, Dr Laurence J Peters explains:

'In many social situations, we sit for long periods so that respiration becomes shallow and circulation becomes sluggish. The physical activity of laughter contributes to conversation because it increases circulation and respiration and brings about a feeling of euphoria or wellbeing. This restores our zest for mental activity and social interaction.'

Laughter builds relationships.

The most constant use of humour communication in a business setting is the joking relationship between work colleagues. First identified by Radcliff-Brown (1940), it comes under the superiority theory of humour. He describes a joking relationship between two people In which, by custom, one is allowed to, and at times is coaxed into, teasing or making fun of the other. The recipient is required not to be offended. This is light-hearted insult humour where the people involved like and know each other well. It is a game that is fun to play at work. It serves a vital function in certain work conditions. It releases competitive tension, saves face for the users and prevents divisions by uniting everyone in laughter. The *The Eleven Rules of Joking Relationships* follow. Issue employees with these and a joking Relationship Licence. If they don't abide by the rules, they are banished for a period from the group and its activities.

The Eleven Rules of Joking Relationships

1. Make sure that your face and eyes express a genuine *Humour Attitude*.
2. To start with, only joke about people for what they do, never for what they are. Even if, in time, they show they can laugh at what they are, you still need to tread carefully.

3. When you insult, smile! Make sure your face, voice and posture show no sign of hostility.

4. Structure the insult so that as well as insulting, you are also saying that you like the person.

5. The tone of the insult should have a touch of irony so that the recipient feels important because you have picked them out to send up. Your tone should show that the recipient has a sense of humour and can laugh at him/herself.

6. The put-down will work better if it is an obvious exaggeration and not just insulting truth. This will reassure the recipient and the listeners that you are joking.

7. Insult about things that in no way resemble the truth or the subjects that the recipient uses to put themselves down. Use the insult to draw the recipient into the group.

8. Be careful about using insults you have heard other people use. Put your own perception into your put-downs. This adds empathy to your insults.

9. When the insult is returned, try to top it in good fun. Be on guard not to go beyond the court of discretion. Just in case you do, have a *Saving Line* ready.

10. Insult humour does an important task and in some settings it is the most fitting humour, but stop yourself getting a reputation for using only insult humour. Use other forms of humour and let other people joke about you.

11. A sure-fire way to get a laugh without offence is to use a *Roast Insult Line*. For example, a mate told George (point to George) about a businessman whose family spent $35,000 on his funeral. So George said: 'if they spent another $500, they could have buried him in a Mercedes!'

Humour is a big part of successful conversation.

Because conversation is such a big part of our business lives, and humor is such a big part of successful conversation, spend some time asking yourself the following four questions:

1. What sort of humour do I use?
2. What effects does it have?
3. What considerations are involved?
4. In what situations do I often find myself and should I prepare spontaneity?

To help you give useful answers to these last four points, here are 10 basic techniques used in successful conversations. The list is not complete, but will give you some understanding of what you can do to master the use of humour in conversation.

1. Shakers

Humour can be the first common denominator between people leading to lasting friendship and lots of future profitable conversations. When you are introduced to someone, you can add humour through:

> An enthusiastic handshake
> A friendly smile
> A happy tone of voice
> A twinkle in your eyes
> A cheerful attitude

The verbal humour should contain self-putdown, something that fits your *humour identity* like:

> 'G'day, I'm Pete Crofts, the man of the week. Shows you
> what kind of weck it's been!'

2. Openers

First impressions are lasting impressions. Here you are not trying to be funny but to show you have sense of humour and do laugh. Use humour to mirror the mannerisms and mirth of the person you meet to show you like them and you are just like them. One I like to use is:

> 'How are things? I must say things are gradually falling into place... on top of me!'

3. Honesties

> 'There is a great man who makes every man feel small but the really great man is the man who makes every man feel great.'

So wrote G.K.Chesterton of Charles Dickens. In his book *The Laughter Prescription*, Dr Laurence J. Peters mentions *metatalk* and how to read someone like a book. Gerald I. Nierenberg and Henry Calero discuss how the words we say are completely overwhelmed by the feelings expressed in our physical attitudes and movements. These authors urge us to become more aware of these feelings and to put them more honestly into what we say to produce some integrity in our communication. They suggest that the more you use talk flavoured with apt attitudes, the more people you will have to talk to and the more people will want to talk to you. *Positive Humour* creates an environment of honesty and if the humour expresses humility at the same time, you have an emotional connection.

> Say someone asks you: 'What do you do? Respond honestly and with a smile:

> 'I will tell you everything I know... it won't take long!'

Responding with humour is as important as creating it. The honesty will catch the listener by surprise and bring a smile to their face as well.

4. Compliments

Trough the distance between the two is only 11 inches, the results received from a pat on the back or a kick in the pants are vastly different! Practise concentrating on the positive aspects and energies of the person to whom directly or indirectly. Sayings such as:

> 'I haven't seen you for a while. I'm the one who's the loser.'

> 'I like to be kind to my friends. Without them, I would be a stranger.'

5. Changes

Change is another word for transition. At times in conversation, you will want to change from one topic to another. The changes must have purpose and tell the listeners in what direction you are going. Changes build bridges, link ideas and, most importantly, link feelings. Try bridging the gap with sentences like:

> 'To make a long story short, there is nothing like having the boss walk in...'

> 'You know I am the same as most people. I never agree with the boss until he says something!'

Remember, when people laugh, they often stretch, move about, or rearrange their seating. It is a miniature intermission. Develop the skill of using changes to keep the conversation on a roll while allowing people to relax between the laughs.

6. Controllers

These are lines that allow you to stay in control and keep the conversation moving in the direction you have planned. Weigh up the personalities of the people you are conversing with so that you can:

- Keep them interested
- Make them feel important
- Help them feel involved
- Share their thoughts and ideas

All conversations need a captain and a navigator to get them in the air, dodge storms and land safely after a pleasant journey. A good controller is a startling statement like:

> 'If you want to lead the orchestra, you must turn your back on the crowd.'

Or you can pose a quizzical question like:

> 'How many bosses does it take to change a light bulb? None, he tells someone else to do it.'

Another good controller is a strong opinion such as:

> 'Knowledge is power ... if you have knowledge about the right person!'

Another one is a thoughtful remark such as:

> 'The turtle never makes progress until he sticks his head out.'

7. Strengtheners

Here you use humour to strengthen relations based on shared situations, predicaments and experiences. If someone complains the mail is always late, you can respond with:

> 'They should give the post office control of nuclear missiles. You could bet they'd never be delivered!'

8. Coverers

Coverers or savers are studied lines, quotes, quips, announcements and bits of information that in time become part of your conversation style. They are comebacks to your own behaviour and are ways to recover after bloopers. If you give somebody the wrong name, say something like:

> 'Names have never been my strong point. That's why I always carry this.' Then I take out a card from my wallet which states: "My name is Pete Crofts.' Of course, if your name is not Pete Crofts, use another card.

When you get jumbled in your ideas and expressions, say something like:

> 'I'm not feeling the best today; I have a headache. It happened this morning when I was shaving. I was dabbing my face with toilet water and the seat fell on my head.

When you are asked for free advice that you don't want to give, you can cover the situation with something like:

> 'When somebody comes to me for advice I find out what they want to be told and I tell them.'

9. Closers

You don't have to be a comedian to leave them laughing. Thats what closing lines do. They give you an entertaining, emotional exit. Humour is making connections. At a business lunch, my associate told me he barracked for the Essendon football team, and dared to declare how many points they would win by on that Saturday. Time passed and he had to leave. As he was going I said, 'Don't worry about the bill, I'll pay it out of this', and I held up $100 note. I'll get it back on Saturday when I bet the change on Essendon.' He left laughing. By linking an event to something someone has told you they care about, you not only get a positive high, you give them a subliminal message that says: 'I have been listening to what you said and I care about what you care about.'

10. Leavers

Leavers are the last words of a conversation. When you have shaken hands to say goodbye and your friend has turned to go, laughter can fill the silent gap before you get out of each other's space. Send you friend away feeling cheerful with lines like:

> 'See you later, and remember, if you dance with a grizzly
> bear, let him lead!'

> 'Have a good day and a better night!'

I like to use closers and then for a leaver, top them with my catch-phrase:

> 'Keep laughing; it's good for you."

Using humour effectively in a conversation melts the ice and warms the room. It gives your mental muscles a work-out and your emotional energies exercise. If you find the ever-changing scenes of life fascinating and stimulating, you are well on your way to becoming a champion conversationalist.

Making a point with humour
'Ladies and gentlemen, I use two types of humour. Some is funny and some is illustrative. You'll be able to tell the difference. If you laugh, it's funny. If you don't, it's illustrative.'

This is a line I use in many of my presentations. It always goes down well. By using your *Humour Attitude* to illustrate a point, you help your listeners remember it and enhance the impact of what you have to say, without 'force-feeding' them with your message.

Humour is a spur to learning and retention
One study showed that people who went to a business meeting recalled only eight per cent of what they heard. When the point was made with humour, their recall rocketed to 80 per cent. In an article, 'Take My Boss, Please,' published in *Across the Board* magazine, James Kohne Jr says:

'Dozens of studies have confirmed that humour is a spur to learning and retention. Convey a fact via a relevant joke and that fact will be remembered longer and more clearly than if it had been delivered straight - for two reasons. Firstly, an apt Joke relieves the stress that most people feel when they are back, if only figuratively, in the classroom. Secondly, a joke momentarily leaves us teetering on the edge of the unexpected, alert for an impending stumble, and such heightened awareness makes seeing and remembering easy.'

Use Humour to lustrate Your Point

I read about a man who lectures on tree clearing. Luckily he had the external identity of baldness. To illustrate a point, he would pick up a small jug and pour a little water on his bald head. Then he would ask his audience: 'Did you see how the water ran off the cleared area and got caught in the growth area on the side of my head?' Needless to say, he got a laugh and made a point that would not be forgotten. The point I'm making is that humour does not have to be spoken joke. It can be a sight gag like the bald lecture's or any aspect of humour science that suits the occasion, your identity and the message.

A strong Ha-Ha for a memorable A-ha!

For humour to work well, it must:

- Connect with the idea you want to demonstrate
- Be in harmony with your message
- Highlight your purpose

The stronger and clearer the connection between these three aspects, the stronger the Ha-Ha and the more insightful and memorable the A-ha.

Do you get it: You won't have to ask this question if you use humour to communicate your feelings, visions, objectives and business message. With humour you can easily highlight important attitudes, solve personal problems, pass on in-house information, make facts and figures palatable, explain dull material and get people enthused about your topic. No means of communication is more adaptable and useful than humour. Use the *Humour Point-Scoring Steps* to make your points convincing and memorable

1. Start a joke file based on the subjects, topics and needs you talk about most.
2. Analyse each joke thoroughly for the points it can make and file it under all the possible headings.

3. Study ways of switching so that all the humour you file can be used completely.

4. Expand your humour science by experimenting with as many humour devices and techniques as you can.

5. Understand why you are using your point-scoring humour. Is it to clarify, persuade, digress, cushion or to silence criticism? Go to your list of reasons for humour communication.

6. Look deeply within the humour, past the point you want to illustrate, to the sub-text. What mood will the humour trigger?

7. Do the point, purpose and mood add integrity to your humour identity or do they belittle it?

8. Write a strong, secretive, creative, tension-building transition to credibly link the points you want to make with the humour you are using. Then use a strong transition back to your subject.

9. Always blend the topic of your humour with your message as well as you can.

10. Remember the prime reason tor using humour is to help your listeners understand your points and your whole message. It helps them to vividly recall your ideas and be inspired to act on them for everyone's benefit.

11. Repeat! With change.

    Make your point seriously.

    Make the same point humorously.

    Make the point convincingly and go on.

Get a response to your messages- use humour!

No matter how important or serious your point, it can be made more strongly and clearly with humour. When you use humour for a serious reason, your listeners' resistanceto laughing is softened and even if they do not laugh aloud, they will respond more strongly to your message.

Keep the smiles, chuckles and laughs coming by using a variety of one-line, two-line, five-line and 10-line jokes. They dot any dull spots in your message with a touch of surprise. They tickle your listeners back to attention.

Plot jokes make the best points

For most one-line jokes, you are wise to use the *Rule of three* to give a real punch. Gather jokes that are linked by topic or techniques and present them as titillating triplets to your audience. This builds the laughs gradually and adds impact to the message. For key messages and points, use plot jokes so that the listeners have a chance to warm to your humour. Make sure youhave clear link with the point you are making and build up enough tension to make a lasting image. Over time these jokes can become *signature jokes* as you add your personal style and skills to them. They can become old friends to your audience. Here's one of mine:

> 'Most business people have a sense of morality, but there are the odd few that manage to give business a bad name. The other day, I was walking past a clothing shop and saw a big colourful sign: "Laughat the cold in our fun clothes - 25 per cent off everything!"
>
> I walked in and said to the salesman: "Is that right? Twenty-five per cent off everything?
>
> He said: "Yes, it's because we're going out of business."
>
> So I said: "OK, find me 10 suits, 15 shirts, five pairs of shoes, 50 pairs of socks, 120 singlets, 120 pairs of underpants, Six belts, six dozen ties, six dozen handkerchiefs, six cardigans, six sports coats, three dinner jackets, three

dressing gowns, three pairs ol slippers, two raincoats, two overcoats, and two cravats. How much will that be?"

He added it up and said: "$12,000 please.

I said: "Just a moment, what about the 25 per cent off?"

He said: "That was when we were going out of business. Now you've bought this lot, we're back in business again!

Fortunately, there aren't many business people here with the morality of that person!

Making a point with humour exercise
Carefully read the joke below half a dozen times then analyse it by answering the questions which follow it.

> Tarzan was broke. He needed money in a hurry. For a while he had been thinking of going into the used crocodile business. He decided on the name Corporate Crocodiles Pty Ltd'. Keen as mustard, he got up the next morning very early and swung down to the river bank. All day he bargained, bustled, bought and sold crook and crummy crocodiles. That evening, he walked home; he didn't have the energy to swing through the trees. He fell through the door of the tree hut and shouted to Jane to bring him a martini. He gulped it down and demanded another one, threw that down and pleaded with Jane to get him another.
>
> 'Tarzan,' she said, 'this is no good for you.'
>
> Jane, you don't understand, Tarzan sobbed. 'It's a Jungle out there!'

Now ask yourself these analytical questions:

1. What are the humour elements in the joke; the essence of what makes funny; the key words; the things that are linked; the idea under the joke's plot?
2. Could it be switched to another place or topic?
3. Think of three points you could illustrate with the joke as It is or when it is switched.
4. Return to your list of things you talk about most and see if you can connect with any of the points or topics the joke would illustrate. If so, good. If not, file it under the three headings you recognised.
5. Could anything else be added to it to make it easier for your particular identify with? Could you change the subject, add some personal words, and create characters which are more interesting to your audience?
6. Classify this joke under one of the four styles of humour – Philosophical, sexual, nonsensical or hostile. This will help you work out whether the joke is positive or negative (look in chapter three).
7. Does the joke fall within the boundaries of your humour identity's point of view. What would your identity say or do?
8. If you like the joke and have a point to convey with it, 1S it good enough to spend the time to rewrite it using your own words, idioms, rhythm and rhyme?

Invest time in learning and rehearsing the Joke and perfecting it by adding other humour elements such as dialect, sound effects, humorous gestures or props. Could you use the joke without too much trouble to make the following points:

- Business Is tough
- New business opportunities

- Drink is not the answer
- Don't panic!
- Analogies are funny
- Creative thinking

Pick out half-a-dozen jokes and practise making a point with each. You will find it comes easy with a little work and the more creatively you make transitions into the humour and out into your serious message, the better the response. Look for as many techniques and devices as you can find to use in your talking, public speaking, training, writing and conversation. Build your own point-making system to convey messages and sell ideas.

Humour can make your point indirectly

The following example comes from Esther Blumenfeld and Lynne Alpern's marvellous book, *The Smile Connection*.

> 'People Related Aggravations - When people work closely together, handling minor irritations and diverse tensions requires tact. Humour can make your point indirectly without provoking retaliation. Used in this manner, humour becomes a verbal shield. For example, Mary was a smoker in a tiny office with a non-smoking office mate. Although she was out of the office a great deal and had many opportunities to smoke elsewhere, she still smoked in the office. Sally, her office mate, instead of triggering a confrontation, offered an acceptable substitute in a humorous way. She gave Mary a jar of hard candy with a funny poem accompanying it.
>
> "The smoke you blow into the air is mucking up our comfy lair,

I hope you'll substitute this candy tor the cigarette you find so randy

If you won't smoke, I won't spit, You'll live longer and I'll keep fit."

An alternative method is to offer a whimsical substitute such as a rubber cigar which may be strong enough to make your point.'

Humour opens up your opportunities to make your point effectively whether you choose the direct or indirect method. When difficult situations can be handled smoothly and your day-to-day communication made easier, our team will work together better and your customers will be leaving with a smile. Your HA HA Skills will bring FUN AND PROFTT to your working environment every day!

Chapter One Summary
Humour Improves Your Business Communication

1. Humour-cation means business.
2. HA HA skills bring fun and profit
3. Positive humour communication generates good feelings
4. Listening with a sense of humour radiates warmth
5. People with a sense of humour are more employable
6. Use hunmour to communicate with yourself before Communicating with others
7. Positive ego enables you to tackle your dreams and goals
8. Effective humour-cators use humour that is laughing with, not laughing at
9. Build into your *Humour Attitude* the energies and elements of positive humour.
10. Learn to distinguish between positive and negative humour
11. Accentuate positive humour - eliminate the negative
12. Leadership is an art that needs to be practised, experienced and applied
13. Humour helps managers manage themselves
14. Top managers and a sense of humour go together
15. Build a reputation of having a sense of humour by listening to others
16. Humour makes you memorable
17. Humour is a spur to learning and retention
18. A strong Ha Ha brings a memorable A-ha!
19. Humour helps you make a point
20. Humour disarms conflict and confusion

CHAPTER 2

How Humour Can Work For You In Business And Life

People do not laugh or use humour without reason. Every time somebody laughs, it serves a function. We will now look at eight functions where humour can benefit you.

- Coping with survival
- Handling stress and burnout
- Enhancing self-image
- Building relationships
- How to motivate and increase productivity
- Gaining attention
- Selling successfully
- Caring for customers

Coping with survival

Marvin R. Koller, in his very comprehensive book *Humour and Society*, says:

> 'The single concept that subsumes all the social functions of humour is survival. In social bonding release from stress and strain; expression, aggression or hostility; celebrating life, self-effacement; social correction;

upholding honesty over pretence; provoking thought; balancing pain; reinforcing or undermining stereotypes; therapy and defence against threats or attack, humour helps humanity endure. When the substantive areas in which humour operates are examined, the thesis that humour is a survival mechanism can be documented.'

Humorous Survival Sayings

A *Humour Attitude* operates as a complete support system, helping us cope in the fragile, unpredictable chaos of corporate absurdities.

Build up your own personal repertoire of humour survival sayings and practise repeating them so that when you do, they act as a switch from one perception or mood, to another. A negative frame of mind to a positive one:

> 'I don't have time to be confused, I'm too darn busy trying to figure out what's going on around here!'

> 'Don't try to make a fool out of me, I'm doing all right myself!'

Coping support send-up
Here are a few survival sayings to give you an idea to create your own for your own personal circumstances.

> 'This is a non-profit organisation; we didn't plan itthat way, but that's the way it turned out!'

Another practised behaviour to incorporate into your humour mentality is the coping support send-up. When you foresee a difficulty or a negative aspect of your personality surfacing, in a meeting or a one-on-one discussion, prepare a send-up line to cope with the trouble.

If you tend to get hot under the collar, have some readily available lines to send that situation up.

> 'I'm a pretty relaxed sort of person; I had a portrait painted once and it turned out to be a still life!'

Using humour successfully boosts your confidence, helps you maintain Objectivity, and best of all, it's a pleasurable, usable technique for surviving and coping on the job.

Handling Stress and Burnout

> 'You think your job is stressful; at my last job they passed out the desk calendars in weekly instalments!'

Dr Joel Goodman, who created a special humour project, says:

> 'Humour can control stress. Stress 1s not an event, but a perception of an event, and by using humour, we change our perceptions, Our attitudes and our behaviour, and how we approach a situation. The people who have trained themselves to use humour, whether consciously or subconsciously, to cope with the day-to-day conflicts and confusions, do not show the kind of psychological or physiological response to stress as the humourless ones do.'

Humour Stress Busters

Humour is a stress buster: you can't feel humorous and stressed at the same time. So when you feel yourself becoming anxious, angry or tense, the logical thing to do would be to put yourselt in a comical frame of mind.

Hyperbole Hassle

I owned a bookshop in Sandringham, a very quiet suburb of Melbourne. When we had a quiet day, I'd use an exaggeration technique that the philosopher Aristotle called hyperbole.

> 'The only way to make money in Sandringham is to put a cyclone fence around the town and charge people to come in!'

Deflating tension

If you can develop the skill to deflate tension, then you will be welcomed everywhere by everyone - it's a prized ability. There is a true story about a man who had gangrene in his arm, and had to go to hospital to have his arm removed. The thing he loved most in life was sport. Friends didn't know how the illness would affect him, and they were all anxious and nervous when they went to see him in hospital after the operation. When he woke up, he saw his friends standing around the bed. He rubbed his eyes, shrugged his shoulders and said: I didn't get a bit of sleep last night because of the dogs fighting over my arm. Everybody broke up laughing. Humour was his way of signaling that he was coping. Learn to make it your way of defusing tense situations.

Aggression recession

The beauty of humour as a stress buster, as opposed to meditation or exercise, is that its spontaneous. It addresses the crisis as it happens. Some time ago, business was slow at the book shop and my ex wife went into town and came back with boxes of new clothes I didn't think we could afford. She also bought some fish for her fish tank. I didn't say anything until she said: I'm going to put the fish in the fish tank. I couldn't contain myself. I screamed out from the bottom of the stairs: Drown the bastards! It was amazing how much better I felt when I thought of the humour of that line; I chuckled to myself for an hour. Humour has always been my way of releasing aggression.

Pleasant imagery

Humour can turn stress into mental success. For instance, it you're standing in the bank and the service is slow, you do have a choice. You can allow yourself to get stressed, causing emotional and physical harm, or you could use pleasant imagery to make yourself feel good. Every time you breathe in, suggest to yourself that you are feeling less stressed, more cheerful and more relaxed.

Then imagine that all the people in front of you are comedians. You are the bank clerk and he is the last one on your queue. As the comedians come up your window they tell you their favourite jokes. Of course, if you go on share the jokes too, you will not only relax, you'll have half the bank joining in the chuckles.

Humour Stress – Busting Chart

Make a list of all the stressful situations and conflicts you are experiencing in the main parts of the life – professional, financial, social, creative, cultural, personal. Then list the three situations in each part that cause you the most frustration and stress. Now list the humour stress – busting techniques you are to apply to each, and you will have a chart like the following one:

Major Categories of Life	Three Stress Aspects	Stress Busters of Life
Professional	Finding preparation time Maintaining credibility Customer service	Hyperbole Hassle Pleasant Imagery Deflating Tension
Financial	Paying Bills Buying new equipment Unpaid bills Not having enough time	Hyperbole Hassle Pleasant Imagery Aggression Recession Pleasant imagery
Social	Groups wanting me to speak Not enough teenage centres Noise when thinking	Deflating Tension Hyperbole Hassle Aggression Recession
Creative	Silly distractions. Writer's block. Australian identity.	Hyperbole Hassle Pleasant Imagery Pleasant Imagery
Cultural	Racism in humour Drunks and yobbos Understanding children	Aggression Recession Deflating Tension Aggression Recession
Personal	Taking my family for granted. Slow personal growth.	Deflating Tension Pleasant Imagery

As we know, some stress is good for us. And let's be honest, most people get emotionally stressed at some time. Teenagers are because they live in a world dominated by nuclear weapons. The adults are stressed because they live in a world dominated by teenagers

Gain Attention

Thirty years ago, television gave us 24 hours a day of show business. It also brought our attention span down to cight seconds. Today, we have business show to gain and maintain that attention. Humour, comedy and laughter are three of its major strategies.

Four Humour Attention-Getting Methods

Dr Virginia Tooper tells us in a magazine Laugh Lovers News of how flight attendants are usng humour to get the passengers attention. During the first part of their announcement (done straight) the flight attendants welcome the passengers who may be sleeping or reading. They use methods designed to get them to listen, such as:

> 'Smoking is not permitted in the aisles or the toilet; it you are caught smoking in the toilet, not only will your potty privileges be taken away, but you will be asked to leave this airplane, immediately.

> And in the unlikely event of a water landing, you may use your seat cushion as a flotation device. There will be no lifeguard on duty and the women with long hair will be required to wear bathing caps.'

By now the passengers are grinning and chuckling, and of course listening It you want to arouse interest, and get people to listen and remember your messages, train yourself in the skills and tactics that humour offers. Whenever you have to pass on important information, people automatically listen because they know that there's something in it for them. Try these three ways to get attention:

1. Ludicrous Instruction

Sometime ago (choose any year) postal costs rose again, and a local company sent around a memo to teach the staff the thriftiest ways of using the post.

To gain attention, they opened with:

> 'A new method has been devised to handle all outgoing mail. Carefully loop together the rubber bands provided, and then stretching out the window as unobtrusively as possible, lasso the nearest passing bird. We suggest:

- First class - Pigeon
- Second class Sparrow
- Recorded delivery - Parrot
- Special express service - Swift

2. Information Impersonation

Robin Williams in the film, *Dead Poets Society*, uses this method quite successfully. When you are continually informing people, you sometimes need to change the method of delivery, to gain attention. The information could be delivered in the voice of a local politician, a movie star, cartoon character or a unique personality in the organisation. Here we are getting into a more sophisticated form of humour use. The following piece could be delivered in a Humphrey Bogart style. Put a hat down over your eyes, turn your collar up, push your hands deep into your pockets, give a quick unemotional grin atter every few words, keeping your mouth closed as tight as you can while you are speaking:

> 'All right you squealers, get this. The object of all dedicated company punks should be to analyse thoroughly all situations, checking for a double cross. Anticipate all problems before their occurrence, watching for stoolies, and move swiftly to solve these problems when called upon. Without putting a hit on any goons.'

(Raise your voice and go out of character ere and deliver the following line quickly.)

> 'However, when you're up to your ass in alligators. it's difficult to remind yourself that your initial objective was to drain the swamp.'

3. Synonyms Messages

In this device we overuse synonyms - those words that have the same or nearly the same meaning as another word. Labour and toil, for example, are all synonyms for work. Of course, we choose funny ones.

> 'The way the economy is today, not too many of us are going to work our way up to the upper crust. Well, who wants to? They're only a bunch of crumbs held together by a bit of dough. You know what dough is, money! That green folding stuff that hubby brings home every week. You know what a hubby is, a husband! A blob of biological humanity that takes the garbage out and spends Sunday hitting a little white ball with a croquet stick over potholes and into water.'

Humour adds a human emotion to your messages and unlocks the comfort zones and prison cells people build in their minds from prejudices, beliefs, fear and prior knowledge. Humour blasts through rejection, grabs attention and shouts: Listen, you'll love this!'

Building Relationships

> 'Humour is a great thing, the saving thing; after all, the minute it crops up, all our hardnesses yield, all our

irritations and resentments slip away and a Sunny spirit
takes their place.'

Mark Twain

Think of the people you know who have a sense of humour. You like
them, you easily establish a rapport with them, and you find you are
more willing to listen. Humour becomes a path that leads to mutual
understanding. Business friends is not an oxymoron, it's a relationship
based on trust, Common purpose and a humorous helpfulness.

Humour bonding device
To have a friend, you first have to be a friend. Humour is the ideal means
to ffriendship - it softens harsh, argumentative, competitive behaviour.
It can be used to introduce aspects of your personality and value system
in an enjoyable, non-confronting way.

Self-disclosure satire
Here you pass on information and details about what you think and feel
by honestly expressing your point of view.

> Two business executives, Johnson and Harrison. were
> discussing a mutual friend, Johnson said: 'He used to
> work for me; I would not trust him with my money.
> He lies, steals, cheats, does anything for a quick buck.'
> Harrison said: 'How well do you know him?' How well?',
> answered Johnson, "I taught him everything he knows!'

I use self-disclosure satire when I don't know a person's point of view for
example, a company's IT policy. I say something like:

> 'I don't worry about computers if they get too powerful,
> I'll just organise them into committees.'

I haven't expressed a strong View in this situation but I have hinted at the issue and made it easy for them to give their view.

Humour, used successfully, is a powerful social lubricant, which foster harmonious growth. Humour is a fun fertiliser that nourishes relationship so they can withstand disagreement, jealousy and selfishness. You can see how this happens when you study the next humour-bonding device.

Group gripes
In this situation you identify a shared frustration and then express it using humour; at the same time gauging the level of discontent. If you have been involved with others in a successful project and company appreciation ls not forthcoming, you could remark:

> 'Doing a good job here is like wetting your pants in a dark
> suit: it gives you a warm feeling but nobody notices.'

Corporate culture is infested with segregation and aggravation. A priority for any company wishing to rejuvenate their ethos of personal relationships would do well to spend some time and money on humour R&D. For as we all know, the people who can laugh together, can work better together.

To Motivate and Increase Productivity

One of the most important and constructive applications of humour in the world of high achievers, is the use of its power to motivate, and increase productivity. Humour stimulates an atmosphere of mateship, intensifies group cohesion, and enhances self-confidence. It alleviates personal inhibitions, making it possible for peeople to enjoy the camaraderie of capitalism.

Take the two blokes who were working digging a hole and the foreman said, 'Look Jack, and you too, John, jump out ot the hole up here, and they did. The foreman said jump back in and they did, jump up, jump back, jump up, jump back and this went on for an hour.

Finally Jack said: 'What the heck's the idea? And the foreman said: "You're bringing up more muck on your shoes than you are on your shovels!'

Corporations spend a fortune on accounting, marketing and the latest technologies, but are blind to the needs of their most important resource their employees! Needs is another word for motives. What are your people's motives? Personal gratification, wealth, prestige, power: One thing is for Sure: they all want to achieve. Even the ones who don't think they do, but have not been motivated correctly. Corporate culture has not caught up with the concept of personal growth because of its cognitive involvement and its group co-operation qualities. Humour has the force to inspire personal motivation and increase productivity.

Try applying the following humour motivational methods to tap into your teams maximum potential.

Running group joke
If something goes wrong and the boss comments in frustration, "That's the Almighty Murphy's Law again', turn it into a running joke, and use it, or a variation of it, whenever other things go wrong. If someone leaves a window open and rain splashes on some important papers, you could say: 'That's the almighty Murphy's Law again: never leave thin wood under raining windows.'

The possibility of personalising running jokes into your work environment is unlimited and very worthwhile.

Motivational mottos

These are short, sharp quips that are repeated at appropriate times, If you have just been loaded up with four jobs at once, you could say, 'Nothing is impossible if you don't have to do it yourself.

Motivation comes from having learly identifiable goals, the patience to endure frustration, the knowledge that success only comes with hard work and the *Humour Abilities* to overcome all obstacles. An example is the sales manager who could motivate hundreds of people but couldn't get his son into a barber shop.

Enhancing self-Image

Having a healthy *Humour Attitude* is the same as having a strong self-image Dr Walter E O'Connell says in his chapter, 'Natural High Theory and Practice', in the *Handbook of Humour and Psychotherapy*:

> The theory that guides me (Natural High theory) follows from the clinical and research observation that those with humorous attitudes are self-orientated but not ego-constricted. That is, the humorist knows that self-esteem (SE) is an intuitive process of inner development. Self-esteem carries the well-practised message that, in spite of my mistakes, I am guilt free.'

Humour self-image exercises can be used as mental trigger signals for moving into the humour mode. One such exercise is the *I'm not guilty farce* or (the water-off-the-ducks-back syndrome)

The moment you fteel yourself being targeted by someone, use humours a shield to protect yourself from these emotional invasions. Use lines like:

'Come on, stop showing oft, I'm here for a few laughs.' And: 'That's right, you graduated from the Spike Milligan Psychodrama School!' Or: 'I disagree with what you say, butI will defend to the death your right to tell such lies.'

Novelist George Meredith defined true humour as the capacity to laugh at the things one loves, including one's self. And to continue that love because the topping of self-deception and the development of appropriate self-regard are two basic objectives of all forms of insight psychotherapy.

Past pratfalls
As we mature, we learn not to scare ourselves, to be kind and tolerant, and to support and praise ourselves. When an attitude of the past surfaces in your present behaviour, learn to laugh it off. See it as a past pratfall and start to play with it; do a parody of your former self.

Jackie Mason I know who I am
My favourite comedian, the mind-boggling Jackie Mason, says: 'When I tell you I don't care if a person laughs or not, it's because I know who I am. That's not arrogance, that's mental health. Any psychologist will tell you that if you know who you are, it doesn't matter what other people think of you. The measure of yourself should be within yourself. You should have enough confidence to know who you are and not care what other people think, because all great men were always rejected, neglected and even hated in their own lifetime. I'm talking to you personally.'

Mason goes on to say:

> 'That's why it doesn't bother me that you might think
> I'm nuts because I know who I am. That's right! This is a
> great trick in life to know who you are. There was a time
> I didn't know who I was; thank God now I know. I don't

know if you heard about it, but I went to a psychiatrist and I'm not ashamed to admit it. It was because I didn't know who I was. He took one look at me and said right away: "This is not you." I said: "If this is not me, then who is it? He said: "T don't know either." So I said: "Then what do I need you for?" He said: "To find who you are." I said to myself: "If I don't know who I am, how do I know who to look for? Even if I find me, how do I know it's me? Besides, if I want to look for me, why do I need him? I can look myself or I could take my friends; we'd know where I was. Besides, what if I find the real me and I find out he's even worse than me Why do I need him? I don't make money for myself; I need a partner? Ten years ago I'd be glad to look for anybody; now I'm doing good, why should I look for him? He needs help? Why doesn't he look for me?'

The psychiatrist said: "The search for the real will have to continue. That will be $100 please. I said to him: "If this is not the real me why should I give you one hundred dollars? I'll look for the real me and let him give him a $100. But what if I find the real me and he doesn't think it's worth a hundred dollars? Then I've stuck my money with the real him." Then I said: "For all I know the real me might be going to psychiatrist altogether. Wouldn't it be funny if you're the real me and you owe me $100." So I said: "I'll tell you what, I'll charge you $50 and wwe'll call it even."

Dr Vera Robinson says in her book *Humour and Health Professions*:

'The belief that humour is necessary to human welfare and as a survival mechanism to cope with the heavies of living, is shared by many. In the enthusiasm and urging that we not lose this great benefit, we may end up appearing to propose a prescription or recipe which may seem too mechanical. Actually, these prescriptions are the plant food and fertiliser to aid in the growth of humour. 'The key word to remember is cultivate. We can teach or facilitate the learning of, the knowledge about, the concept of humour. But the attitude, the sense of humour must be inculcated. Cultivation implies the right atmosphere, patience and loving care, with the occasional application or artificial aids for revitalisation and stimulation.

A companion concept is that of habituation. The cultivation of humour requires consistent exposure and practice, and together with the understanding of the concept of humour, the sense of humour comes into bloom.

Humour and Health

The only medicine that needs no prescription, has no unpleasant taste and costs no money is laughter. Research has proven that people who laugh a lot, resist disease much more than the glum ones. Which only goes to prove that the surly bird always catches the germs!

(My jokes are all original – it's just that the people who originated them died years ago!)

Humour means health
Humour means health and it always has. The Latin word 'Humure' means to flow or be wet. The word 'humour' is derived from this. The doctors of

the past believed there were four fluids in the body that affected health and these were called Humors. The four fluids were blood, phlegm, yellow bile and black bile. If you had a happy-go-lucky attitude, it was because of your abundance of blood. If you were an emotional midget, it was because you had too much phlegm. Too much yellow bile meant you were irritable and an overdose of black bile made you melancholy. The correct balance of these Humors gave rise to the term In good humour. Today, if a work colleague behaves irrationally and obnoxiously, you might be well advised to humour them.

Doctor of laughter

In his book *Anatomy of an Illness,* Dr Norman Cousins describes how he regained his health following the development of collagen disease, which weakened the connective tissues of his muscles. He was given a one-in-500 chance of living. He regained his health through a program of Vitamin C and laughter therapy, which consisted of comic conversations with friends, and watching Marx Brother's films and *Candid Camera* TV show.

Dr Cousins theorised that if negative emotions could cause changes in body chemistry leading to ulcers, skin rashes, respiratory problems and even cancer, then positive emotions, laughter in particular, might change the diirection towards healing. He calls laughter 'internal jogging', a healthy massage of our inner organs – something like the effect you get from those magic- finger beds in motels, but without the coin box!

We have to take laughter seriously in two ways: first, psychologically, where we laugh at our own assumptions of ourselves: and second, physiologically, where we can gain health just through the exercise of laughter.

Dr Laurence peters agrees with this view. He states:

> 'Humour and laughter control pain in four major ways. One by distracting attention. Two by reducing tension. Three by changing attention. Four by increasing production of endorphins, the body's natural pain-killers.'

Dr William Fry, a psychologist at Stanford University, has been studying humour and laughter for more than 40 years. Through his articles shed in many books, journals, and magazines and his information presented on television shows, he has been educating the world about the bodily benefits of laughter. He states that laughter makes heart rate and blood circulation soar, just as effectively as an aerobic workout. Afterwards, the rate drops below average, providing relaxation. While this is happening, laughter is also stimulating the adrenalin flow, generating and sharpening your mind power. A buffo belly-laugh exercises the lungs and stimulates your circulation. Your heart and arteries benefit from the deep breathing that accompanies it, putting more oxygen in your blood. It's great to know that something that feels so good can be so good for you!

The healing professions have taken humour and laughter seriously. At present, we have an ever-growing number of laugh therapists and humour programs in hospitals and nursing homes. Dr Joel Goodman has helped hospitals set up "Humour Rooms equipped with humour trolleys, which carry books, tapes, games, magazines and props to patients in their beds. The idea is that when you make sick person laugh, they feel more comfortable. Besides, it makes them hopeful, even optimistic. This fosters self-healing.

From what we know about the healing value of laughter, its filtration in business life becomes more important. The following scenario becomes a possibility:

The Vice President of a large company went to inspect a new company building. On the way, his car collided head-on with another vehicle and he suffered concussion. Undaunted, he arrived at the building site and proceeded to suffer a series of incredible accidents, culminating in his falling 14 storeys and impaling himself on a massive wooden spike. He staggered back to the Head Office, bruised and battered, with this rather noticeable spike embedded in his chest. His boss said: Johnson, I've always known you have had stamina. Doesn't that hurt?' The weary corporate battler replied: 'No, only when I laugh.'

A Laughter First Aid Kit

With these obvious health benefits from humour and laughter, it's only natural that I suggest you start your own office *Laughter First Aid Kit*. Get a large briefcase, then ask each member of your team to bring something humorous each week. This way, you are continually replenishing the laughter gear. Enjoy each item for a while. When the fun fades from a particular item, store it in a special area called the laughter place'. Bring it out again from time to time, especially when new members join the team. Use your own touch of lunacy to build the laughing stock so that it suits the needs and fulfils the functions of your particular work environment. Your team might also enjoy the following:

- Creating a list of all the crazy and absurd excuses that are given. Record these in an exercise book or on a computer database so that everyone can contribute.
- Collect bizarre badges and wear them from time to time.
- Hang a sign over your visitor's chair stating: Please don't sit without telling a joke.' Then insist all visitors join in.

- Collect all the amusing business cards that you see or design.
- Print weird professional posters and have a poster gallery. Like the optometrist who hung this poster in his waiting room: If you don't see what you want, this is the right place to be!
- Have a photo album with photographs of everyone on the team - as a baby.
- Include a copy of Arthur Bloch's *Murphy's Law* in work library. This treasure of wisdom includes Heller's Law in its 'Hierarchiology Section' which states: The first myth of management is that it exists!'

Let your sense of fun and jocularity run wild and you will have no trouble coming up with comedy content.

> 'A sense of humour 15 a philosophical state of mind. It tells nature that we take her no more seriously than she takes us.'
>
> Renan

Laughter and More Laughter

If you laugh with people, you can work with them. Write a Ha Ha memo and pass it out to your team members. Ask them where they fit on this list:

- An *Ageist* is somebody who never laughs
- A *Geologist* studies the science of laughter
- A *Humorologist* studies the science of humour and is interested in the cause of humour
- A *Humorist* makes people laugh and iS interested in the effects of humour
- A *Megalaugher* is somebody who laughs 150 times a day
- A *Healthy Happy Person* laughs 20 times a day

I'm never short of laughs. Sometime ago, I went to see a real estate agent and asked him to show me some houses he had for sale. He did, then he asked me how much I had to spend. We both had a good laugh ... and then he showed me a whole new lot of houses!

Psychologists tell us that people laugh for many reasons: for example, after we have a victory or when the joke is on someone we don't like. We also laugh to give ourselves confidence, when we recognize ourselves in others, and when we are shocked, nervous, undecided or feeling friendly.

The laughter comes in various expressions – a smile, a chuckle, a titter, a scoff, a smirk, a giggle, or a belly-laugh. Observe your own laughter and listen to its sound. Play around with the pace. When you're

Laughing with someone, look into their eyes and laugh together. It seals a shared moment.

Laugh when you are alone. Laugh when there is no joke, just because laughter is good for you. You don't need a reason to feel good. You can develop the ability to laugh at and out of everyday situations.

Spend time with people who make you laugh, and laugh a lot themselves. It is important to work *Laugh Breaks* into your lives. Laughing is living in the now, and now is all there is. Laughter is the end result of a lifestyle of *Humour Attitude*. **It's the best HA HA skill of all!**

Humour and Selling

> He has a salesman's mentality. I once saw him add 15 and 15 and get 100. I asked him about the extra 70 and he said: 'Follow on potential.'

Being a salesperson and being a comedian are very similar. You have to respond to the way your audience responds to your performance. You need to think on your seat, and feet. You need Prepared Spontaneity With your carefully rehearsed material up your sleeve, you sense the situation then improvise, all the time adjusting and adapting your content and techniques, to build an emotional bond with the 'audience.'

Buying and selling are emotional and logical processes. Two great quotes from *The One Minute Manager* say it all:

> 'My selling purpose is to help people get the good feelings they want about what they bought and about themselves.'

> The wonderful paradox. I have more fun and enjoy more financial success when I stop trying to get what I want, and start helping other people get what they want.'

Used positively, humour can create a caring feeling between people. It can be a friendship that changes the traditional customer/ salesperson relationship.

Selling runs in my family. My great grandfather jumped ship in Sydney Harbour with only a penny in his pocket. He didn't spend that penny: he borrowed a bucket of fish and peddled them, door to door, for 20 years around the nooks and crannies of Botany Bay. When my great grandfather died, he ... still owed for the fish.

10 Ways to Sell Successfully.

These cover the stages from the pre-sale attitude to the post-sale behaviour.

1. Have a sense of Humour Attitude about your selling and yourself.
2. Use humour to warm up the prospect.
3. Use humour to explore and find out what they want while building rapport.
4. Use humour to display your product knowledge by selling your prospect's benefits.
5. Use humour to give examples of how they can benefit.
6. Use humour to overcome objections.
7. Use humour to maintain interest and attention during your sales presentation.
8. Use humour to test the buyers' response to your sales presentation.
9. Use humour to close the sale successfully.
10. Use humour to build a follow-up selling relationship.

It's hard to sell if you take yourself, your product or your profession too seriously. Selling begins with liking yourself, selling yourself, then selling your product or service.

Tom Hopkins says in *How To Master The Art Of Selling:*

> 'If you're the one who has the PhD degree for being a pessimistic, humourless depressive, there's hope. You can change yourself by learning to laugh and enjoy living again, anytime you decide to pay the price of laughing.
>
> The price of laughing I hat's right! Everything in the world has its price. You have to give up whatever has been stopping you from being healthier, enjoying life more, and living longer.
>
> Part of the price of laughter is that you have to stop enjoying bad habits. You have to give up your daily fix of

bad news. You have to decide that looking on the bright side of life, not the dark side, is what you do. You have to start looking for the chuckle that's hidden in every situation. You have to start finding and enjoying the good that's in everybody. Then you have to give up the pleasure of grumpiness, of putting people down, of having ulcers.

Start with a Warm Smile

Warming up the prospect and warming up the environment starts with a warm smile. Follow this with a *self-putdown joke* appropriate to the situation. When I sold books door to door, I would start off with conversational comedy to create a friendly mood. Something like:

> 'Being a door-to-door salesman has its moments. When I was being trained, my sales manager and myself were walking past a house, when we heard a woman crying for help! We dashed in and found her in all sorts of pain screaming: "Help me! Im having a baby." The sales manager said: "I don't know anything about this." She said: "Quick, the baby's coming: pull it out, pull it out, please." So he pulled it out and said: "What do I do now?" She said: "Slap it." He did and said: "And don't you go in there again."'

I would follow this up by saying that I hoped u there is no one having a baby in this house tonight. With the ice broken, I joked all the way through my sales presentation.

Be yourself by honestly sharing aspects of your life as a salesperson customer. This builds customer relations and helps find out what want so that you can then provide it. By using humour as the set-up line, and the probe question as the punchline, you can discover the information you need. Start by saying something like:

> 'Being a salesman is sometimes like being an accountant these days. You have to be as flexible as figures in the hand of a statistician. It can really add pressure. Jim, what are some of the extra stresses of your profession today?'

Once they relate specific problems, no matter how simple, you can now use humour to exaggerate the consequences of that problem if something is no done about it. I was discussing with an advertising executive the possibility of training him to improve his pitch response rate. He said: "One of the problems I have is finding time to do any preparation. I said: "It's a good thing you're not a builder then; there is no way you could sell anyone a penthouse in your new condominium.

You must have a blueprint; you have to do the preparation.

A Picture Sells More than a Thousand Words

When you know what your customer wants, sell the benefits of your product or service to fulfil those 'wants'. I use a lot of illustrations when I sell my *Humour In Presentation Programme*. The right humorous illustration can be worth the sales benefits. Build a small collection of humorous pictures that buyers would enjoy looking at.

Use humour to give examples of how they can benefit. Historically, pictures came before words, so spend a little time studying the way graffiti wit has been used. In advertising and selling it can add a wonderful touch or humanness into a selling situation. A good book to read for this research is, *Graphic Wit, The Art Of Humour In Design* by Steven Heller and Gail Anderson. In the book they talk about the difference between written and graphic humour.

> 'Though graphic humour shares many fundamental attributes of verbal humour, it is not encumbered by similar emotional complexities. Unhampered by the numerous light and dark psychological turns endemic to written or spoken humour, graphic design humour's primary agenda is to attract viewer attention and make a client's message more memorable. How this is done is indeed varied and fascinating, but sometimes comparatively simple to achieve.'

Graphic humour is under-used as a sales tool. Since we are in the media, driven by a see-it, feel-it, buy-it world, it's only natural that we demonstrate our products and services through the use of graphic humour. There are many ways to do this:

Posters	Slides	Comic Labelling
Funny Faxes	Bugs Bunny Socks	Joke Watches
Key Rings	Funny Photos	Silly Stickers
Comic Lettering	Business Cards	Daffy Duck Shirts
Cartoon Coasters	Colourful Braces	Comical Displays
Brand Badges	Picturesque Pens	Ties and Socks
Drinking Mugs	Novelty Note Pads	Signs

These are great ways to add some fun touches to your selling identity. Traditionally, humour and selling was all about a travelling salesman with a bag of jokes. Today, the consumers want the jokes, along with other techniques of humour, like graphic humour.

Objections Lead to Sales

Learning to love objections is one of the major breakthroughs a communicator can make. When your client objects, they are demonstrating that they die listening and emotionally involved in your selling process. While they are objecting, they are weighing up and evaluating what you are saying.

I love objections. When I was a stand-up comedian back in the early days of my career, I was working in striptease clubs. After I was introduced most nights, all you could hear was silence, or get oft and bring the girls back on'. I learnt early on not to take this personally, because when people collectively object to being somewhere, there's probably some strong emotional reason for it. I trained myself to love the non-response to my introductions to such an extent, that when I came out on stage and got a round of applause, I felt I had nothing to achieve because they were already sold. I wanted to earn the applause.

You can overcome objections by using your *Hunmour Atitudes and Actions*. See yourself as a slapstick comedian and the objections as a custard pie in the face. Learn to see the pie coming and prepare for it. Don't try to duck it: take it firmly on the face with a smile, and as a reminder of what business you're in. Learn to handle objections with a spirit of play.

> Like the suave salesman who was copping every objection in the book from the client. He put his *Humour Attitude* into action and said: 'Sir! This is a wonderful suit. I guarantee your best friends would not recognize you in this suit. Just have a bit of a walik outside in the sunlight.' The client went outside and came back in a few seconds later. The salesman darted upto him and said, with a big smile on his face: 'Good morning stranger. How can I help you.'

The Philosophy of Prepared Spontaneity

Earlier, we briefly looked at how humour can be used to gain and maintain attention. The performance philosophy - Prepared Spontaneity - can also be used here. Prepared Spontaneity involves being sensitive to your client, how they are behaving and how they are responding to your sales presentation. By having a range of one-liners, funny anecdotes, jokes and other humour devices 'up your sleeve, you can be prepared tor any event. By rehearsing these pieces well and choosing humour, which suits your personality, it will appear that you have a 'natural humour style. The customer need never know that you have used these devices to regain their attention and to send the discussion in a chosen direction.

You can use humour to *Test the Buyers Response To Your Sales Presentation* by becoming skilled in using what I call, *roving pieces*. These are 30-second pieces of humour you can use to pull back attention, or test your buyer's response. It's important to have roving pieces on as many different subjects as you need. Roving pieces are client appeal grabs that allow you to monitor and challenge your client's responses.

Roving pieces can be

- Humorous
- Entertaining
- Emotionally moving
- Motivating

This depends on how your client is responding. Each client is different in their response, their comprehension, attitudes, values, needs and wants. Having a variety of roving pieces that you can weave in and out will allow you to zone into your client's specialties and build a bond with the buyer. The secret is to spend time preparing your range of roving pieces.

Make a list of areas in which you need to get attention.

- Different buyers' response behaviours
- Product benefits and advantages
- All the possible needs and wants of buyers
- Write roving pieces that relate and identify with them

Some examples would be:

- Self-putdown
- Self-disclosure
- Identity trustability
- Embarrassing moments
- Lovable subjects
- Emotional impact
- Community opinions
- Current events

Reactive Buyer Relate Lines

Your buyer's response continually changes depending on what you are saying and how you are saying it. When you notice a subtle negative change in the response, think back to what you said that caused the negative response.

Then use what I call reactive buyer relate lines to turn that negative response into a positive one. These lines help bring the two points of view back together again. If you realise that a statement may have appeared political, your reactive buyers relate line could be:

'I don't usually make political references and I never tell political jokes, because most of the time they get elected.'

By continually using a variety *of reactive buyer relate lines*, you are responding positively to your buyers. You are saying: 'I know how you feel; your opinion is important.' This prevents a communication gap, allowing you to move on with your sale.

Self-Deprecation Humour Sells

The last thing you want to do is confuse the buyer when closing, so deliver your product information clearly. Ask for the order sensitively and smoothly. When your buyer completely understands the situation, you can use humour to soften the tension and reinforce that this is what they want, or to highlight certain facts.

The best humour to use is *self-deprecation*. Create self-deprecation humour on a variety of different subjects to use as roving pieces when closing. Money, age, duties, children and time all make good subjects. For example, if you are my age, fifty something, you would bend down to open your brief ca to get the contract out, and as you straighten up you might say:

> 'You know when I was 26 the creaking of the bed is what woke up the kids. Now that I'm 50, it's the creaking of my bones when I get out of bed that wakes up the kids.'

> When I bend my arm to put on my singlet, it sounds like a safe door locking.'

> When I bend my back to put on my socks, it sounds like a musician playing the xylophone.'

With self-putdown humour, you are signalling to the buyer that you know who you are, that you have a certain inner confidence and feel secure enough to laugh at yourself. Never put down your pride in your job, nor anything you are too sensitive about, and never sound self-abusive otherwise the buyer will think you don't like yourself

Self-Deprecation Humour Chart

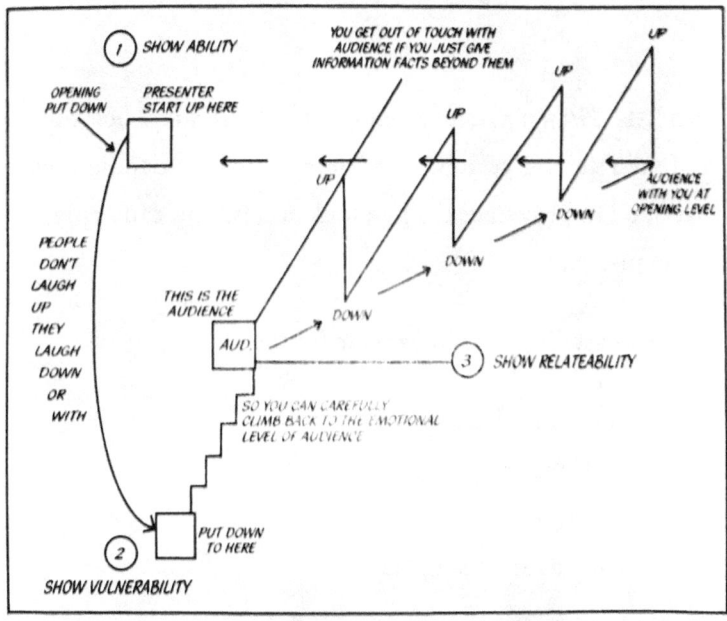

1. Start by using an opening putdown line
2. People will laugh down' with you. Use another putdown line to show your vulnerability, so you can carefully climb back to the emotional level of the audience.
3. This shows the audience that you can relate to them. You then continue to build yourself up and put yourself down to keep them moving with you. Be careful not to build yourself up too far or use information that the audience cannot relate to because this will make you go beyond your audience's level of appreciation and you get out of touch with them.
4. Begin the process again.

Humour Opens an Ongoing Selling Relationship

When you close a sale, you open a relationship. The same can be said when you use humour in selling. It's used to establish an atmosphere of honesty and empathy. You can refer to them as a new friend and look at using humour as a way of building a trusting, joking relationship with them.

Make two lists: *Humour Action and Humour Attitude.* Look through all aspects of your selling communication and make a detailed list of the areas that need improvement. Then look at how you can apply *Humour Action* to do just that.

Humour Action selling area improvement List:

- Questioning to discover wants
- Small talk between product information
- Negotiating
- Presenting a range of options
- Quality line
- Selling to different people
- Putting feeling into communication
- Stopping your mind from wandering
- Asking for the order.
- Poor listening skills.
- Handling objections.
- Lack of confidence in your use of language.
- Timing
- Building rapport into the relationship.

Different Humour Selling Techniques

You are now ready to pick the priority areas to improve through the use of humour. One salesman I know collects and uses different techniques of humour to use with different types of people.

He had quite a lot of success with the you know it's going to be a bad day when...' technique.

He uses them at appropriate times during the presentations. For example:

> 'You know it's going to be a bad day when ... you forget your mother-in-law's birthday, and she's a major shareholder in the business.'

> 'Your taxi driver turns out to be a kamikaze pilot who's still trying.'

Humour Attitude Selling Improvement List

Explore your *Humour Action* options; selling is also about being creative. Now make the second list, the Humour Attitude selling areas of improvement. When you can demonstrate that you have a sense of humour about yourself, your performance and products, people feel much more relaxed in your company. Look at all areas of your life as a salesperson, and list all aspects of it that cause you stress, frustration, fear, unhappiness and anger. Some of these could be:

- Being kept waiting
- People not phoning you back
- When you miss a surefire sale
- Keeping some customers happy

- Telephone call resistance
- Solving problems that could have been prevented
- Ignoring your buyer's personal prejudices
- Making small group presentations
- Getting stuck in the traffic, making you late for an appointment
- Rude people on the telephone
- Not being able to motivate yourself
- Being rejected
- Receptionists who play games

When you have completed your list, then prioritise it, and go to work looking for *Humour Attitude* ways to put more fun back into your sales lifestyle could be the frustration of working on a large account over a long period. What you could do is put $5 aside for every hour you work on it, so have more to fall back on if you don't get it. You would still have money to take your wife on a night out. Esther Blumenfield and Lynne Alpern say in their book *The Smile Connection*:

> 'Selling successfully requires a high level of enthusiasm. If you carry over negative feelings of rejection, frustration, or anger from one customer to the next, your effectiveness will suffer significantly. Therefore, let humour help you unwind, take a few minutes in between appointments to look for humour in your situation, put your aggravations in proper perspective, and create an optimum frame of mind for successful selling.'

No matter how well you develop your sense of humour, there will come a time when you will suffer as a result of your customer's lack of humour.

A clothing shop proprietor, called Harrison, had a suit he had been trying to sell for years. He called his head salesman in and said: 'Frank, we have had this suit for seven years. I'm going on a holiday. When I get back I want the suit sold, or you're fired. When he arrived back, the suit was gone. As a smile flashed across his face, he heard groaning and moaning from one of the changerooms. He walked in and there was Frank, covered in blood and bruises, lying on thee floor with his clothes ripped to shreds. Frank what happened to you? he asked. 'Mr Harrison, I sold the suit. Thats wonderful. Harrison said. 'But what happened? Well, sir, a blind man came in and I got him to buy the suit. "That's great, but what happened to you? "His seeing-eye dog didn't have a sense of humour.'

Humour and Customer Service- Creative Customer Service

Stew Leonards is a 100,000 square foot grocery store in the US known as the Disneyworld of supermarkets. The dairy store owes its success to a combination of tough business practices and uncompromising service to customers. It personifies Paul Hawken's statement that laughter and delight produce a bond with customers because they build trust and support, together with good quality, good prices, and by providing an entertaining shopping experience.

We can use humour in creative customer caring to keep customers happy. Happy is a metaphor of humour. A happy customer is a satisfied customer, one who, along with purchasing products or services, purchases good feelings. Therefore, customer service is about selling good feelings.

To make someone feel good, you have to feel good. To truly achieve total customer service, an organisation has to focus its attention on making all it's employees feel good.

> A manager got out of the lift at work. Instantly, a band started to play, an orchid was pinned to his suit, a cheque for $10,000 was pressed into his hand, he was photographed on all sides, and a TV camera beamed down on him. 'You are the most cherished manager, the Master of Ceremonies told him, smiling broadly. 'Now, can you tell us what you are going to be doing today?' 'Yes,' said the manager, 'I'm going to the CEO to resign. I can't stand all this attention.'

Creative customer caring means using humour and its metaphors to first get customers, then convert them into loyal customers. This can be achieved by taking the following six steps.

1. Develop a Customer-Centred Corporate Culture

One company I know has a two-sided sign, which says, 'I am your customer; treat me special', on the front and, I am your livelihood; treat me special. on the back. Each person in the office has to treat the employee who is wearing the sign that day, as if they were a real customer. This leads to a lot of comic situations and allows the staff to focus continuously on improving their customer care.

2. Create a Happy Environment that Empowers Your Employees

A lot of companies are using a theatre sports team to run an improvisation workshop for those employees in the front line who have to offer constant. courteous service. This has two positive benefits:

- The service staff get to re-create stressful situations, and play around with them
- They are being taught to think creatively and humorously on their feet, so that they can handle any situation with an appropriate response

3. Research Your Customers. What Are Their Wants?

This is done in many ways. Two aspects are qualitative and quantitative research done by the marketing department, and the employee customer interaction in the front line. This cannot be over done. I don't really like the term front line; it's too much like war terminology. May I suggest that these people are called the 'friendly line'.

A friend of mine was thinking about opening a shoe store in Caulfield, Victoria, which has a large Jewish population. As he was doing the research on the business plan, he learned to speak Hebrew and study the Jewish customers. Specifically, he studied the wonderful Jewish sense of humour, so he would have fun with them, before he opened the store. I can assure the anti-Semitic lobby that for years he went diddle-diddle-liddle-lowing all the way to the bank.

4. Make Your Customers Feel Special and Appreciated

Customers need to feel important and wanted. The idea is to make their experience of doing business with you a positive one. Focus on being friendly, take a thorough look at your work environment, and remove all objects and procedures that affect your 'friendly line of employees humouring their customers. For example:

An expensive gift shop was having a lot of items broken from customers handling the merchandise. So instead ot putting up a sign that said, 'Do Not Touch, the sign read: 'Lovely to look at, delightful to hold. But if you drop it, we mark it sold.

Another aspect of humouring your clients is to get your friendly employees to take part in humour awareness workshops. Telling your employees to smile just doesn't work. Teach them not only to smile, but to keep smiling, even when they make mistakes, and they will.

Take the airline hostess who had just finished a two-week course in pleasing customers. She was having trouble with a man who kept insulting the lady sitting next to him. He was saying: Lady, your baby is the ugliest baby I have ever seen. And the woman was terribly upset and kept screaming: This man is insulting my baby. On the third attempt, the hostess said: 'Look, calm down madam. Don't get upset. I will remove the man. Get a drink of water for yourself, and a banana for your monkey and everything will be all right.'

5. Have a System to Service Your Customers Properly

It takes months to find a loyal customer; if you keep them waiting you can lose them in seconds. A big part of treating people importantly is treating them promptly. Meeting deadlines is one of the pressure points of customer service, and can also be a unique selling point. Comet Couriers promise: Absolutely, Positively Overnight.' At lunchtime Pizza Hut says: "Your pizza in 10 minutes, or it's free.' When you are delivering jokes, and you don't get a laugh, you use what I call a 'saver'.

The same techniques can be used when you are delivering goods to a customer. If, because of a technical hitch, they will arrive late, have a customer service saver.

In my business, I sometimes have to cancel seminars and workshops, thereby inconveniencing people. When this happens, I send them two tickets to a Comedy club, with the updated program schedule and a little note explaining the situation. I deliberately don't use humour in the note, as I don't wish to appear uncaring. For such occasions, I have a permanent table booked at a comedy club, on a Tuesday night. If I don't have to change my schedule, I send the gift tickets to a person who referred people to me, or a loyal customer.

One of the many professional speakers I have trained, Laurie Smale, speaks about achieving excellence in customer service. He tells the story of the managing director of one of Melbourne's large bulk-buying stores who was awakened at two o'clock in the morning by a telephone call. The man on the end of the phone said: 'I just called to tell you how much I appreciate your goods and your services. There are not many stores these days that give you such excellent terms and swift attention. I bought a washing machine from you about four months ago and it's an absolutely fantastic piece of machinery, a real marvel! If you ever want me to do any advertising for you, just let me know. My name is Tom Wilkins. The manager was still very groggy from sleep and was trying to get his bearings. He muttered: 'Mr Wilkins, do you realise it's the middle of the night? Did you have to wake me up to tell me about something you bought from us months ago?'

'Well, sir Wilkins replied, 'it's just been delivered!'

6. Develop Methods of Getting Regular Customer and Employee Feedback

One important aspect of creative customer caring is to get your custom to tell you the aspects of your business about which they are unhappy. Jim Cathcart, in an article in *Successful Selling*, says:

'In the late '70s, a study of customer satisfaction was done by Technical Assistant Research Programmers, I & C Tarp. Among its findings were:

- 96 per cent of the unhappy customers of an average business, never tell the business of their dissatisfaction
- Dissatisfied customers typically tell nine to 20 other people about it.

Your customers have the answers to your success: through the ongoing process of servicing them. Make them feel comfortable enough about your company to give you vital information about their dissatisfaction. There are many ways to do this:

- Suggestion boxes
- Checklists
- Focus groups
- Questionnaires
- Feedback sheets

Humour in one sense is a method for all positive experiences. If you come away from a situation where you are feeling good, some aspect of *Humour Action* was involved.

Develop a Humour Method Questionnaire to pass on to your customers to get the information you need from them about the experiences of doing business with your company. Ask questions like:

1. Did you experience any discourtesy?
2. Do we have the ability to admit mistakes?
3. Was there any indication of a lack of tolerance?
4. Were you treated with the utmost friendliness?
5. Were the staff smiling from the inside, or the outside?
6. Did you find any unwillingness to help
7. Was teamwork evident from our staff at all times?
8. Did you feel that you were treated cheerfully at all times:
9. Was doing business with our company a joyful experience
10. Did you get the sense from our staff that doing business with us is fun?
11. Were you offended in any way with our service?
12. Would you say that our company demonstrates an attitude of humour during the service process?

C.W. Metcalf and Roma Felible say in their book, *Lighten Up*:

> 'Keeping customers happy is such an important part of a flight attendant's job that South West Airlines has made humour part of the job description. The airline recruits people with a strong sense of humour who, along with serving well and smiling and communicating well, have been known to recite the safety regulations in rap, bring out a guitar and sing, and wear costumes on Halloween flights. According to the Wall Street Journal, a standard interview question asks job candidates to divulge their most embarrassing moment, and how they got out of it with humour.'

What do the customers think of the happy attendants? Do they long for increased gravity in the air? To find out, in April 1991, South-West began having their frequent flyers interview flight attendant candidates, and almost across the board, they said the Wall Street journal's frequent flyers choices were almost identical to the airlines.

Over the years I have trained many close-up comedians: comedians, with extra skills like juggling or magic, who walk around tables in a restaurant, or mix in with the guests waiting to go into the meeting or conference. It's a highly sensitive and skilled aspect of communication. One thing they must all have is a passion for entertaining people, backed up with a passion please. In close-up communication, both the attitude and action aspects humour are necessary. Creative customer caring must be a major part or a organisations purpose as it leads to your customers feeling good about doing business with you.

Chapter Two Summary
How Humour Can Work For You In Business And Life

1. Humour helps you survive the pressures of the corporate world.
2. Humour helps you survive life's stresses.
3. A Humour Attitude operates as a complete support system.
4. Humour is a great way to gain attention.
5. Humour builds relationships.
6. Humour motivates and increases productivity.
7. Preparing a send-up line helps you cope with trouble.
8. It's hard to sell if you take yourself, your product or your profession too seriously.
9. Having a healthy Humour Attitude is the same as having a strong self-image.
10. Being a great salesperson and being a comedian are very similar.
11. A warm selling environment starts with a warm smile.
12. Humour, used successfully, 1s a powerful social lubricant.
13. The best humour to use in selling is self-deprecation.
14. When you close a sale, you open a relationship.
15. Use Humour Action and Humour Attitude.
16. Customer service with humour makes creative customer service.
17. Humour helps to develop a customer-centred culture.
18. A happy environment empowers employees.
19. Develop a Humour Method Questionnaire.
20. If you want to be a successful professional, you need to use humour successfully.

CHAPTER 3

Developing Your Humour Attitude

'Humour retlects the character, personality, intelligence, cultural background and social class of a person. The kinds of jokes you tell and enjoy, even the tone and fullness of your laugh, mirror your personality. A study of humour is a study of people, how they feel about themselves and others. The temper of their times, their outlook on life.'

Harvey Mindess

Harvey Mindess has greatly influenced our humour outlook on life, especially through his breakthrough book *Laughter and Liberation*.

In business, we are trained to take our seriousness very seriously, but true Success means developing your sense of humour and taking your seriousness humorously. This gives you the capacity to see yourself, your problems, your responsibilities, your challenges and your behaviour in general, seriously and humorously at the same time. If you're in a meeting with important clients you start to take the negative remarks of one of them too seriously, It can affect your natural responses and sour the situation.

Thinking humorously, you might visualise the agitator as Groucho Marx in a movie and you as one of the audience members. This would prevent you from taking the sarcasm personally and enable you to enjoy whatever humour it offers. There is humour in any situation, so stop your negative responses and view it from the *Humour Attitude* angle. A lot of people have a sense of both how to use humour and the art of humour. Because of this, their external personality, their humour persona, is developed to a certain level. They are intelligent and have an innate understanding of the science of humour and the structure, components and psychological functions humour serves. However, they have not developed their *Humour Attitude*, which is the most important part of using humour successfully.

A *Humour Attitude* is a way of perceiving, seeing, feeling and enjoying the uncomfortable, unpredictable realities of life as well as the mundane, ordinary, everyday, boring activities of life.

A woman executive friend of mine knew how to use her *Humour Attitude*. Her husband had been unemployed for 18 months and she had been eating his attempts at cooking. Then one morning at breakfast she said, I'll have cold eggs, burnt bacon and fruit not in season. She got them!

It's a well-known fact that most of us use only 10 per cent of our brain. I believe we only use five per cent of our *Humour Attitude*. Again, we all know how valuable it is to have a sense of humour. Imagine what a personal and competitive advantage you would have it you nourished your five per cent towards 25 per cent.

A sense of humour is:

- An acquired attitude
- A practised perception
- A trained tolerance
- A learnt lifestyle

You weren't born with a sense of humour. It is made up of your beliefs, values, judgments, character traits, feelings and thoughts, which are formed by environmental conditioning, and patterns of learning. They can be enhanced and even completely changed if you desire. I believe that shaping your *Humour Attitude* is as important to your personal enjoyment and your professional success as your honesty, education and IQ. Your *Humour Attitude* controls and influences the way people act and respond to:

- What you do and how you do it
- What you say and how you say it

The Qualities of the Humour Attitude

'Our psychological abilities develop gradually affected by a host of factors. lo whatever degree of excellence they attain, neither our intelligence, nor our compassion, for example, is entirely innate. Nor can either be turned on by a simple act of will. Our sense of humour is no different. While inborn qualities nmay predispose it and conscious effort may facilitate it, in the larger sense it waxes and wanes as part of our psychic economy. It is determined by our other means and in turn contributes to them. A Humour Atitude is made up of many qualities and moods.'

Harvey Mindess

A list of qualities and moods of the *Humour Atitude*

Accommodation	Adaptation	Affection
Balance	Celebration	Controversy
Consideration	Courage	Contradictory
Derisive	Diplomacy	Delightfulness
Empathy	Enthusiasm	Equilibrium
Flexibility	Freedom	Fun
Generosity	Happiness	Harmony
Honesty	Humility	Incongruous
Iconoclastic	Imaginative	Intelligence
Impulsive	Irreverence	Impertinent
Kindly	Joyfulness	Lightheartedness
Nonsensical	Off-beat	Optimism
Playfulness	Provocative	Reasoning
Reconciliation	Resiliency	Respect
Ridiculousness	Sincerity	Spontaneity
Tolerance	Trivial	Unconventional
Unpretentiousness	Vital	Whimsically
Zaniness		

Some of these we have already discussed and others we will look at later, but I have chosen 10 of the above qualities on which to expand. I feel they represent a broad spectrum of a sense of humour; what I refer to as 'Humour *Attitude*'.

The Top 10 Qualities of a Humour Attitude

1. Flexibility
2. Enthusiasm
3. Unconventionality

4. Optimism
5. Courage
6. Balance
7. Humility
8. Adaptation
9. Fun
10. Freedom

1. Flexibility

We have to learn to be as flexible as figures in the hands of a statistician. A flexible attitude saves your back from breaking when you're out of your comfort zone or being forced to bend over backwards. The only alternative if you want to climb the corporate ladder, is to backflip out the back door or to sky-dive from the boardroom window.

To improve your flexibility, begin by re-evaluating your values, beliefs traditions, thoughts, processes and behavioural patterns. By looking a yourself through the magnifying glass of flexibility, you can see the blemishes, blotches and blackheads that are distorting your appearance, as seen by others. Ask them how you appear to them: the way you look, your body language, and the way you phrase what you say. It's important to be open to all their suggestions and all their suggestions about suggestions. Now apply the same magnifying glass to your pet issues, ideas, judgments, customs and goals.

Once you can see your blemishes, you realise how they block the way in which others see you. Don't be afraid to use your blemishes. Just apply a flexible attitude to these aspects of yourself and you'll begin to see them in a different way. A *Humour Attitude* makes it possible to think things through, around, about, over, in and out!

You have the flexibility to see your imperfections through a kaleidoscope of humour sides:

Exaggeration:

There was a fellow who was a little bit like myself - 40 and fat. He wasn't worried about his portly posture. "The good thing about middle-aged spread, he used to say, 'is that it brings people closer together.

Reversal:

I don't want to complain about mother nature but wouldn't we business executives be a lot more attractive if she had given us middle-aged flat instead of fat.

Mistaken Identity:

The workshop leader said: 'Having a huge middle-aged spread can be embarrassing. Once I walked in front of a group with a white shirt on. The audience, as one, screamed, "The projector screen has arrived"!

Frustrated Expectations:

The middle aged manager promised himself he Would diet to lose his middle-aged spread. He couldn't do it; he now has an old-aged ranch.

2. Enthusiasm

Are you enthusiastic and work 10 hours a day? Well, Don't worry in no time you'll be the boss and work 15 hours a day and do all the worrying!

Enthusiasm, like all attitudes and activities, can be positive and negative. So having a sense of proportion has a lot to do with developing a sense of humour. We need to be enthusiastic about all the vital areas of our life: family, health, spiritual, personal, community, financial. For most of my life I have been enthusiastic about money - mostly to do with spending it; not too enthusiastic about learning about it or how to invest it! Some time ago, I went to a seminar on financial management and the cashier who was taking the money had run out of change and we were all lined up waiting to get in. Everyone was becoming tense and angry. The fee was $50. When my turn came, I gave the cashier $100, and with a friendly smile and in a loud voice said: 'Here's $100; I'm paying for you to join the seminar. We are as enthusiastic for you to learn about financial management as we are for ourselves. We want this seminar to start, right?' The crowd agreed with me, the cashier laughed and relaxed, and people began helping by getting the right money among themselves.

Don't hold back on being enthusiastic and using humour communication. Let your impulses, instincts and insights free up your enthusiasm. Enthusiasm expressed good-naturedly through humour can free your creative fortitudes and feelings and do the same for those around you.

Having a sense of humour Is having a go in lite. Be eager to do your best and succeed, but don't crucify yourself because you didn't win; be fulfilled because you gave it your best shot. You know your enthusiasm will motivate you to begin again.

And if life has zapped your enthusiasm, try this mental exercise:

Imagine you are walking along the silver sands of a sun-kissed, secluded beach, and you bend down and pick up a $2. Under the coin are two more

$2 coins, and under those are four more and then eight more. You load your pockets, you load your car, you're jumping about. What will you do now What are you thinking? How are you feeling? How enthusiastic are feeling now? Keep this enthusiasm ticking over.

3. Unconventionality

Impulsive, iconoclastic, provocative, off-beat, zany and contradictory are all ways to describe the attitude of unconventionality. How many of these are you known for? When you're sober I mean! Most of the great business thinkers, achievers, innovators and entrepreneurs were unconventional in their thinking. Walt Disney, Rupert Murdoch, Henry Ford, Lee Iacocca, could all do things contrary to popular belief. As you see, a *Humour Attitude* is cost-efficient and the lack of it can be a serious business liability. The exciting thing is that these days it is quite conventional to have a sense of humour in corporate life.

A *Humour Attitude* begins when you can break free from your own personal and social conformities. This is best done by taking part in some of these unconventional practices:

> Humorous Customs:
> It can be as simple as combing your hair with the opposite hand to what you normally use.

> Comedy Customs:
> When you shake hands with someone, dont let go!

> Burlesque Beliefs:
> Never drop names, ! never do! I only said that to Bill Cosby, Tom Peters and Edward De Bono the other day.

Rules About Humour:
Never tell a joke before breakfast, and if you have to do
so, have your breakfast first!

Our life is spent imprisoned by morality, reason, seriousnes, time, self-image and profession. Unconventional behaviour can be the key to letting out your creativity, energy, vision and humour.

When you behave differently you start to:

- Think differently
- Feel differently
- Act differently Spontaneously

Let me relate what happened to me one day. My now ex-wife Edith came down from her office upstairs and was going to the supermarket to get some stationery. I glanced up at her and looked back at my writing; she walked out of the shop into the street and a smile came to my face. I had noticed a big blotch of blue biro running the length of her upper lip, resembling an untidy moustache. My behaviour of not telling her was unconventional. If I had I would have spoilt all the fun for her. She came back giggling and laughing.

Bring some humour into your life intentionally by taking a vanity, an idea, a passion, a work situation, or a person and lavish unconventional action on them. This kind of humour experience brings the power to homour and enjoy all areas and aspects of yourself and your business life as you send up your 'usual belief and behaviour.

4. Optimism

You have a choice in life, either to be humorously aware or cynically detached. The choice of feeling happy or unhappy, to be an optimist or a pessimist, is not something you make once but a thousand times a day. You can get into the habit of letting your subconscious make these decisions for you. However, to train for HA HA skills, you first have to take control consciously, optimistically. A humorous optimist is someone who is aware of the negative but lives in the positive, someone who invents the aeroplane and then invents the parachute. He or she is someone who looks into a tunnel and sees the light at the end of it, then thinks: "That could be a train coming towards me! Under no delusion that the bad things in life exist, the humour optimist sees the good in the evil, the beauty in the ugly, the best in the worst.

Australians are the ultimate optimists; we know when the insects take over the world, they'll remember with gratitude how we took them along on all our picnics. It's a practical, resourceful, creative, self-confident optimism. There was a cartoon some time ago about a farmer driving through the bush when the fan belt broke and the car stopped. He turned to his passenger and said: She'll be right, mate!' He then jumped out of the car, ran into the bush, killed a snake, skun it, tied the two ends together, replaced the fan belt with it, started up the car and drove off. Daily successes like this in the early years gave the Australian the optimism and confidence to approach any situation with an attitude of, 'No worries!'; 'No Problems!"; 'She'll be apples!' She'll be Jake!'; and the much misunderstood 'She'll be'right mate'! Australians know they can use their innovation and inventiveness to come with an answer. As a last resort, they're left with the optimistic answer: 'You gotta laugh, mate!' The following joke explains this humour optimism attitude:

An English migrant walked up to an optimistic Australian friend and said: 'I'm bankrupt, out of business, I've lost my house and car. I don't have a cent coming in! His Aussie mate said: Be thankful you aren't one of your creditors!'

5. Courage

> Courage l have love, faith, trust, gratitude and courage.
>
> Phillip Young

Courage is a word that not only relates to humour but all our endeavours. Taking a humour attitude towards trouble is a creative and surviving way to show courage. It's an acquired mental and emotional strength that gives you the fortitude to overcome the fears and frustrations blocking your path to personal mastery and professional happiness, and to make your own fare. Courage has a role to play in both aspects of the HA HA Principle. The second 'HA, Humour Action, is risking rejection continually! And you can benefit from the first 'HA', *Humour Atitude,* in most of life's troubles. Overcoming sickness, unemployment, divorce, sexual anxieties, bankruptcies, disappointments, and all kinds of inescapable stress takes courage. wallowing in your own pain can become pleasantly safe.

Allan Klein, in his courageous book, *The Healing Power of Humour,* mentions some humour-coping strategies such as.

The Joke Jitsu
In this exercise we reverse the good news - bad news humour type. Start with your bad news and turn it into good news.

> The bad news is that my suitcase fell apart as it came of the airline; the good news is that it was the first one out of the baggage chute!

Trivialising Humour
Take a major fear and turn it into humour by trivialising it.

> I hope there is not a third world war; I don't think I Could handle rock 'n roll war songs!

The Round Circle

Dr Walter E. O'Connell says: If you are passionately pursuing guilt, try feeling guilty about feeling guilty!'

The Defence

I read somewhere that Oscar Wilde, on his deathbed in a shabby untidy room, said: 'Either that wallpaper will have to go, or I will!' Then he died.

The Exaggeration

Start taking control, instantly wiping out negative thoughts by magnifying them beyond the limits of reality. You need the courage to ask the boss for a rise. Imagine that he says no, then he stands on his desk, takes a megaphone and begins screaming to the world why he can't afford to give it to you. This goes on for five minutes, then two men in white coats take your struggling boss away. Then, of course, you're offered his job.

The Mistaken Identity

Norman Cousins, who showed tremendous courage by healing himself with the help of others and a *Humour Atitude*, used this technique: A nurse came in at his breakfast time with a specimen bottle. When she wasn't looking, he poured his apple juice into the bottle and passed it to her. She took a look and said:, 'We are a little cloudy today, aren't we? After taking a swig from the bottle, Cousins said: by George, you're right. Lets run it through again.'

To be a leader making decisions and accepting responsibilities so that you set examples to others, takes courage. An expanded awareness of the *Humour Atritude* can give you the courage to go closer to the edge, the techniques and tactics to tackle your personal future, and the vision and wisdom to win.

6. Balance

> If a man goes after money he's 'Money Mad'! If he doesn't go after it, he lacks ambition. If he keeps it, he's a miser. If he spends it, he's extravagant. If he inherits it, he's a parasite. It he earns it after a lifetime of hard labour, he's a fool who's got nothing out of life.

This humour formula is called "The Pendulum' where you swing backwards and forwards from one perception to another. The *Humour Attitude* is to maintain a balance between one paradoxical point and the other, between one extreme of behaviour and the other.

A balance between seriousness and nonsense

- Work and play
- Striving and relaxing
- Performance and peace
- Challenge and calm
- Discipline and letting loose
- Tears and laughter

It's about being who others want you to be and being who you want to be

A *Humour Attitude* means balanced behaviour and a practised perception to see the ludicrous side of life. Using this saves you from losing your poise as you go about your restricted daily rituals in the mirror maze of reality. It also keeps you from falling into the "Too Serious Zone'. This ability gives you both the weapon and the shield as an outlet for your anger, disagreements and criticisms, in a way that's socially acceptable. Eliminate those frustration and feelings and you are again centred, focused and balanced.

Finding harmony between the fears, stresses and challenges of achievement and the enjoyment, laughter and relaxation of self-indulgence is vitally important to your health, happiness and success. One way to find it is to reward yourself, psychologically, biologically and physiologically.

Put time aside to watch a comedy movie; take your children to that pantomime; listen to your favourite political satirist on the radio; buy yourself a humour book, executive toy, or surrealistic painting.

Use the Pendulum formula to study a crisis, conflict, challenge, responsibility or decision to help you move from one course of action to the other. This gives you an overall view of the circumstances and Situations involved and can only help in making 'zero defect decisions'. A great example of this pendulum pondering comes from a conversation between two executives.

> One executive says: 'We can always hire a marketing manage, he will boost business.'
>
> 'That's good!'
>
> 'Yes, but we don't have an office for him and that's bad.'
>
> 'Well, we could put him with Jones; he needs motivating, that's good.'

'Yes, but it would make his office too crowded and could push one of them out the window, that's bad.'

'Well, the swimming pool is right under the window, that's good.'

'Yes, but there is no water in the pool, that's bad.'

'Well, if he knew what I hope he knows about marketing, he will fall into a hole in new territory and that's good.'

The bottom line in business is balance. Balance the team, balance the behaviour, balance your attitudes, balance the books!

7. Humility

There is one saying which sums up humility for me:

'The higher the monkey climbs, the more you see his backside!'

As humans, our ego requires that we are taken seriously. As professionals, our self-image requires that we consider ourselves great. Our pride requires that other people look on us as important. Otherwise, we feel inferior and a failure, and we fear we will amount to nothing. However, this is not really the way it works. You don't have to be seen as sombre and over serious to feel powerful, successful and worthwhile. If you spend a little time observing the greatest leaders of our world, you will see leaders who practise humility. These are people who know they are human, vulnerable, imperfect, at times impatient, troubled, angered, aggressive and stressed. They also know that for most of the time they are tolerant, modest, unpretentious and humble.

The funny thing about humility is, that the moment you think you have it, you've lost it! It's like being proud about not being proud.

The lack of humility in certain businesspeople can be funny and very entertaining for the rest of us, as beautifully demonstrated by John Cleese as the owner of Fawlty Towers. But a lack of humility in oneself can be tragic.

It fogs our perception, derails our performance and can prevent us from fulfilling our purpose. To top it off, it prevents us from seeing the funny side of ourselves.

A *Humour Attitude* sees every side of every side of ourselves. In my case, I'm lucky, I can't feel anything but humility! Only last week I was at this really 'toffy' cocktail party. I've never seen so many famous successful people in one place at one time. In fact, I was the only person in the room I'd never heard of!

Here are some Humour Humility Activities to implement:

Intelligence Comparisons
Write down your most insightful philosophy to do with life. Then buy a book of quotations and compare it.

Humour Achievement
Buy a copy of *Who's Who* and *The Guiness Book of Records* and check to see if your name is in them. If not, write down your most important achievement and compare it.

Expressing Kindness
Find, re-write and learn three jokes based on kindness and compassion. Then use them as many times as possible.

Humility Record

Make a list of 10 people in whose company you would feel humble. Make a second list of 10 people in whose company you don't currently feel humble, but will the next time you are with them.

Humility Remembrance

Think of the time in your life when you felt most humble. Write a 200-word humorous story about it and use it when the occasion arises.

8. Adaptability

I think this well-known joke will show you to what length we will have to adapt to survive.

> The Lone Ranger and Tonto were galloping along the prairie, when all of a sudden a bunch of hostile Indians appeared at the front of them. They turned to the right - more screaming savages! They turned to the left - more wide-eyed redskins! They turned completely around and were confronted by more bloodthirsty savages. The Lone Ranger and Tonto were completely surrounded by hostile Indians! The Lone Kanger turned to his faithful companion tor 25 years and said:, 'Well Tonto, it looks like this is it. And Tonto said: 'What you mean? Paleface.

A *Humour Attitude* is the medicine for the disease of change, adjustment and adaptation. A sense of *Humour Attitude* helps you adjust and adapt. It encourages us to enjoy the unavoidable changes in our lives. Adaptation is our survival skill in remodelling and reshaping our attitudes and actions to suit all circumstances.

One man who could do this was the guy who had been evicted from his office so many times, he had curtains to match the footpath!

During the Crusades, we could always tell the atheists - they were the ones who wanted to negotiate.

When you train your mind to accommodate the incongruity between the set-up line and the punchline or a joke, you learn to swap one mental image for another. You have changed your mind and been rewarded for it. Humour justice has triumphed! If we did not take ourselves, our superstitions and our prejudices seriously, we could re-evaluate our behaviour to change and learn to adapt in an instant. 1he old expression, 'You only change when it hurts too badly to stay the way you are', could be switched to, "When you can laugh at yourself and the way you are'.

Try the following adaptabilities to exercise your *Humour Attitude:*

Impersonation Progress
Observe somebody whom you admire because they adjust to change well, then impersonate their behaviour.

Sitcom Conversion
Video-tape three episodes of a situation comedy, particularly one that you detest. Then watch them with the view of identifying what attitudes and actions you don't like. Then try to see them as funny.

Sacred TabOo Tall Tales
Pick a personal prejudice then write a 200 word nonsensical tall tale about how you learned it.

Once you begin applying your developing sense of humour, the experience of change becomes a celebration. And a Humour Attitude becomes a strategy for personal sanity and corporate success.

9. Fun

'Work is more fun than fun.'

There are, in fact, three fundament degrees of fun - serious fun, creative fun and fun fun.

They are all degrees of the feeling of fun. They make all the difference to your appreciation and use of humour It can turn a simple humorous remark into a hilarious line. Use your humour as a warm-up tool before networking with people.

Just a little while ago I was walking down the street and saw a group of people standing around a mess of shopfittings on the footpath. I thought I would build some rapport with the chap who had taken over the business. This fellow was standing in the centre of the mess on the footpath, dusting and brushing down a log of wood. He was taking pride in this piece of nature. He took it into the shop and ran straight out to have a look at hie creative work, through the window. To get past, we were forced to wall between him and the window. He saw me and said: "Hello!' I didn't answer at first, letting the tension build. Then I turned and said: "Hello! By the way how much is that loggy in the window? Everyone burst out laughing. With one single line, my feeling of fun had spread throughout the whole group! Later on that week, I rang him and said: "I would like to buy that log in your window and when I come down, I would like to have a chat about some business with you.' He laughed and I had a new, friendly contact.

For humour to succeed, a feeling of fun must replace a feeling of fear. A sense of self-fun makes it possible for you to come to terms with your own imperfections, as well as the imperfections of those around you. Both are necessary for *Humour Attitude* and *Humour Action*. Life can be a fight for survival or a fun-filled game. Remember, if you find yourself caught up in the fear of making mistakes, appearing awkward, getting embarrassed, showing signs of nervousness - forget lite, and consider death!

Fear can have a devastating effect on your self-image and the outcome or your career. People don't mind seeing you in awkward or embarrassing Situations if you have fun with them. When I sat down at my brand new Computer for the first time, my staff, who were well aware of my difficulties With writing and spelling, gathered around supportively. I cracked my fingers in an exaggerated way, dusted the screen and declared: 'I'm as comfortable doing this as a duck is at pole vaulting!' This eased the tension and we were soon having fun and learning at the same time. This technique is called refocusing with fun and can be applied to any personal difficulties, leadership demands and management chaos. Here, humour alleviates the pressure momentarily and provides a whole new insight and solution.

Other techniques under the banner of Fun-Changing Methods are:

The Bingo Shout
Copy a list of all the swear words you know. Give each a number, and when frustration next strikes, shout out the numbers!

The Fun Affirmation
Whenever I am going into a stressful situation, suffering rejection or walking on stage to perform humour, I repeat to myself: "I'm breathing, I'm relaxed and I'm having fun!

A Humour Attitude is the invigorating feeling that the sense and spirit of fun injects into our personal power. It becomes a source of strength and stamina, an advantage in the competitive corporate world.

10. Freedom

Freedom to act, think and feel the way I wanted to in life has been my biggest challenge. Running amok with regulations, breaking rules, defying authority, ignoring traditions, laughing at seriousness, is the life of the comedian. When I worked as a stand-up comedian, my gimmick was to grow half a moustache. If the half-moustache became so popular in 10 years that everyone had one, and five years later another fella came along and grew the other side as well, everybody would say: There goes a bloke with two moustaches

As a stand-up, I learned how to say what I saw without claiming to have 20/20 vision. I became a miniature folk hero as well as a verbal vampire. I was a humour sponge, soaking up the discomfort of those around me. By coupling it with my own ignorance and anger, then attacking chosen targets and delighting in their discomfort, I got the audience laughing at life and not at me.

Luckily, sometime later, I walked away from my existence as a user of negative humour and began seeking freedom again, this time in the direction of a *Humour Attitude*. I discovered an inner sense of freedom from our own restrictions and disciplines. Dr Harvey Mindess devoted the first section of his book Laughter and Liberation to freedom from conformity.

He says: To get with our sense of humour, then we must learn to accept. Accept not injustice, hypocrisy and foolishness but life. Life which includes all these things, which is in fact pervaded by them. To accept life and to accept ourselves, not blindly and not with conceit but with a shrug and a smile. lo accept in the end, existence! Not because it's wonderful, nor because it's divine, not because it's just or reasonable or even satisfactory but simply and plainly because it's all we've got!

Laughing at Yourself

> A Humour Attitude is a mirror, that lets you see yourself
> the way others do!
> Pete Crofts

Laughing at yourself should become a permanent hobby; it's one of the basic rules in the game of life. Using this *Eye Witness Humour,* you see yourself from an emotional distance, training yourself to step out of your sensitivity, consciously letting loose your ego and appreciating your humorous second self.

First self-humour is when you deliberately try to be funny; second self-humour is when you have no control of the conditions or environments and you appear foolish, ridiculous and downright laughable. It's a cultivated skill that lets you enjoy your external human behaviour, internally, with warmth and amusement, rejecting any feeling of guilt or embarrassment. We should not have to forgive ourselves for being human but celebrate our bumbling, delight in our clumsiness, and on those special moments, laugh out loud when we have the opportunity of glimpsing our pompous absurdity.

Every human being on our paper maché planet - from politicians to priests, managing directors to factory hands - is a walking comedy duo, comprising the internal straight man and the unintentional comedian. Learn the skill of laughing at yourself. A person with a true *Humour Attitude* merrily submits when other people laugh at them. Develop this habit because if you don't there are lots of others who will do it for you!

I know how important this is, because I couldn't laugh at myself. I took my point of view, beliefs, image, conduct and general behaviour too intensely.

That is until I went through a program similar to the way an alcoholic gives up drinking. He tells himself a hundred times a day, 'One day at a time'!. I told myself a hundred times a day, rule number six. There's no rule number five, no rule number seven, Just rule number six: 'Don't take yourself too seriously because if you do, you're missing the biggest joke of all – yourself!'

Practise the following self-humour strategies to observe the amazing ambiguity of yourself.

Family Option
I video-taped the most important lecture of my life, raced home, sat the family down and turned on the video. By mistake, the lecture had been recorded without sound. The picture came on and I burst with pride; the family watched the silent me silently for five minutes. By this time I was very impressed and I said: 'What do you think of it? And without blinking an eye, my 12-year-old daughter Charly said: '"You sound great, Dad'

Awake to Mistakes
Observe yourself in the mistakes you make, see the humour in them and share it with those around you. For example, if you drop a bundle of papers bend down to pick them up and trip over deliberately.

Joke Licence
Intentionally let other people know you can take a joke on yourself by sayingthings like: Am I really that funny? Make a mock joke licence saying: "The person who has this licence has the right to joke about me.

A Humour Attitude is broader than just laughing at yourselt. It's a permanent, constant giggle because you know you have the ability, knowledge, confidence, persistence and commitment to achieve your goals and enjoy he journey.

Humour Appreciation

Have a look at these examples:

> I was thrown out of NYU in my freshman year; I cheated on my metaphysics final. I looked within the soul of the boy sitting next to me.

> Did you hear about the process server in Fort Wayne, who's getting altogether too cocky to suit his colleagues? They don't like the way he's been putting on the 'Writs'!

> The Mulla went to see a rich man. 'Give me some money!'

> 'Why?'

> 'I want to buy an elephant!'

> If you have no money, you can't afford to keep an elephant!'

> 'I came here,' said Nasrudin, 'to get money, not advice!'

> A young executive we know recently spent three months finding a suitable secretary. He knows it pays to have a good head on your shoulder.

Did you enjoy any of them? These jokes would be appreciated by different people, in different situations, experiencing different levels of anxiety. How individual audience members respond is a personal process, controlled by numerous levels of perception and environmental forces.

To help you understand the different aspects of your humour, begin taking notes on your own humour actions and actiVities. Do this weekly under the headings on the following sheet:

Humour Action and Reaction Sheet
Write the humorous experience in some detail.

Where did the humour happen?
The situations and locations: business, home, social, other occasions; office, dinner table, cocktail party. Give details.

Who was involved?
Business associates, family members, strangers, customers, hierarchy structure, ethnic group, etc. Give details.

What was your emotional state?
Relaxed, enthusiastic, stressed, happy, annoyed, frustrated, other details.

How was the humour introduced and executed? And by whom?
Spontaneous, planned, throwaway, friendly, angry, deadpan, expressive, physical, other. Give details.

What was the function the humour served?
Joking relationship, release stress, gain attention, impart information, give confidence, attack authority, putdown, Others. Give details.

What affect did the humour have?
You enjoyed it, everyone laughed, everyone smiled, stopped action, unresponsive, people listened, got the message, embarrassed, improved humour use, other. Give details.

List what you learnt from exercise.
About yourself, others, humour, using humour, other details.

Other thoughts, remarks and observations.

Svebak (1974), identified three essential ingredients of a sense of humour:

a. Metamessage sensitivity or the ability to recognize humour and situations.

b. Personal liking of humour or the enjoyment of humour and the humorous role.

c. Emotional permissiveness or the tendency to freely express ones emotions.

The way we experience, interpret and respond to humour has an effect on the way we express, perform and use humour. This, in turn, effects the quality of our communication, relationships and leadership style, and eventually our success and fulfilment. With this in mind I think the next exercise is appropriate. The idea for it and some of the questions came from Svebak's *Sense of Humour Questionnaire* and Dr Joel Goodman's exciting publication, *Laughing Matters*.

The Ha Ha Internal Expedition

Humour and laughter are signposts to personal enjoyment and job satisfaction. Before you make a positive decision about the role humour can play or could play in your life, it is necessary to take some time to navigate through the mirth maze of your humour and laughter beliefs, patterns and values. This list of questions is designed to help you diagnose your own sense of humour by giving you an insight into your own humour history, vulnerabilities and values. It is a jolly journey for judging your jocularity.

1. I find when I look for something humorous in a problem I can see it in a new light.

2. I have or have not developed a Humour Attitude as an efficient way of coping with my problems.

3. I often lose my sense of humour when I have problems.

4. I am often/seldom the butt of others jokes.

5. What percentage of people you meet do you make laugh.

6. I don't think you have to tell jokes to develop a Humour Attitude in life.

7. I know all there is to know about the difference between laughing at others and laughing with others.

8. I do/do not like attacking, putdown humour.

9. I am/am not regular at taking myself too seriously.

10. When I am in a tense situation I have trained myself to think of something humorous to say.

11. I find it hard to keep a straight face in a situation that I find funny even if no one else sees the humour.

12. I regularly join in and laugh in a humorous situation then wonder after what was so funny.

13. I was sometimes or always the class comedian at school.

14. I do/do not have a joke/quote cartoon file.

15. I do/do not always carry something humorous in my briefcase or wallet.

16. There are not many circumstances in which I can't see something humorous.

17. Sometimes I am slow at seeing humour and getting jokes.

18. Tickle fights are fun/not fun.

19. I have enjoyed humour today, once, twice or more.

20. Humour often opens my eyes to aspects of life I seldom think about.

21. I want/don't want to build the amount of laughter in each day.

22. I can't remember jokes.

23. I can laugh at myself when others are laughing at me.

24. I can laugh at a humorous situation over and over again.
25. I can recognise cues such as a twinkle in the eye, change of voice and raised eyebrows as signs suggesting humour intent.
26. I often laugh when laughter is not appropriate.
27. I think people who overdo humour have a poor self-image.
28. I do/do not laugh at other peoples jokes.
29. I am impulsive or I plan my humour use.
30. I am afraid of laughing too much and having other people think I'm an exhibitionist.

Think of some other questions yourself, and then answer the following five questions in detail.

I discovered that I was...

I realise now that I have to...

I found I need to more.

I can see where I have been going wrong.

The first thing I am going to do is..

Getting and maintaining control of your life only comes when you can use your *Humour Attitude* to laugh away your outdated actions, Ideas, concepts, fears and values, then replace them with *Humour Action*.

Humour Attitude Appreciation

> Having a sense of humour is like having a shower. You have to have it otherwise your business wont prosper and people will avoid you.
>
> Pete Crofts

Making better decisions
Understanding your humour history will give you an insight into your strength and weaknesses. It will highlight areas and attitudes of your internal behaviour and personality and help you feel humorous in tense situations when you are making decisions. To help you accumulate your humour history:

Start a humour ad lib album
Write in your *humour zappers*- the lines that zap into your mind and you use without thinking. I get a lot of my best material this way. Just recently in a workshop I said: 'If I was in the humour business only for the business I wouldn't be in the business. Not a great line, but good enough to use.

Have a humour selection journal
In this you keep any humour you read by cutting out or photocopying and sticking them into your humour selection journal. This file is an excellent resource when making business presentations. By deliberately making an effort you will grow your Humour Attitude and you will accumulate a great resource you can call on.

Develop a humour diary
Daily, write around 300 words about your thoughts, feelings and actions a humorous way. This will keep you in touch with yourself and your as well as improve your humour writing. You can edit the best and add into your humour joke file.

Just recently I wrote this in my humour diary:

The white trouser mystery.

I wanted a new pair of white trousers. I'm always embarrassed and anxious when I'm shopping for myself. I picked a pair of white trousers, took them into the fitting room, tried them on and they fitted perfectly. The next morning, I was delighted to find that my then wife had laid the white trousers on the bed ready for me to wear. I had been on a diet, but the night before I had a meal that was far too big. I put my right leg into the trousers and thought there was something wrong. Then I squeezed myself into the pants, drew my breath in and just managed to button them up. I looked like a sausage that had burst its skin. I couldnt figure it out. Yesterday they fitted perfectly; today I was a tight arse. You can imagine the dumbfounded look on my face. I hat was when my wife came in laughing hysterically. She had been watching in the mirror and said: 'Happy April Fools Day, darling, they're your old pants; here's your new ones.'

The Humour Attitude Appreciation Pyramid

> Humour is like weightlifting. If you show an interest, exercise and practise, your *Humour Attitude* will become stronger and your skill at pumping punch lines will improve.

When I had my humour bookshop, customers would first come to buy a joke book. The second time, they would buy a 'how to' book on humour. The third time, they would be looking for a book on the academic analysis of humour and the tourth time, something to develop their own sense of humour. I knew that their *Humour Attitude Appreciation Pyramid* was working for them. By applying this pyramid you will discover a strange and interesting phenomenon. The more you practise your humour, the more curious you will become.

The more humour activities we build into our daily lives, the quicker our *Humour Attitudes* and *Actions* will mature.

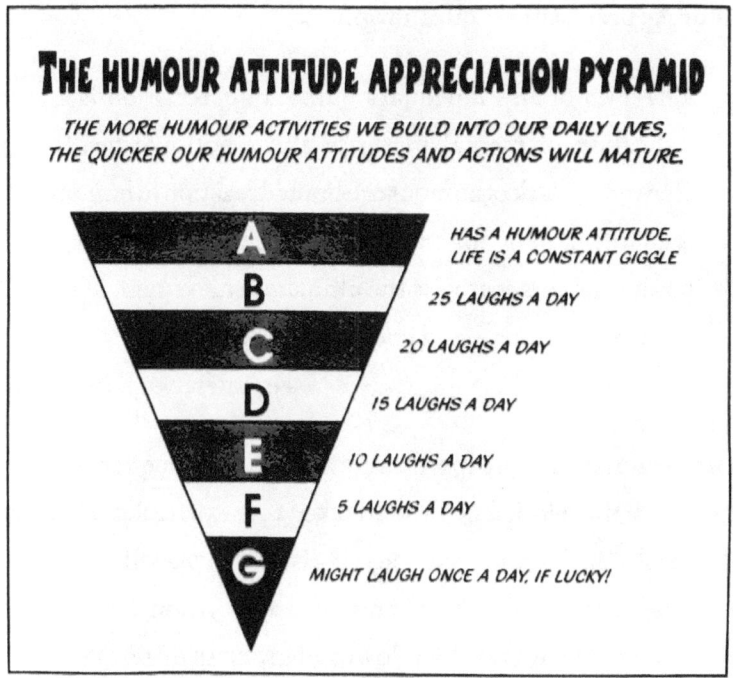

G. Discovering a need and turn it into an interest.

F. Takes humour notes; buys humorous material; looks for humour stimulus.

E. Chooses to use more humour; buys how to books; practises skills.

D. Communication improves; reads academic books; wants to be effective as well as funny.

C. Begins building *Humour Attitude*; uses constructive self-putdown humour; laughs more at other people's humour.

B. Some understanding of the theories, energies, functions, formulas and nature of humour. Seeks to use positive not negative humour; continually laughs at self.

A. Becomes a humour asset. Uses humour to motivate, instruct an inform. Exerts creative co-operation; releases stresses appropriate with laughter and humour; finds life and work fun; has unlimited potential; can laugh at self.

Humour Appreciation Examination

> The level of an individual's humour appreciation is an indication of mental maturity and emotional health. Conversely, lack of humour or a limited reaction to humour is an indicator of inhibition, or a restrictive lifestyle. The humorous perspective is the ultimate achievement in the quest for happiness and good mental health.
>
> Dr Lawrence J. Peters

My own personal humour appreciation has been through many developmental stages: the selt-defence, the attacker, the sexual release, the satirist, the philosophical, the confused, the self-discovery, the self- improvement. I have travelled the ftull circle of humour appreciation, first using it as a defence from the insults and putdowns of my class mates. When I was a child, I was sensitive, short, freckled, with a mop of red hair, and my eyes were too close together. When I got excited I stuttered; as well, my mother owned a milk bar and some of her staff charged too much for the lollies. So the other kids had plenty of targets to attack. I would go home, write some lines, come back to school the next day and let loose.

Is that your nose, or are you eating a banana?

You have the type of face that grows on a person; I'm only glad it didn't grow on me.

As an outsider what do you think of the human race?

I got very good at preventing myself and others from getting too close to the real me. My humour is now a personal force, expanding my self-understanding and providing me with the power to reach my full potential. I practise living my life through my humour attitude.

AS Dr. Harvey Mindess says: 'The jokes and humour we laugh at and appreciate most are keyholes into our mental makeup and one way of getting a better insight into ourselves.' With that in mind, let's do the humour appreciation examination.

Here are 12 jokes. The concept belongs to Harvey, but the jokes are mine. I would like you to read through them and make an immediate decision about how funny you think each joke is. Rate them from one to five following this guideline.

Sadly unfunny	1
A bit funny	2
Reasonably funny	3
Very funny	4
Hysterically funny	5

Just mark whatever number you think is appropriate next to each joke.

A. A Lawyer is an expert on justice as a prostitute is an expert on love.

B. The bloke in Perth who raced across the street and said to a lady pointing to the sky: 'Is that the sun going up or the moon going down She said: How do you expect me to know; I'm from Melbourne.

C. The very pompous Englishman who was looking for a subway in Sydney. He said to an Aussie: Excuse me old fellow, can you tell me how to get underground. The Aussie said: 'Sure can. Drop dead, you pommie bastard.

D. The story about the three bears. She was bare, I was bare and her husband was grizzly.

E. There's a new deodorant that's so effective, people don't even know you're around. It's called vice president.

F. The two prostitutes who went into business on the second floor of the brothel. In a week they were bankrupt! Too much … overhead.

G. A boss sent the office boy to get the portable computer. 'Make sure you don't drop it, he shouted and gave the boy a whack behind the ear. 'Boss, asked one of his executives, 'why did you whack the boy: He hasn't done anything" "You bloody fool, said the boss, 'It would be too late to punish him after he broke the computer.!'

H. Did you ever wonder how unfair it is that only one hole in your watchband gets all the action.

I. The lusting businessman who, after six months, finally persuaded his secretary to get undressed and bend forward over his leather couch. When he got home that night, his wife shouted: And what have you been doing, arriving home at this time of night?' He said: I've been down at the office, darling, working like a dog!'

J. A team of scientists fashioned the supreme computer. When they asked it the ultimate question, 'Is there a GOD?', lights began flashing and clicking, and the whirling was deafening, and finally it's message appeared. It read: "There is now!

K. What's black and yellow and very, very dangerous? A shark-infested custard!

L. In the Garden of Eden there was Adam, the first man, Eve, the first woman, and snake the first consultant.

The above jokes fall into four *Humour Attitude* classifications:

- Hostile c.e.l
- Sexual d.f.i
- Philosophical a.gj
- Nonsensical b.h.k

Don't let analysing these jokes cause you any aggravation. For, like the Leaning Tower of Pisa, it depends on which side you stand! Look through them and see which ones you marked the highest and the lowest. You will discover that you do have a specific liking or disliking for a certain category.

Hostile and sexual humour come under the classification of emotional humour, while philosophical and nonsensical come under the classification of intellectual humour,

When you find you have an obvious preference or an aversion to any of the classifications, give some thought to what it's saying about your attitude and personality. And consider the way it's limiting your personal growth and humour appreciation, and how it is affecting your humour communication. One of the myths of humour is: 'only use humour you like yourself!' That's all right if you enjoy all categories that humour content covers. If you're like most of us and you don't, then you're preventing yourself from getting maximum humour response. You've heard the old expression: 'I'm doing comedy over here and tragedy over there! It could mean you are hostile humour all around, when you should be using some nonsensical or philosophical humour. If you constantly mock and attack with sarcasm satire, then you're venting excess feelings of aggression; likewise if sexual humour is your forte.

If, on the other hand, you find sexual humour extremely distasteful, it's a Sign that you might be unable to come to terms with the fact that you have these feelings. Escaping emotional humour completely by enjoying nonsensical and philosophical humour indicates that you re someone who is proud of their mental capacity and none too pleased about exposing your feelings and emotions.

The most truthful insights into our humour psyche are the zappers we ad lib in our daily lives. They pop out of the depths of our subconscious anxieties and shine as a beacon to our insecurities. Our off-the-cuff witty remarks in moments of pressure or relaxation are innate human reactions. They are a way of coping or communicating with, or expressing, our instinctive feelings.

This following humour exercise is worth spending a little tume on.

I call it *Come out - whoever you are?*

Pick out five favourite jokes, five humorous experiences and five zappers, and dissect them to discover:

1. The Humour Attitude classification.
2. The sub-text message given.
3. What they reveal about you.
4. Where did the motive behind it come from?
5. Do I still feel comfortable about the humour?

This form of humour analysis is more fiction than fact, so don't take it too seriously. You will, however, get a better insight into your *Humour Attitude* and become aware of areas for expanding your humour appreciation and expression.

Develop Your Humour Attitude Habits

Spending time building a *Humour Attitude* is just the opposite to building sandcastles in the sky. Its cultivating characteristics of sanity and forging behavioural patterns for survival. Learning to respond to your situations, predicaments and challenges in a creative cognitive fashion, as opposed to emotional immaturity, leads you to discover your personal genius. It provides you with the silence to see your vision and the energy to achieve your destiny. A Humour Attitude becomes a process for living your life.

Formula focusing- become so familiar with humour formulas that you can see an idea, problem or decision with the multiple perception that formula focusing invites.

Comedy control- take personal control by monitoring your moods. Humour evaporates when you're too stressed, tired, bored, drunk, egotistical, worried or self-absorbed. Fanaticism and perfectionism are laughed at by the *Humour Attitude.*

The gleeful challenge - a sense of Humour Attitude is a sense of sensing things in a new sense. It has nothing to do with complacency; it has more to do with self-stimulation, excitement, stretching and risking, while gleefully challenging yourself to do your best and enjoying your worst until the next time.

The laughing cause - learn the methods then wait for the moments to make others laugh. When we make others feel good, we feel good. Making people laugh through friendliness, as opposed to aggression, is self-contagious.

Humour Attitude *affirmations* - whatever we think or say, or what others think or say about us, that we accept, becomes an affirmation. Start by writing a humour affirmation for each day of the week and repeating them a dozen times a day. Then write one for each waking hour of the day and do the same. Example: My eyes, ears, mind and emotions are open to the universal humour around me. I will celebrate it and share it with others at every opportunity.

Positive paranoia power- behave with positive paranoia; practise seeing the humour in the difficult people with whom you come in contact. There is no doubt some people will try to take you down, but when in doubt assume, that people are out to help you achieve and succeed.

The Positive Nature of Humour in Business

> I take humour seriously but not so seriously thar I lose my
> sense of humour about the seriousness of it:
>
> Peter Crofts

The best known aspect about the nature of humour would be its power in the face of adversity. Like the business entrepreneur who said: 'The only way to have a successful small business nowadays is to start out with a successful big business.' The nature of humour thrives on chaos, clogged channels, clutter, cold calls, credit crunches and customer service – especially to customers who make unnecessary demands.

Humour can be used as a tool or as a weapon:

> An overworked tailor said to his client: I will make a suit
> for you, but it won't be ready for 12 days. The customer
> was shocked; he said: "What? Twelve days when the good
> Lord took only six days to create the entire world. The
> tailor replied: "That's true, but have you taken a good
> look at it lately?"

In business, humour shouldn't be used in a clown-like fashion, merely to communicate that you have a sense of humour. It should be used to demonstrate that you are a warm, responsive, intelligent and considerate person. Often humour brings a chuckle, grin or a smile. Humour for entertainment's sake wants maximum LPMs (Laughs Per Minute). Humour in business requires maximum SETs (Successes Every Time) and must create a cheerful, receptive and positive mood.

Humour expands your perceptions and boosts creative potential. Its cognitive properties assist innovative executives with limitless possibilities for morale-lifting, decision-making and problem-solving.

> A union official stomped over to a building site, to where a giant bulldozer was at work. He said to the Site manager: Look, 100 men with shovels could be doing that job. The manager said: "Yes, that's true, but why not a thousand men with teaspoons

That's one of the powers of humour. It can take things so far out of proportion that it brings them back into their proper perspective. Positive humour alleviates stress, tension and pressure. We subject ourselves to the pressure because society has trained us to think one way- straight-ahead, with the left side of your brain. Pressure cause anxiety, which prevents clear thinking. Thinking humorously can free your mind from anxiety and help you think more creatively. Attributes alone can affect your entire business career.

Humour is multi-dimensional. There are many attributes, which include:

1. The incredible buzz you get when you laugh uncontrollably (release)
2. The relaxed state that descends upon you when the laughter ceases (peace).
3. The freedom that a prolonged feeling of humour provides (mood).
4. The sharp realisation of humour when you first see the joke (surprise).

5. The revelation you receive when humour gives you an insight into yourself (awareness).
6. The internal laugh you have when you make a clever connection in a conversation and deliver an ad lib (satisfaction).
7. The surge of strength you feel when you make people laugh (power).
8. The sense of evil contentment that comes over you when you have put somebody down with sarcastic wit (revenge).
9. The snap back to reality when somebody says something to make you laugh when you're depressed (hope).
10. The useful tool of self-debasement when you are in a position of authority (empathy).
11. The joy of playing with your children when you come home from work (love).
12. The pleasure of laughing along with your workmates on the job (fun).
13. The deliberate use of humour to divert attention (triumph).
14. The complete confidence in yourself that no matter what happens you can always laugh (natural high).

Humour means having a perceptive insight into what is going on around you, then having the flexibility, spontaneity and vision to control it and profit from it. HA HA skills for fun and profit!

The two most important and effective humour qualities are:

- Being able to enjoy it
- Having the ability to create humour and use it

These are the essences of *Business Show. The HA HA Principle* brings two abilities:

The first HA stands for *Humour Attitude,* which helps you to:

- Develop an internal sense of humour
- Laugh at yourself
- See life through the various lenses of humour

The second HA stands for *Humour Action,* which enables you to:

- Use your internal humour externally in a positive way
- Communicate better with others

You need to take a practical, honest approach to both aspects of the *HA HA Principle.* You can discover your personal attitude to humour by reflecting On, researching, then recording your experiences with humour. This helps to:

- Get some insight into what does and doesn't make you laugh
- Determine what humour comes easily to you and what doesn't
- Transfer the information into affirmations

One of the affirmations I use to help me stay open to understanding myself more is

> 'I enjoy criticism and feel excited that I can learn something important.'

I treat everything with a sense of lhumour -that's my *Humour Attitude,* I use things such as humour cushions, visualization and a variety of other techniques to help keep my *Humour Attitude* in place - that's my *Humour Action.* **After putting your HA HA skills in place, all you need is patience, patience and patience!**

Humour Action starts by understanding some of the structural elements of humour.

Evan Esar says in his marvellous book, *The Comic Encyclopedia*, that popular comedy may be diagrammed like a tree, with the principal classes of humour as its boughs, the sub divisions and types of humour as its smaller branches and twigs, and the specimens of humour as its leaves.

Dr Laurence J. Peters, in his book The Laughter Prescription, says: 'Many fears too much investigation into humour will destroy their capacity to enjoy it. But there is no evidence to support this point of view. The psychologists, medical researchers, sociologists, comedians and others who study humour have not lost their sense of humour. In fact, my own experience and observations suggest that their sense of humour has been heightened through learning more about the subject, gaining new know edge about the nature and uses of humour and applying it to life's problems. There is no other activity that can be as rewarding in so many areas of your life.

> I recall the story of a young college graduate with a PhD in Corporate Management. He got a job with a large financial institution. On Monday morning, he was met by the managing director and, as the day progressed, he was passed further down the line. By morning- tea time, he was on the shop floor with the foreman who said: Righty-oh mate, grab this broom and sweep this place spotless. Ihe young graduate threw his head back and said: "I beg your pardon, you've forgotten something, I have a PhD in Corporate Management.' The foreman laughed and said: I'm sorry, I forgot. You put your right hand here and your left hand there and you push.'

You need to re-evaluate the restrictive rules and misleading myths that govern business such as, 'you can't be funny and be taken seriously'; 'anyone who smiles a lot is a fool'; or 'business is about making money not having fun'. You need to re-educate yourself about the value and advantages of humour. End the secretive use of humour and see it for what it is: our most effective human resource that functions as a social safety valve and whose very nature is to inspire and inform us, to improve our personality and profits, and to educate and entertain.

Use all these strategies to develop your Humour Attitude and apply them through your Humour Action. Your HA HA skills will add meaning to your life while building your professional skills.

Chapter Three Summary
Developing your Humour Attitude

1. Humour Attitude enhances your business success.
2. True success means developing your sense of humour and taking your seriousness humorously.
3. *Humour Attitude* is a way of perceiving, seeing, feeling and enjoying the uncomfortable, unpredictable realities of life.
4. Shaping your *Humour Attitude* is as important to your personal enjoyment and your professional success as your honesty, education and IQ.
5. A flexible attitude helps when you're out of your comfort zone
6. You need to be enthusiastic about all the vital areas of our life.
7. A *Humour Attitude* is cost-efficient and the lack of it can be a serious business liability.
8. Let your impulses, instincts and insights free up your enthusiasm.
9. Unconventional behaviour can be the key to letting your creativity, energy, vission and humour out.
10. You make the choice to be an optimist or a pessimist a thousand times a day.
11. A *Humour Attitude* means balanced behaviour; a practised perception to see the ludicrous side of life.
12. Use your humour as a warm-up tool before networking with people.
13. For humour to succeed, a feeling of fun must replace a feeling of fear.
14. Laughing at yourself should become a permanent hobby.
15. How individual audience members respond is a personal process, controlled by numerous levels of perception and environmental forces.

16. Understanding your humour history will give you an insight into you Strengths and weaknesses.

17. The jokes and humour we laugh at and appreciate most give an insight into ourselves.

18. Develop your *Humour Attitude* habits.

19. Humour can be used as a weapon.

20. Your HA HA skills will add meaning to your life while building your professional skills.

CHAPTER 4

The Nature of Humour

The Mind of Humour

> 'The fun in life comes from exercising humour energy and the best humour exercise is to bend down and help yourself or somebody else up.'
>
> Pete Crofts

H umour is an energy:

It can help you fight fear, uncertainty and sadness, and give you the strength to reach your goals. It can assist you in the growth of your personal power. You will need to store it and use it whenever necessary, spiritually, intellectually or emotionally.

Humour is a creative energy that can wash away our mental restrictions and make our imagination soar. It frees our creative observations. It can unlock our cognitive potential.

Humour energy levels the mountain that tunnel vision travels through. However, for it to work, it has to be consciously and continually switched on. Otherwise, we can become like the fellow who was bored with his job in the circus. His job consisted of looking after the elephants. He had to feed, clean, water, walk and wash them as well as take care of them when they were sick!

His mate said: 'Why don't you get another job?' He said: "What? And get out of show business?'

When I worked as a professional comedian in show business, you could say I was like the elephant man in the story above. I used humour merely to deflate other people's egos, I fed my own ego by deflating theirs. I became a verbal vampire looking for weaknesses, vanities and vulnerabilities. I used lines like:

> 'Don't you know you're auditioning for unemployment?
>
> Have you seen his desk? The council has assigned it as an alternative sight for dumping Human waste.
>
> My boss doesn't smoke, drink or gamble. His other bad habits don't leave him enough time!

Then one day I had a revelation. People weren't laughing with me, but at me. If I could have harnessed that negative humour energy, I could have singlehandedly solved the energy crisis. Slowly but surely, over the past 20 years, I have gone from being a person without a sense of humour, to a person with a sense of humour, getting at least 25 more laughs a day by generating my own positive humour energy.

Let's discuss the 10 creative energies of the humour mind:

1. Perspective
2. Imagination
3. Observation
4. Visualisation
5. Memory
6. Thinking
7. Creativity
8. Spontaneity
9. Truth
10. Surprise

THE MIND OF HUMOUR
THE CREATIVE ENERGIES OF HUMOUR

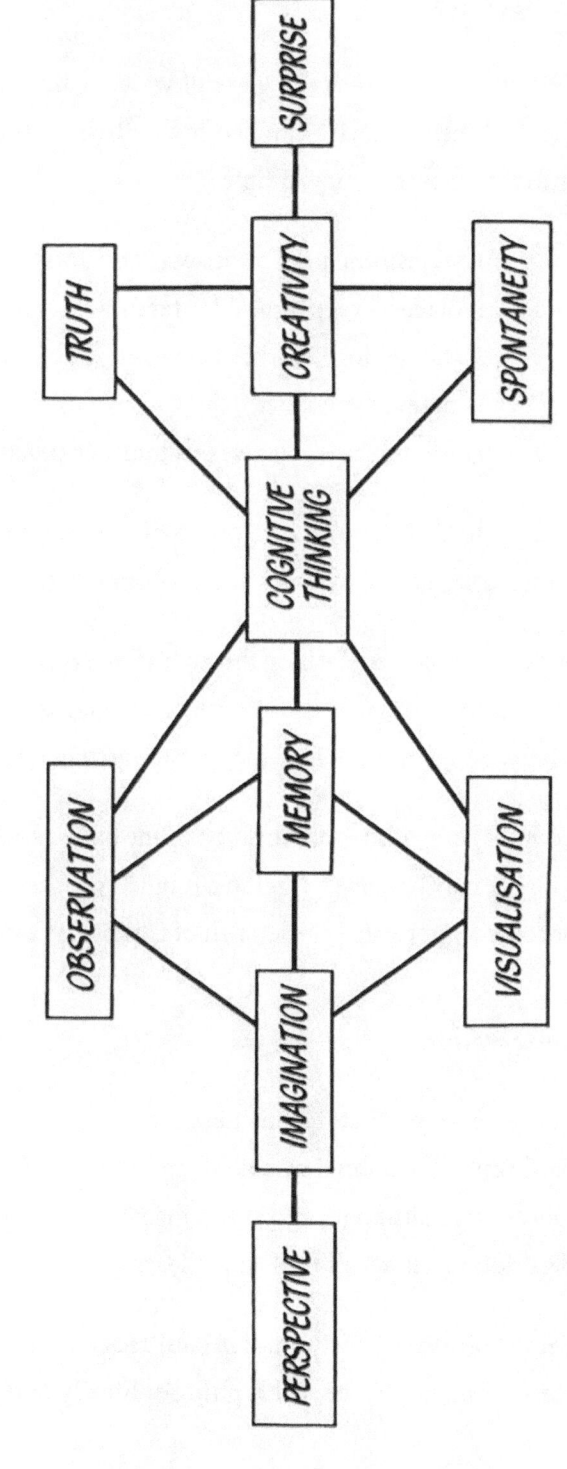

Perspective

The opportunist sees the glass of water as half full. The pessimist half empty. The humorist can see it as either of the above or something entirely different. For example:

> A swimming pool for insects and ants!
> A place to keep your false teeth!
> A shower for a worker who needs to be woken up!
> Whatever you wish!
> Humour thinking gives us multiple perspective.

One of the most important powers of humour is that it makes it possible for us to see crises, troubles and problems in their proper perspective.

When we look at something through a fixed perspective, we shape what we see. An employer may see humour on the job as a frivolous waste of time, whereas an employee may see it as a way to maintain sanity on the job.

People's perspectives are different. One businessman, when he walks into a forest, may become a tiger in a jungle. Another sees the opportunity to become a puppy in a garden full of Christmas trees.

Observation

I have observed that if a businessman comes up with a bad idea, he goes bankrupt. If a politician comes up with a bad idea, he gets re-elected Observing a situation, and reporting it in humorous detail, with startling descriptions, is a skill well worth learning.

Sarah Jobson, in her book on Paul Hogan, says Paul managed to stay close to his audience, both philosophically and physically. He got his humour straight from real life, watching the foibles of real Australians he met.

Paul Hogan's American equivalent, Will Rogers, once said: I don't tell jokes; I just watch the Government and report the facts.'

When you develop your humour observational skills you are not just well. Developing your observational humour becomes a process you can enlarging visual ability, but enhancing your listening and sensory skills as Cultivate the ability to observe a situation in detail, and recall each

ail specifically. Then, when you are relating it, see it as you say it.

Imagination

> A financier is a pawnbroker with imagination.
> Arthur Wingpinero (1855-1934)

Most professional humorists are highly intelligent. They have subconsciously picked up some of the formulas and elements of humour. You can learn those same formulas and elements consciously and they will help you develop your imagination.

Humour trains our imagination to tickle and tease, to unlock and set free and ultimately transform our intelligence. The first step is to lock into your subconscious the words if only and 'what if'.

'If only this were my father's business, then I would be successful.'

'If only the MD were dying of thirst in the desert and I was a camel with a water pack, then I would be appreciated.'

'What if I wasn't as much in debt as I am in love?'

'What if, as well as having wall-to-wall carpeting, I had wall-to-wall financing, instead of having back-to-wall financing"

Practise using humour by stretching your imagination. It strengthens your intelligence.

Make a list of:

- Five risks you want to take
- Five errors that you have made
- Five goals you want to achieve

I have your own private brainstorming session using the four magic words of humour imagination - if only, what if! You will be amazed at the results and the practical ideas that come from this exercise.

Visualisation

We all have our own ways of verbalising and visualising our humour. The most successful humorists are verbal photographers that help you see their verbal pictures by reflecting them off the distorted mirror of reality. At the same time they role-play with images and actions.

When Dick Smith, the successful Australian businessman, went on another incredible adventure, his image became ripe for visual humour.

> Dick Smith has just announced his new first-man adventure. He is going to climb Mt Everest barefoot and blindfolded, in shorts and singlet with a carton of Carlton bottled beer on his back, singing Advance *Australia Fair* through a megaphone with a smiling Kangaroo on it.

I will stop here; I am sure you can see what I m saying.

You can help the audience visualise your characters, actions and attitudes, by painting a picture with sound and by describing in finite detail the scenes, situations and circumstances. This is what Bill Cosby, Richard Stubbs and other great comedians do. Humour visualisation is not only a way of getting a humorous reaction, it can also be used to get attention, maintain interest and sell your message as well.

It's also a valuable personal tool as an antidote tor your anger and to help build a working relationship with people you don't get along with on the job. This humour technique is called 'Visual Sanity'.

Think of any difficult people you know. Make a list of all their disagreeable, nerve-wracking, obnoxious traits. Say the person is overbearing, dictating and snobbish. Visualise them in the office in the morning as if they have just taken the Yarra River and not the train to work. Visualise them at their desk, which is not a desk but a fishbowl full of piranhas. They are not sitting on a chair but in a large bucket of custard etc etc. Then, in detail, write this

Mental picture in your notebook for nasties, so you cojure uo these images in a future conflict and prevent yourself from becoming stressed and losing control.

Memory

> There was once an efficiency expert who said to his doctor: You have to help me, I'm in trouble, I'm losing my memory. The doctor said: Ah, just how long has this been a problem? The efficiency expert said: 'What problem?

This joke is nearly as old as the excuse! I don't use humour because I can't remember jokes. Telling jokes is a very small part of using humour. Telling jokes well is a precise art. It needs to be smooth, comfortable and effortless in its introduction, performance and execution. Our memory for humour is motivated by our interest in humour. An interest in learning the tables at school was motivated by the fact that there was trouble if we didn't pass maths. The method for humour is the same as we remembered the tables: repetition. We need to apply this to memorise jokes.

It is easier to remember humour, which comes from your own experiences because your observations and visualisations are personally motivated. You remember references, feelings and images through association with people and events. You also need to prepare layout, construction and the natural progression of the piece. This makes it easy to remember the opening, the key words and connections, and never to forget the punchlines.

There is another important aspect and it is demonstrated in the story about a young man from Melbourne who was passing a street violinist in Sydney and, being lost, he asked the violinist:

'How do you get to the Opera House:'

The violinist said: 'Practice my son, practice!'

The last ingredient for the recipe of remembering humour is: when you have written out the humour, read through it a reasonable number of times, then tell it to at least 10 people a day for two days.

Motivation, observation, visualisation, association, practice and rehearsal are the keys to remembering humour.

Cognitive Thinking

I think therefore I laugh.
Title of John Allen Paulos book 1985

Harold Greenwald wrote: "One stops thinking about everything in this world as a catastrophe and begins to See the humour in life's event by, by looking at the world as the divine comedy that it really is.'

Training yourself and your statt in humour thinking and humour behavior can be the difference between success or failure and the quality and quantity of your company's products or services. I he more you use the cognitive humour processes, the sooner you develop humour patterning systems that automatically act and react in a positive way. Solving problems, finding Solutions to puzzles, generating innovative insights, and making quantum mental leaps, are everyday behaviours to the person trained in humour thinking.

One of the many humour exercises to stiumulate cognitive thinking is role-playing the 'ridiculous'.

Teams of two players have to match complete opposites by brainstorming the attitudes, accents and actions of paradoxical pairs, such as the following:

A tombstone applying for a job as editor of The *Financial Review*.

A warm, fuzzy, debating George W. Bush on multiculturalism.

A wastepaper basket applying for a job as public relations officer for the State Bank.

Creativity

Edward De Bono says:

> 'Humour is a more significant process in the human mind
> than reason. In practice, reason may be more useful,
> but as a type of process, humour is more significant.
> Reason is a selecting process and is easily carried out
> by a machine, and indeed we have developed excellent
> computers to do just this. Humour involves a switching
> over from one way of looking at things to another. This
> is absolutely essential in a patterning system, for it is
> the basis of creativity, and patterning systems cannot
> progress without creativity.'

Computers cannot laugh. Wouldnt it be sinister if they could? If they
could laugh, they would be capable of creativity. Computers cannot laugh,
because they have no choice but to arrange the available information
in the best possible way, according to the program they're given. If a
computer could break away from the obvious way of looking at things
and find a different way of looking at them, then that would be humour.
If a computer could do this, it would be creative, because it would start
producing answers that went beyond the instruction given.

Humour creativity is an acquired ability. It comes with the conscious
understanding of the structural, emotional and aesthetic elements of
humour. It provides creative insight for us to conceive, see and present
Concepts, ideas and attitudes in a new light.

> There was the executive who went to Surfers Paradise
> for a holiday and spent three weeks laying on the beach.
> He then claimed it on his tax as a creative business trip,

saying he was trying to develop contact lenses that wouldn't pop out.

You can encourage others in creative humour thinking and behaviour just by showing your appreciation of humour.

One manager interested in humour invented what he called creative comedy cards. These were just ordinary pieces of cardboard in the shape of playing cards. Instead of numbers, he had names on them such as frustration, anger friendliness, fear, co-operation and rejection. They were designed around the recurring stressful aspects of the organisation.

To depict the behaviour the cards represented, he used cartoons, drums, doodles, twisted proverbs, humorous quotes and jokes. Then during the course of the day, he passed them out to the office staff when he sensed which one was appropriate to the situation.

For example, when an employee had far too much paper spread across their desk, he would pass them a card similar to this:

> Dear Fred, success in our business Is measured in inverse proportion to the amount of paper used. In government it is just the opposite. Because of this, this card will self-destruct in five minutes.

Ashley Brilliance's extremely clever books of epigrams are perfect for this creative humour exercise. Follow these five humour creative action steps:

1. Creativity and play are closely linked; at the right times play at work
2. You can stimulate creativity by just supplying humorous articles. Pass out copies of Monty Python-type books just before a meeting.

3. Give humorous rewards to people who display unconventional thinking. Diverse thinking is humour thinking.

4. When necessary, use humour to set up a tension-free atmosphere. Creativity bursts when set free.

5. Remember, we all have the essential creativeness as well as the need to be trained and encouraged in creative thinking.

Use humour creative thinking to re-organise, re-value, re-shape, reform, refresh, reinforce, rejuvenate, resolve, rejoice and above all, relax on the job!

Truth

By far the shortest measurable interval of time is that between when you put a little extra aside for an unexpected emergency, and the arrival of that emergency. Ain't that the truth!

When you listen to experienced humorists you will notice that they will often use:

> 'This is a true story.'

> 'It's true this happened!'

> 'That's the way it was, really!'

> 'Hard to believe, but it's true.'

This bases your humour on reality and establishes empathy with the audience. Truth humour hooks hearts no matter how insignificant the truth observation. If it's insightful, it's funny. For example, road maps tell a motorist everything they want to know, except how to fold them up again! Scratching the surface of truth is funny; exploring deep beneath truth's surface is funnier. Exposing your trials and tribulations and identifying the ridiculous aspects of society's rules and rituals is hilarious.

'I know a psychiatrist who has a company director as a client and he tells him to spend more time with his children; he's trying to drum up more business!

Work with the following five humour truths:

1. Share truth humour with others by telling them the funny things that happened to you. Sharing laughter in this way builds up a joking relationship with your workmates.
2. Humour is quite often the expression of a deep-seated stressful, emotional truth which, when recognised, could be healed.
3. There are certain stressful truths that happen again and again. Be ready with a relating line to provide a relief. For example, you might have a boss who likes telling jokes and he does it badly, but everyone feels compelled to laugh. When he leaves say: I aalways laugh at the boss's jokes. It doesn't give me a lift, but it might give me a raise.'
4. Carefully use the energy of truth umour to pinpoint business worries and wrongs, so they can be seen through the light of laughter for the purpose of improvement.
5. Where there is continuous humour directed at a certain target, there is possibly an unspoken truth that, if identified, could be a valuable insight.

As in business, honesty in humour works. Talk about the things that you think, feel, see, hear or have, because people sense it your humour is you.

Spontaneity

> The worst humour at the right time, is better than the
> best humour at the wrong time!
>
> Folklore

I got a phone call from a gentleman one day who said that since he had an operation in hospital he had not been able to laugh or feel humorous. I said: It sounds like you have just had your sense of humour taken out! What you need is a sense of humour transplant, a funnybone replacement. He thought this was funny and burst out laughing. It was the first time he had laughed months. This situation had the qualities of spontaneity including:

1. My voice was relaxed and my attitude was appropriate.
2. The content was personalised, localised and relevant.
3. The telling was free, trusting and friendly.
4. His expectations of what I would say were equalled and bettered.
5. I sounded confident, knowledgeable and undeterred.
6. He was relieved of the embarrassment he would have felt if I didn't answer his question the way I did.
7. There was no hesitancy, forcefulness or pressure.

As well as learning jokes, practise spontaneity. It will enhance the mood and tone of all your communication. In my humour workshop, I advise people to mirthfully marry a spontaneous spouse' where you give one another the licence to behave in an immature way for five minutes every day. You both let loose, act and react, undertaking actions and activities to do with a work decision, office problem, people behaviour.

When you are using humour energy spontaneously, it helps if you can think three ways at the same time: one-third asking what's happening;

one-third asking what do they want; and one-third asking what's the punchline. Spontaneity is a positive way of nurturing belief in yourself because using it involves self-trust, self-image and self-confidence.

Surprise

Life and humour are so much alike: they're both full of surprise and tension.

> A salesman rushed into his bosses office and shouted: Surprise! Surprise! I want a bigger commission or else! 'Or else what? groaned the boss. 'Or else I'll go back and work for the commission I'm getting!

The salesman's energy in this joke built the tension. The energy was frustrated because of the reaction of the boss. The frustrated expectation provided the surprise. No other ingredient is as universal in humour as surprise. It creates the suddenness and sharpness, and jerks us from one trame of mind to another. This is vital to most humour!

As there is a positive and negative humour, the same thing applies to Surprise. We have the unexpected surprise that does not give us time to move from a business mood to a playful mood. The practical joke is a case in point. It is jolt humour. This form of surprise threatens us and we build resentment even if we do not show it. Expected surprise is where there is a at a surprise is coming. This can be in the form of a facial expression, a wink, a slight smile or just verbally saying something to the effect of: "Life funny; do you know what happened to me? All this sets the mood for the surprise of the humour.

It's been said that to be successful in using humour, you have to build and release tension. Surprise releases the built-up energy and replaces it with the pleasureable energy of laughter. The samething applies whether the tension is built deliberately, as in telling jokes, or environmentally, say when the boss shouts at an employee (they are not happy with). The tension there can be released once the boss leaves and someone makes a remark such as: 'Everybody has a good word for our boss, but we have to whisper it behind his back.' Used positively, the humoour energy of surprise can revitalize business attitudes, actions and atmosphere, either by the actual use of humour, or, in the broader sense, by offering others a little light relief to life. This can be done with a thoughtful, caring remark, the sending of novelty humour card, a surprise friendly phone call, subscribing to a humour magazine for a client, or sending a workmate tickets to a comedy club.

There is no doubt that your professional life will be full of human surprises. Make a commitment to deliberately add the surprise of humour to your life. The surprise of humour can include your customers too. A sign was placed in the reception area of a struggling new business: "Customers wanted, no experience necessary.'

The Heart of Humour
(The emotional energies of humour)

Humour is about feeling good, emotionally. This good feeling is expressed by smiling, smirking, grinning or laughing. Laughing is an emotional and psychological act that propels endorphins into our body, making us feel good. It is also a cathartic release for pent-up feelings triggered by a cognitive connection. It is a socially acceptable way to release, but not so in the following story.

A hard-working, never-home businessman was running across a zebra crossing. All of a sudden, a car came whizzing around the corner. He did everything to get out of the way but the car still managed to hit him, tossing him in the air. As the car raced away, a loud cackling could be heard coming from it. A cop who saw the accident raced over to this poor bloke and said: 'Did you see the driver or remember the registration number of the car? The man replied; 'It was my wife who ran over me. The policeman said: Well, how do you know that? The battered businessman said: Simple, I'd recognise that hideous laugh anywhere.

For humour to be, firstly, effective, and secondly, funny, we must be alert to the emotional hooks on which the humour hangs - the subliminal text being said between the lines of the theme. What values, beliefs, feelings, thoughts, meaning, assumptions are we suggesting but not saying? What symbolic 'metamessages are we transmitting within the camouflage of our humour? We must become aware of the emotional energies circulating beneath the surface of our humour, the purpose and functions our humour serves, and the results and effects of our humour. We also need to eliminate our shotgun, self-satisfying humour and re-arm ourselves with heat-seeking emotional-missile humour.

This is one of the reasons humour has been ignored in education, religion and business, because we haven't known the rights and the wrongs, the do's and the don'ts, the positives and the negatives, of humour. Hopefully, this brief insight into the emotional energies of humour will help you in this regard, so that your laughs are long and lasting.

Subtext Emotional Energies

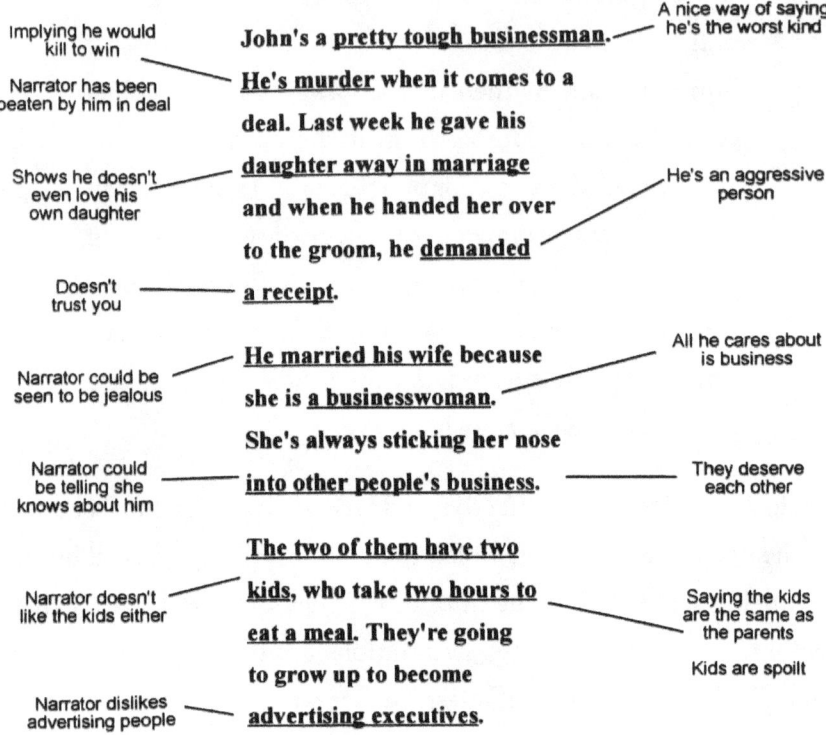

Implying he would kill to win

Narrator has been beaten by him in deal

Shows he doesn't even love his own daughter

Doesn't trust you

John's a **pretty tough businessman.** **He's murder** when it comes to a deal. Last week he gave his **daughter away in marriage** and when he handed her over to the groom, he **demanded a receipt.**

A nice way of saying he's the worst kind

He's an aggressive person

Narrator could be seen to be jealous

Narrator could be telling she knows about him

He married his wife because she is **a businesswoman.** She's always sticking her nose **into other people's business.**

All he cares about is business

They deserve each other

Narrator doesn't like the kids either

Narrator dislikes advertising people

The two of them have two kids, who take **two hours to eat a meal.** They're going to grow up to become **advertising executives.**

Saying the kids are the same as the parents

Kids are spoilt

Let's discuss the 10 emotional energies of the heart of humour:

1. Vulnerability
2. Irreverence
3. Aggression
4. Embarrassment
5. Sexuality
6. Defence Mechanism
7. Discretion
8. Credibility
9. Empathy
10. Enjoyment

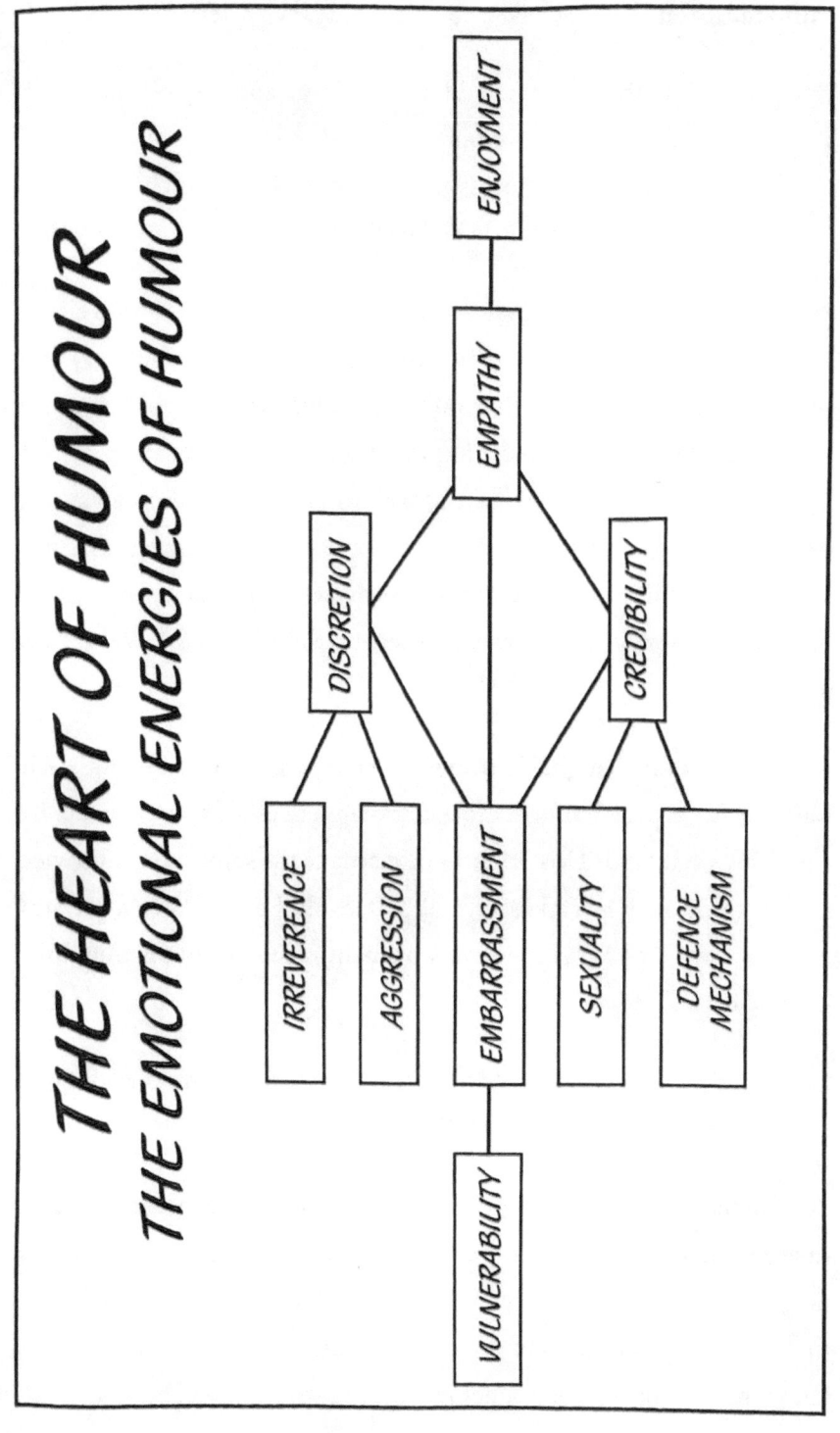

THE HEART OF HUMOUR
THE EMOTIONAL ENERGIES OF HUMOUR

Vulnerabilities

> A funny thing happened to me as I was coming to this
> humour training program this morning. A little bloke
> fell off the back of the bus and everybody laughed at him,
> except me. was the little bloke who fell off!

Professional comedians know that a self-disparaging joke is more reliable
as a humour device than anything else. People don't laugh up; they only
laugh down.' This means that our vulnerabilities become our major
humour assets. A technique for humour users is to achieve an emotional
link with your listeners. It is felt as well as funny. We all do awkward,
ridiculous. laughable things. If we build humour from these natural
experiences of life we will come across as everyday human beings not
figures of authority. That way we are less threatening and more real and
relatable.

An example of the laughable things we all do was when I bought a self-
warning, waterproof, unbreakable, antimagnetic, shockproof watch. Do
you know what I did? I lost it! But I never make the same mistakes twice;
I always find new mistakes to make. It could be you have a physical
imperfection. Dr Wayne Dyer gets brilliant results from putting down
his bald head.

Comedian Rodney Dangerfield has a philosophical self-putdown outlook,
summed up in hiIs catch phrase: 'I get no respect.'

You can show vulnerabilities by sharing an embarrassing moment, like the
time you knocked over your top client's coffee. You could have a behavioral
uniqueness, Like continually blushing. We all have some vulnerabilities
that we can use as targets for our self-putdown jokes. Sharing your
humanness is another way of demonstrating your sense of humour.

In his book, Making Humour Work, Terry L. Paulson PhD tells of a business owner who put a dollar note on the conference table and told his staff one of his recent errors, and what he learned from it. He gained the trust of his staff and each one shared a recent error that evoked laughter. The winning error earned the money and a lot of laughter. Everyone learned from each error discussed.

I must suggest caution here: don't ever put down your skills, talents and abilities to do your job well. You must show you take your job seriously, but not yourself. This develops your internal sense of humour, establishing that you can laugh at yourself, and improves your positive use of humour. As well, you become more approachable. You will notice that people emotionally respond to you from a new perspective. Vulnerability makes us honest and truthful, not secretive and phoney.

Sexuality

Sexual humour in the workplace acts as a floodgate for our pent-up sexual anxieties, desires and fears. It helps to discuss sensitive issues such as impotency, latent homosexuality, premature ejaculation and frigidity. Like one woman who said: "Some guys do strange and funny things in bed. They'll yell: "I'm coming, I'm coming!" Sometimes, I think I'm not there as a partner but as a witness.

Sexual gender conflict is another sensitive issue. As a management tool, humour needs to be understood on a more positive, professional and sophisticated level. It should assimilate and not alienate the sexes.

Sexual humour needs to be studied. It serves an important function, which must be increased not stifled. This means two things:

1. Its use must be improved.
2. You must develop a sense of humour about your sex, and not take it too seriously.

There is a well-aged business leader from whom we could all take lessons in this regard. He said: Tm 80 years of age and I can laugh at my age. Why? I can make love almost every day - almost on Monday, almost on Tuesday, almost on Wednesday!

Sexual humour has a place in the workforce and can be used to deal with sensitive topics and unpleasant situations; resolve conflict; add pleasure to pressure; make the boring bearable; and provide insight into emotional problems. This is evident in the following story:

> A corporate psychiatrist drew a straight line on a pad and said to his patient: What does that remind you of? The patient said: 'Sex! Then the psychiatrist drew a cross, and the patient said: Sex! With that, he drew a square and the patient said: Sex!' By this time, the psychiatrist was exasperated and he said: You're nothing but a sex maniac! And the patient said: I don't know about that; you're the one drawing all the dirty pictures!

The use of sexual humour can be encouraged, but before using it, study the following guidelines and choose what's appropriate for your circumstances.

Be very careful about your use of sexual humour. Re-read the positive and negative content in chapter one regularly.

Sexual Use of Humour Guideline

1. Relevancy - Tie it in with the discussion.
2. Use self-putdown.
3. Select location
4. Think of the subtext of the humour.
5. Consider groups personal relationships.
6. Respond to the emotional state of the listeners.
7. Target opposing company.
8. Send up organisational hierarchy.
9. Choose your content and techniques carefully.
10. Have a saver.

Humour is an effective way to lesson the fearful aspects of our sexuality, by making them appear ridiculous and absurd. One way of achieving this is to play reverse roles. This is a group game that allows us to see our sexual inadequacies and anxieties from an opposite perspective. Each person in the group has two minutes to describe what it would be like being the complete opposite to what they are in sex, appearance, employment and matrimonial status. That means that if a man is tall, with dark hair and is a doctor who is single, he becomes a woman with blonde hair, a patient and is married. We can all imagine some people playing this game.

Aggression

You can us humour as a safety and sanity valve for your hostility and aggression. Seeing the humorous side of things is a way of finding self-control when things are out of your control. The late West Australian millionaire Lang Hancock once walked out of a Sydney hotel and handed the doorman a tip. The doorman looked down and saw a 10-cent piece.

He said: "My God! I don't believe it! Hancock said: 'I didn't tip you 10 cents. I tipped you $10,000 after tax.'

As a leader, manager or an executive you must expect to receive a fair amount of humour aimed at you because you are the authority. Most of it will be unfair, some insulting.

A lot of this verbal abuse can be headed off at the pass, by attacking yourself first. Become aware of the inadequate, illogical aspects of your statements, decisions and behaviour. Then prepare humorous self-putdown lines to stifle pending aggressive upris1ngs. Have your employees laughing with you instead of at you.

We all have to release our anger and aggression. Humour is an alternative to violence and can help you play instead of fight with these feelings and emotions. Hating can become comfortable through humour, as Bill Dana advised in 7he Hostility Handbook.

Think of any co-worker, politician, egotist, enemy, parking inspector or any frustations. Then make a list of targets to attack, and then attack. This is done by putting the appropriate name with the appropriate line, so you sanely get the venom and victim out of your system.

Example:

Name .... has a fat chance to succeed and a head to match!

Name .... tried for a corner on the market, and now he has a market on the corner!

May .... spent most of his life at a compliant counter.

When .... started a business, it did as well as a hat-check concession would at a nudist camp.

If you need to take your humour action further, attack once more. Get some photos of your targets, photocopy quite a few copies of each, then start collecting cartoons from all sorts of magazines. Now you have the pleasure of replacing the cartoon head with skulls of your victims. Over time you could build up quite a grotesque gallery of punishing pictures. If they were all viewed in the one setting, they would resolve the most aggressive hostility.

Humour and laughter offer many playful ways of working out and working with anger and aggression. It can replace them with tolerance and acceptance, thereby re-affirming our relationships with our workmates. Remember, you can't be angry and laugh at the same time!

Irreverence

> An 'Ocker' is a mythical Australian creature, like unicorn or a bunyip. The only person who has ever seen one is Mr Max Harris, every time he shaves.
> Barry Humphries

Irreverence is part and parcel of an Australian attitude, whether it's shooting sacred cows, or verbally levelling pomposity and hypocrisy. Rebelling against rules and regulations are part of our Australian psyche. When you cultivate a sense of irreverence, you're not being negative, you are being positive, because nothing is perfect. In fact, you're stimulating your emotional capacity, making it possible for you to focus flexibly on your fixed views. The emotional humour energy of irreverence has been responsible for considerable social change. It can play a part in your organizational change. You must have a perception of irreverence, as well as an acceptance of it.

However, it must be respectful irreverence. You might like to organise a company 'irreverence day' in which employees are invited to come work dressed the way they like.

Give them a licence at the door to say whatever they like and so protect them from management backlash. Or, instigate the oath of irreverence, where employees receive a management oath that there will be no retaliation about what they would like to say. On one such day an employee walked into a director's boardroom meeting and said: ' Do you know what it means walking into a happy office, seeing smiling executives, and being greeted by friendly management? Do you know what it means? It means I'm in the wrong office, that's what it means!" Fortunately, or unfortunately, I was born with a sense of irreverence.

The new Harris Tweed sporting jacket I m wearing now is testimony to this. It's amazing! The wool for it was grown in Australia, spun in Japan. The jacket was made in Iraly with thread from Taiwan. The lining was woven in France from silk produced in Egypt. I bought it in Singapore. What really amazes me is, the people who have made a living out of it and I haven't paid for it yet.

Embarrassment

Dr Annette Goodheart, in *Laughter and Relationship*, one of her series of brilliant cassette tapes says:

> 'The most marvellous thing you can do, which will take care of your past energies and traumas and connect you with the people around you, is to start sharing your embarrassing moments. We are all walking around as if we don't' know how to walk; as if we don't have pins

in our underwear; as if we have it all together; as if our lives are running smoothly; as if we know exactly what we are doing. And we all get Caught up in our postures, posing and pretence. A Woman came up to me and said: T laughed all by myself once! I was hiking up a canyon, I was struggling up this canyon. I looked up on the side of this canyon and there was this flower growing out of the rocks. Incredible!' She scrambled up the cans wall, scraping her knees. She gets to the top, she bends over to smell the flower and all the petals off. That was a "Chaplinesque moment!'

The fear of being embarrassed, making a fool of ousekves and being laughed at has prevented so many ordinary people from becoming a f=great people. A genius is a crackpot until he or she hits the jackpot! Once we have mastered the art of being comfortable when we are embarrassed, then our wildest dreams and goals, no matter how outrageous, become possible. Stephen Wright, the American comedian has a line.

'Do you know the feeling when you re leaning back on a chair and for a split second you feel you are going to fall? Well, I have that feeling all day!'

Using humour and not getting a laugh is a similar feeling. It starts with that pregnant pause and gives birth to embarrassment. This fear stops a lot of people expressing their personality in a humorous way.

Having prepared spontaneity can prevent embarrassing moments. When you get into trouble, people don't mind if you have fun with it and take the laughs on yourself. You can do this by developing a collection of controllers.

These are lines, expressions or character traits you use when something unexpected happens. They control the situation, keep the attention and maintain the emotional hook with the listeners.

For example, if you're involved in an intimate conversation and the phone rings. Say: 'I'd better answer that, it could be the phone. Same situation and there is unexpected noise or sound. Say: 'Do you notice how noisily I talk? Same situation. Say: "The termites are taking dancing lessons. These lines aren't that funny, but they keep control of communication flow in formal or informal situations.

Begin by making a list of all possible embarrassing happenings, comprising circumstances and unpleasant situations. Then prepare control line for them. In no time you will become skilled in the spontaneous use of control lines. However, be careful not to find yourself in the same situation as the manager whose wife was complaining at the dinner table saying: 'All you ever talk about is golf! Everything you do has something to do with golf!' 'That's not true dear,' he said. 'Now, would you please pass me the putter.'

Defence Mechanism

> Coming to work doesn't hurt, it's the long wait to go home.

> I like my job, it's the work I hate.

> I really enjoy work; I could sit and watch it for hours.

These three statements are examples of defence mechanisms. They make it nossible for you to joke about your work anxieties and difficulties. They help you mentally and emotionally escape, to protect yourself from the technological conformity of your work environment. Humour operates as a defence mechanism by providing countless pleasurable methods of dealing with job dissatisfaction, uncertainties and responsibilities.

Some humour defence mechanisms are:

Superiority:

> He's the only bloke I know who can sleepwalk to work and back.

Denial:

> I don't have to work here; I have enough money to last me the rest of my life. That's unless I want to buy something.

Rationalisation:

> I haven't got any money. It's because of my neighbours; they are always doing something I can't afford.

Acting Out:

> Have a managing director auction where employees bid, either with petty cash money or minutes of their time. The winner gets to do a farcical impersonation of the managing director, at his choice of place and time.

Defence mechanisms are a natural part of Australian humour. They are used as an adaptive device, expressed through self-disarrangement about subjects such as apathetic attitude, lousy lovers, shame of cruelty, non-existing culture, geographical isolation, and harshness of the environment. The following joke is indicative of how humour was used as a defence mechanism by the Australian bushman, to come to terms with his environment.

A local farmer's wife had a baby and the farmer came into the hospital to see them for the first time. The nurse said with a smile: "You have a fine boy. As vou now he was premature, so he is very small, but perfectly well.'

The farmer pushed his hat back and said: 'Ah well, in a season like this youre lucky to get your seed back!?

This form of humour, which made outsiders laugh, was a statement of the reality of life in the bush. Australians use it as a philosophical handshake with nature, a joking relationship with their environment.

This same humour attitude needs to be nurtured and practised in corporate life. Our survival depends on our ability to change ourselves rather than our environment. Humour is the agent of change. It is a survival skill that can show you how to remodel and reshape your attitudes and behaviour so you can fit in with, and enjoy, all circumstances.

Enjoyment

To a large percentage of the workforce, the words 'serious humour appear to be an oxymoron. It means not just waiting for joy to materialise but to engineer enjoyment, consciously and deliberately. Think of three real feelings of enjoyment that you have expressed recently at work. Was one a unexpected cheque in the mail, a phone call to say you had just won a hard-fought account or just the enjoyment of the simple realisation that you are alive, healthy, with friends, and happy doing what you are doing?

Whatever your three are, just thinking about them gives you pleasure and satisfaction. You only had to exert the energy of thought to receive the energy of enjoyment. That's how easy taking humour seriously is! Put yourself in enjoyable situations and give yourself injections of enjoyment.

Use anything from a family photo on your desk to a drawing of your boat on the wall. Begin an enjoyment drawer with favourite funny photos, cartoons, games, ridiculous documents, bizarre proposals, badges, signs, collectable rubbish and useless nonsense. Dissatisfaction leads to boredom, boredom leads to meaninglessness. This is the disease of contemporary corporate life. It is brought about by an outdated ideology that there is a distinct separation between enjoyment and employment.

Throughout many years of serious training, people have only managed to mildly introduce enjoyment on the job. Here are a few enjoyment exercises on the job. Here are a few enjoyment exercises that I consciously employ during my working day:

1. Finding as much enjoyment in the challenge as I do in the achievement.
2. Affirming that enjoyment is a state of mind and removing barriers that cloud my perception of this reality.
3. Making a contract with myself, that if somebody that I don't get on with at work uses humour and is funny, I will enjoy it, and give myself the pleasure of laughter
4. Encouraging others to use their humour for my enjoyment, not just using my humour for their enjoyment.

Discretion

As Dr. Joel Goodman says: We must develop our sense-activity to our sense of humour; becoming alert and alive to its elements, energies and expressions and most important of all, its effects.' Humour can either be a toy (just for laughs), a tool (positive and purposeful), a weapon (attack), or a (defence). The most successful humour users have a heightened discretion; they can diplomatically tell someone to go to hell in such a way that they are looking forward to the trip. They have acquired an awareness people's personalities and feelings. They analyse the situation, then choose the time to use the humour carefully.

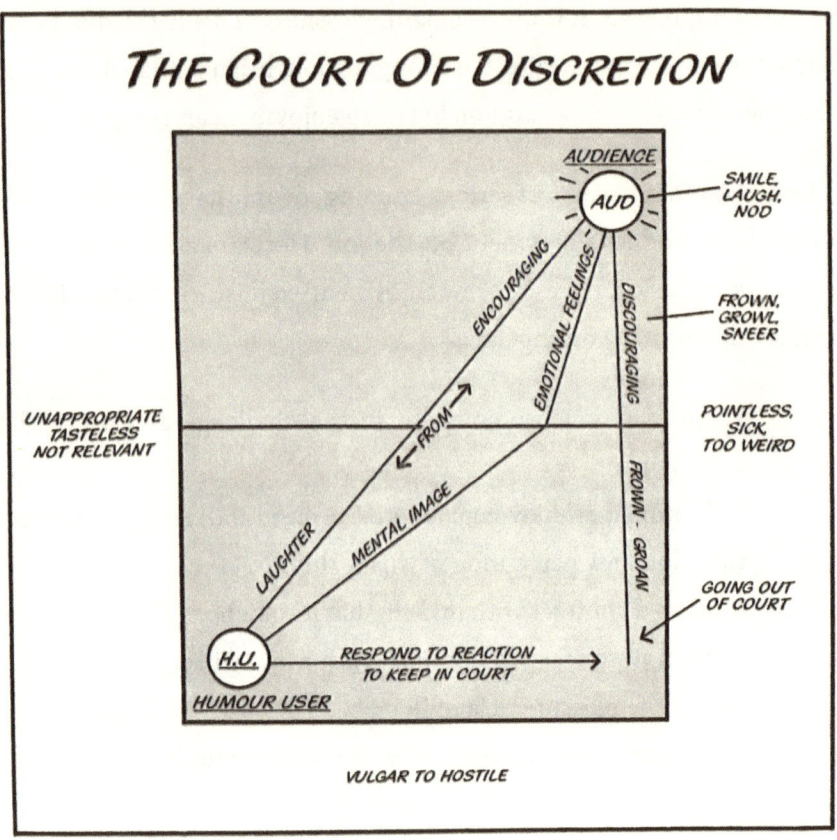

Once the decision is made to use humour, they are very sensitive to the response it receives. If the listeners are strangers and are responding with slight smiles and nods, this is an indication to the user of his direction, depth and delivery. Using humour that will be accepted and appreciated is like playing energy tennis. You send an idea that stimulates a mental image, which surfaces as an emotional feeling. The response is either for or against: this is hit back. From then on you must play fairly and tactfully to keep the humour ball in court, balancing between aggression and empathy, between vulnerability and embarrassment.

Using humour discreetly means understanding how the listener will feel after the instantaneous reaction of laughter has worn off and they have had time to think about what they were laughing about. It means developing a sixth sense, a humour sense.

Being human and being discreet is sometimes impossible. Alan Dundes and Carl R. Pagter, in their book, *When You're Up to Your Ass In Alligators*, under the heading, "Situation Adaptability Evaluation for Management Personnel, asks this question:

> You are making a sales presentation to a group of corporate executives, in the plushest office you have ever seen. The hot enchilada casserole and egg salad sandwich you had for lunch react, creating a severe pressure. Your sphincter loses its control and you break wind in a most convincing manner, causing three water tumblers to shatter and a secretary to pass out! What you should do next is:
>
> a. Offer to come back next week when the smell has gone away.
> b. Point out their chief executive and accuse him of the act.
> c. Challenge anyone in the room to do better!

People laugh out of shock, uncertainty, nervousness, fear, embarrassment indecision and enjoyment. This laughter comes in various degrees -a smile, a chuckle, a belly laugh. So if you're going to elicit this magical elixir, laughter, you need to learn the steps that lead to discretion.

Humour Discretion Steps

1. Give thought to the person you want the laugh from.
2. Analyse the situation you are in.
3. Prepare for the problems that could arise.
4. Find the most relevant way to approach the subject or occasion.
5. Assess the best form and technique of humour to use.
6. Observe and react to responses, whether discouraging or encouraging.
7. Be open and non-defensive.
8. Explore balance.
9. Employ politeness, fairness and tactfulness.
10. Expect the unexpected
11. Listen to your humour sensitivity and sixth sense.

Credibility

You must be experienced in using humour in a one-off formal occasion or a one-to-one intormal occasion. More so if you are continually using humour to the same audience over a period of time. Here we must establish five credentials:

- Humour Dynamics
- Likeability
- Trustability
- Responsibility
- Dependability
- Credibility

These belong to what I like to call Humour dynamics, the science dealing with the flow of feelings from, and responses to, your humour by an audience. Likeability is to win affection and keep it.

Trust is important. You must think your audiences believe you so that they can trust you not to shock, frighten or embarrass them, without adequate warning, and so they have time to prepare themselves for your message. If you are delivering the end-of-year financial report, in the boardroom, you don't say to the company directors: Gentlemen, this year's financial repo is proudly brought to you in the colour red!

Remember, your responsibility to your audience. You must make your humour understandable, non-offensive and acceptable to them. This might sound easy but it's not. A little knowledge is a dangerous thing. A little success with humour goes to your funnybone. The next thing you know, you are shooting from the hip with a shotgun. Anyone can get hurt! Take the responsibility of using humour seriously. It's like another truth that needs to be learned: never agree with your boss until he says something. Once you achieve dependability when using humour, your audience will gain confidence in you. Taking responsibility for your use of humour is harder in the short term, but once an audience can depend on you, they start smiling and responding to your humour. The above qualities go on to establish and maintain our humour credibility. You will enhance your credibility as a leader when you ensure the staff feels secure and satisfied in their employers building their confidence, respect and support.

When you use humour you are putting your credibility on the line. However, this is something you do every day when you're employing people, solving problems or making decisions. You already have the intelligence and communication skills to use humour.

The following number of don'ts will help you maintain your credibility when using humour:

1. Don't try to be anything other than what you are. Stretch carefully.

2. Don't use humour if you have any doubts about its effectiveness.

3. Don't be caught unprepared. Research, Rehearse, Remember.

4. Don't carry your humour too far.

5. Don't add pressure by trying too hard. When the effort shows, the humour goes.

6. Don't forget to make yourself the target and to look at the subtext of the content.

7. Don't laugh at others, but with them, unless you know they can laugh at themselves.

By understanding the nature of humour and making it a natural part of the way you do business, you add fun and profit to your life!

Chapter Four Summary
The Nature of Humour

1. Humour is a creative energy.

2. Humour makes it possible for us to see problems in their proper perspective.

3. Developing your observational humour becomes a process you can practise.

4. Humour trains our imagination to ultimately transform our intelligence.

5. You can help the audience to visualise your characters, actions and attitudes, by painting a picture with sound and by describing in finite detail, the scenes, situations and circumstances.

6. Telling jokes is a very small part of using humour.

7. It is easier to remember humour, which comes from your own experiences.

8. Motivation, observation, viSualisation, association, practice and rehearsal are the keys to remembering humour.

9. Humour is a more significant process in the human mind than reason.

10. Humour creativity is an acquired ability.

11. Use humour creative thinking to re-organise, re-value, re-shape, reform, refresh, reinforce, rejuvenate, resolve, rejoice, and above all, relax on the job!

12. If its insightful, it's funny.

13. As well as learning jokes, practise spontaneity.

14. To be successful in using humour, you have to build and release tension.

15. Make a commitment to deliberately add the surprise of humour to your life.

16. Our vulnerabilities become our major humour assets.

17. Show you take your job seriously but not yourself.

18. Humour has a place in the workforce and can be used to deal with sensitive topics.

19. Seeing the humorous side of things is a way of finding self-control when things are out of your control

20. When you cultivate a sense of irreverence, you're not being negative, you're being positive because nothing is perfect.

CHAPTER 5

The Secrets of Humour

When we use humour in corporate life, law, politics, selling, marketing, education or just in general communication, there are basic humour principles that apply in its application. Only by understanding the structural and functional aspects of humour can we make it a potent skill to be applied in business life.

Most people believe that knowing what humour is and how to use it is a pretty simple matter. But as Arthur Asa Berger pointed out in a paper at the first International Humour Conference, there's so much more to it. Berger's model drew attention to eight points:

1. The creator of the humour (the sender.)
2. The information sent (the content of the humour.)
3. The audience (the receiver of the humour.)
4. How it is transmitted (the medium.)
5. The kind of humour (the forms and formulas.)
6. The methods employed (the techniques.)
7. The consequences of the humour (the effects.)
8. The purpose the humour serves (the function.)

To use humour well, we need to study the structure. We now need to understand the structure so we can answer the 'what, when, why and how' of humour. This chapter will give you a better understanding by making you familiar with some of the formulas and forms of humour. These are the elements and essential properties of the chemistry of humour. Learning them is much harder than studying systems of any other subject, but it's a lot more enjoyable because of the laughs it provides. These formulas for the skeleton that binds your humour. I call them the *formula frames* because they are mostly mathematical.

Humour Formulas

'A formula is a formula is a formula most of the time.'
Annoyed Anonymous

There is a mathematical equation of humour:

Formulas x Imagination
+ (Discipline & Dedication)
- (Fear & Frustration)
= Creative Humour Success.

Keep your sense of humour fresh as you study the humour formulas. Don't become concerned that a lot of humour uses more than one formula. Complication never stopped a chef using a variety of spices or a lawyer applying a complexity of laws to a case. Imagine you have been a gold prospector for 20 years and found nothing but a few ounces, a few grains at a time. Then one day you hit a large reef of gold. The grains are the jokes and stories you already know, and the reefs are the formulas. They are pure comedy gold!

Of course, you need more than formulas to guarantee that you will profit from humour. You need information and the desire to develop your *Humour Attitude*.

From the abundance of humour formulas available, I have chosen five to examine and give examples of. These are:

1. Exaggeration (blowing things up)

2. Understatement (blowing things down)

3. Reversal (the opposite).

4. Interrupted Catalogue (1,2,3…a)

5. Mistaken Identity (getting it wrong).

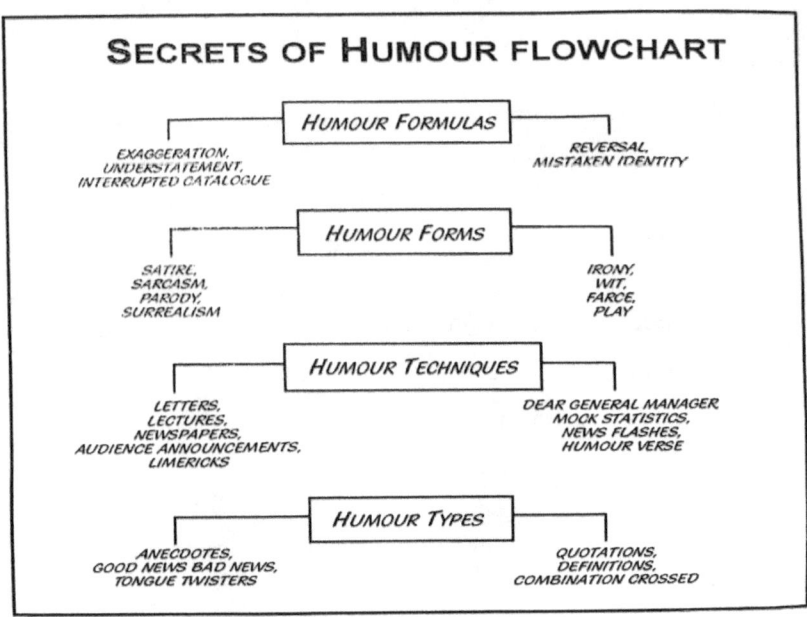

Exaggeration Formula

One of the first things I remember hearing as a child was: 'I have told you 10 million times not to exaggerate. 'Statements like this program us to avoid using exaggeration, but programming can be reversed! It's just a matter of exercising your mental muscles, stretching your imagination, thinking big... then bigger … then enormously big!

Ask yourself what else can be done to make your statement outlandish, more far fetched, and more ridiculous. The following joke demonstrated the extremes:

> I would not say that the new Sydney Entertainment Centre is big, but I believe Michael Edgley is flying out the entire Chinese nation to walk from one end to the other in a remake of their 20-year march.

The idea is clearly overstated, yet it was based on truth. Anything can be exaggerated or understated and we have all used the techniques at various times.

Joel Goodman, in Volume 1 No:3 of *Laughing Matters*, gives an example of one exaggeration structure you can practise. I know a bloke (subject), who is so rich (adjective) that the finance company owes him money (exaggeration.)

Exaggeration works wonders during conflict. I own a book shop and some books arrived damaged, so I rang up the managing director of the company, introduced myself, and said: 'I don't wish to complain, but that load of books that I received from your company looked like they had gone eight rounds with Mike Tyson. And he said: And lost. Our mutual humour dissolved whatever conflict could have begun.

All too often we exaggerate conflict way beyond what it really is. The truth to realise this, and exaggerate it even more consciously, by making fun of it. This gives you the capacity to see it as it really is.

Understatement

The opposite of exaggeration is understatement. I once saw the following sign on a bankrupt business: 'We under sold everybody. Instead of saying too much you underplay the situation.

Understatement is a form of humour that fits the controlled, contrived, sophisticated traditions of corporate life. In his book, *How To Speak And write With Humour*, Percy H. Whiting, gives this example:

> From a notice to employees (Doubtless imagery)

> Due to increased competition and a keen desire to remain in business, we are asking that somewhere between starting and quitting time and without infringing too much on the time devoted to lunch period, coffee breaks, rest period, storytelling and ticket selling. Each employee endeavour to find some time that he can set aside to be known as the work break.

Reversal Formula

> Anyone can sympathise with the sufferings of a friend, but it requires a very fine nature to sympathise with a friend 's success.

> Oscar Wilde.

The *Reversal Formula* is turning things around, flipping things over. It turns the tallest into the smallest, the fastest into the slowest and the most successful into the most unsuccessful.

Evan Esar said:

> 'Humour is universal and one of the universals of humour is reversal.'

P.G.Wodehouse once wrote:

> 'I am going to start at the bottom and work my way down.'

Here are three samples of the Reversal Technique:

Wordplay Reversal

> Take the burglar's wife, who would not stop nags her husband for money. In the end he said: 'Righto, righto, cut it out, stop whingeing, I'll get some money as soon as the banks close.

Sentence Reversal

> My boss is really progressive. Some companies have the four-day working week; he believes in the four-week working day.

Cause and Effect Reversal

> General Motors Holden has just made the biggest automobile breakthrough in years... a windscreen wiper which won't hold parking tickets.

The ability to think in reverse is Vitally important in the quick and critical decision-making world of business. Sometimes, by recognising a mistake you made, and reversing that mistake, you can prevent any acceleration of the error. Remember, admitting your mistakes is part of your *Humour Attitude*!

In 1984, when US President Reagan was debating Walter Mondale for the second time, Reagan knew the age issue would be brought up and he had his humorous answer ready.

> 'I will not make age an issue of this campaign; I am not going to exploit for political purposes my opponents youth and inexperience.'

The reversal is a creative way to explore and expose your fears, goals, passions and prejudices. Just choose half a dozen of your most bizarre attitudes, then Work with the reversal to re-evaluate or resolve them.

Interrupted Catalogue Formula

> 'I don't ask much out of life. All I want is to be so important, so successful, so powerful, that if Somebody yells "hey you", I don't turn around.'

This formula has been called many things: the broken set, the series, the Humorous catalogue. It's the simplest humour formula to master. You build a set up line with similar ideas, attitudes, phrases or words and then surprise with an unexpected punchline. The technique behind writing your interrupted Catalogues is easy. Just research a list of events or habits and tie them together in a group. Then add an incongruous, nonsensical or preposterous thought. It must be suitably surprising to get the laugh response.

> The executive who had just come back from a business trip to Japan said part of his money went on liquor, part on gambling and part on girls. The remainder he spent foolishly.

As you repeat the sameness of the Content, you can raise your voice and pace. This builds tension so it is only natural that your listeners will laugh when you startle them with the opposite to what they expected. The interrupted catalogue can also be a wonderful conversational humour devise. For example: 'My hobby is gardening; every Sunday I put on my old trousers, my old jumper and tell my wife where to dig.'

If you are writing a speech, planning a presentation, or just preparing the opening to a conversation, the best way to add humour is with the *Interrupted Catalogue Formula*.

> 'I played golf with the boss yesterday but that's the last time. Would you play with somebody who cheats, shouts out, changes his card? Well, neither will the boss.'

Mistaken Identity Formula

This is the formula of getting things wrong.

> The policeman asked the rushing salesman who was Going the wrong way up a one-way street: Where are you off to? The salesman replied I don't know, but It can't be much good because everyone is coming back.'

Mistaken identity is the humour of puzzlement and confusion brought about by faulty judgments, inaccurate decisions and failure to be observant.

> The way some people in advertising are dressing these days is dangerous, especially if they are waiting on a corner for a lift at seven o'clock in the morning. One fellow was picked up three times by police and twice by the garbage truck.

Mistaken Identity covers blunders brought about by incorrect or wrong identification of problems, emotions, actions, locations and objects. It's ideal for a variety of characters and character traits.

> A managing director was called down to the taxation office. The tax auditor told him: 'Some of these deductions look funny! The managing director said: Well laugh!

Forms of Humour

Humour is an appreciation and expression of both conscious and subconscious emotions and thoughts. You need to have a knowledge of its principal forms to use humour effectively in a specific environment. These forms set the mood and climate that influences the emotional reactions of the receivers. Understanding them helps you plan your tactics and execute your approach. Here are eight humour forms that invite analysis and action:

- SATIRE
- IRONY
- SARCASM
- WIT
- PARODY
- FARCE
- SURREALISM
- PLAY

Satire

This form of humour comes out of our everyday lives. Its popularity and performance are assured because of its licence for social criticism. *Satire* exposes, mocks, sends up and attacks pomposity, hypocrisy, and immorality, as well as nedative habits and customs. A true satirist combines the painful realities of like with pleasurable experiences and can heighten our personal and social harmony.

Lenny Bruce said:

> 'People should be taught what is, not what should he ...
> all my humour is based on destruction and despair. If the

whole world was tranquil, without disease and violence, I'd
be standing in the bread line, right back of J. Edgar Hoover.'

Satire twists, bends and sends up the values, traditions and customs of
corporate life.

'A business executive must be knowledgeable, diplomatic,
a workaholic and have the stamina and the digestion of
a camel.'

Irony

The irony of life is, that by the time you have money to
burn, the fire has gone out.

Irony can be a forceful communication tool. You make a remark that
can be the direct opposite to what you are thinking. For example, when
somebody uses negative humour, you respond by saying: Thats very
funny. We have all been involved in some of life's little ironies:

Just recently, I did an in-house humour presentation
workshop with audio visual equipment and a radio-
controlled microphone. The equipment failed, which
ruined my presentation. Two days later, I received a bill
for $200 for the hire of the equipment.

Australians are a nation of ironists. We are creative battlers fighting droughts,
flood and fire, yet our national catch phrase is: 'You've gotta laugh, mate.'

Sarcasm

Sarcasm is like sunlight: it can keep you warm but it you
don't look out you can get burnt.

The incorrect use of sarcasm can be devastating and build barriers that can't be penetrated The 'Laugh Professor', Doctor Virginia Tooper, founder of Sarcastic Anonymous, says: 'People don't like being laughed at. Sarcastic laughter can be painful and cause low self-esteem, prevent success, inhibit creativity.'

You can use it to be assertive and protect yourself.

> Like the secretary who said: "In our business you have to
> have a lot of experience with shorthand and long arms.'

With care, sarcasm can be used in a positive way, if the one who uses it is correct and the remark itself is humorous.

> Like the minister who said: "The poor are welcomed in
> this church, and I can see by the collection plate that they
> have come.'

But generally, sarcasm and sarcastic people should be avoided. It's superiority humour, based on ridicule, vindictiveness and aggression, and unless harnessed correctly, should not be used in the workplace.

Wit

> It's not enough to be witty, you must have enough wit to
> avoid having too much.
> Andre Mavrios

One of Australia's greatest wits, Sir Robert Menzies, once said:

> 'One thing about bureaucrats is they never swallow
> their young - leave them alone and you will find them
> increasing every year.'

Wit is without doubt the most admired form of humour. Yet humour originates from emotions and wit from intellect. Wit is the brilliant, cognitive connection between an idea or an attitude, a subject and a target, or a situation and a person.

> When a despised boss died, an office wit was heard to remark: 'He took his first holiday in 40 years yesterday, and picked out a cemetery plot!'

A natural wit has high intelligence and has subconsciously trained their humour mind. A practised wit has normal intelligence and has consciously trained their humour mind. The worst wits of all are the punsters, who should be punished. (apologies for the pun!)

Parody

> If you can keep your head when all those around you are losing theirs, you will eventually find yourself a head taller than everyone else.

This, of course, is a parody of Kipling s famous verse *If*. Parody impersonates, mimics and mocks well-known writings, songs, plays, films and television shows and any well-known set of words. It's a good place to start when creating humour, as there is already something there to model, imitate or build on. We have all been parodists and parodied at sometime or another, or been spoofed at an office party or business function. The John Cleese training films are a successful example of the art of parody. They aim to stop people doing the wrong thing by making them realise that the way they are behaving is incorrect. They are humorous and relaxing. The audience laughs while they learn.

Farce

When the boss says, I don't like yes men; want you to tell me what you really think, even if it costs you your job, the boss is being farcical. The basis of farce is simple. A ridiculous idea is accepted as being true, then is acted on logically. Farce is older than comedy and much more ridiculous than satire and can include slapstick and burlesque. Therefore, it is often called broad' or 'low' comedy, as distinct from more sophisticated comedy similar to wit, which fits easily into a setting of normal behaviour.

Farce is an escape from reality. The use of exaggeration, mistaken Identity, improvisation and eccentricities makes it a genre appreciated by people looking for a good belly laugh. Bureaucratic bungling, embarrassing moments, absurd management policies, indeed, the basis of corporate life, feeds farce. Farce is also a form of meditation that can help you take a menta break from work. Takea couple of minutes everyday to put on your farcical hat, imagining that what you see is a film and you're in a theatre watching it. Have a good Captain Cook at some of the weird, strange and unreal behaviour of your fellow workers. Behaviour which, just a few seconds earlier, you were taking so melodramatically, takes on a convivial perspective, This is a real ulcer reducing exercise! Learn to see beyond the sombre and serious to the ridiculous behind.

Surrealismn

> Sometimes, we can see the real sense, by making nonsense.
>
> Pete Crofts

Surrealism combines outrageous exaggeration, impossible contradictions, zany assumptions and free associations. It brings together the most improbable objects, activities, virtues and vices, juxtaposing them to create verbal fantasies and dazzling mental images that have nothing to do with real life but often show its limits.

> Johnny's feet are so big, he has to put his trousers over his head.

Notice that this is a good farce joke too. Mind you, with the kind of trousers I wear, this is impossible!

The brilliant American comedian Stephen Wright tells this surreal story:

> 'One time I was right in the middle of a job interview and I started reading, and the guy said: What the hell are you doing?" I said: "Let me ask you one question. If you were in a vehicle and you ere travelling at the speed of light and then you turned your lights on, would they do anything?" He said: "I don't know." So I said: "Forget it, I don't want to work for you!"'

Surrealism frees you from 'the system. With freedom from rules or regulations, it demonstrates the limitless capacity of right-brain thinking. It's a form of humour from which we could all benefit putting into practice. For example, if you're facing a seemingly insurmountable situation, you could eliminate some of the stress by seeing it in the surrealistic way.

Like the manager who was caught up in a difficult union dispute. He was heard to say: I met Karl Marx in my sleep last night and he said he wouldn't talk to me unless I joined a dreamers' union.'

We all need to expand and escape our rational thinking and do a little *surreal thinking.*

Play

> To be playful and serious at the same time is possible and
> it defines the ideal mental condition.
> John Delvey

A playful mood helps remove uncertainties and inhibitions; allows for errors; freezes embarrassments, criticisms and rejections; opens up the comfort zone; and makes room for the risk-taker and creative thinker.

> You know it's time to initiate play in your workplace
> when executives start wearing combat gear to work;
> when employees are bringing attack dogs to chain them
> to the desk; and when you have to hire armed guards to
> pass out memos.

In his book *Enjoyment of Laughter*, Max Eastman wrote: "The condition in which joyful laughter most continually occurs is that of play.

A playful attitude helps you put problems, challenges and change into perspective. The executive who had a playful attitude said:

> 'I'm not worried about the problems of my job; if they
> were any less difficult, someone of less ability would have
> my job.'

To foster a playful attitude:

- Adopt a playful frame of mind
- Become skilled at play
- Make a play commitment
- Get permission to play

Humour Techniques

Humour techniques are styles used for delivering humour. They are simple to use, but like most humour in the hands of the practitioner, success comes when you apply the four principles.

1. Preparation.   2. Practice.   3. Performance.   4. Persistence

1. Preparation: Don't be in a hurry to get tons of humour techniques. Do a little research and find what suits you. Then spend time preparing to use it to the best of your ability.

2. Practice: Once the preparation stage is complete, practise the humour technique a number of times before you use it.

3. Performance: This is where you use the humour techniques in an important presentation or meeting to achieve the result you want.

4. Persistence: Keep developing it until you get it to the stage where you feel very comfortable with it. Don't give up; persist until you get it right.

All these devices can be used as prepared savers:

Humour Letters

Humour letters are a great device to use in presentations. They can be any size and have many advantages. They add a touch of humour, which can be personalised and/or topicalised.

Letter to the Income Tax Department.

Dear Sir,

I cheated on last year's return and haven't been able to sleep. Enclosed find cheque for $1000. If I still find I cannot sleep I will forward the balance.

If you forget what to say or blank out, just pull out a piece of paper and say: 'I got a strange letter the other day; it says':

Dear Sir,

Your humour caused my wife to die laughing last night. Tonight I am sending my mother-1n-law to your presentation.

There is a distinct style of humour letter which asks advice from someone of knowledge or authority. It appears in many forms under such titles as Letters to the Doctor, 'Dear Aunt Sally. The technique is to read the letter and the advice in a sympathetic, emotional way. To add realism, you could put your glasses on thoughtfully.

Dear General Manager,

I am writing to ask you the wo qualities I need to find success in business.

Signed Young Enthusiastic Entrepreneur.

Dear Young Enthusiastic Entrepreneur,

The two qualities are integrity and wisdom. Integrity means always keep your word no matter what your manager or supervisor says, and wisdom means you don't give it in the first place!

Newspaper

Take out the local newspaper and read headlines, items and the 'for sale' ads. Example:

> A managing director, retired due to stress, wishes to sell 15 in-trays and one out-tray. Please phone Jacked Up.

This flexible humour technique is reliable and simple to use.

> Widowed farmer's wife, aged 36, wishes to meet man, same age, with tractor. Please enclose photo of tractor.

Business Neus

> A businessman has been thrown out of his office so many times, he had curtains to match the footpath.

Humour announcements

These can also be a statement you share with your staff at meetings or over the loud speaker. For example:

> When you are driving home tonight remember to drive carefully, and remember that humans are the only beings to drive a mortgaged car down a bond-financed highway using credit cards for petrol.

Humorous verse

Sometimes called comedy poetry, the humorous verse comes in many types and styles and can be read in conversation. The verses get giggles instead of laughs, and add variety to your methods of delivery. They should be short and sharp with a strong rhythm and rhyme.

> First came the hearty pioneers with rifles, ploughs and taxes.
>
> Then civilisation followed close with muggers, debts and axes.

Sometimes I will make a point illustrated with a joke, then reaffirm it with a humorous verse.

> The world is like a mirror, retlecting what you do, if your face is smiling, it smiles right back to you.

News flashes

This technique is simple and reliable, if used sparingly and carefully. It Comes under the banner of Card Humour. Have the news flashes written on cards; it's then just a matter of taking them from your pack and readings them when it's appropriate.

> A businessman today was awarded the OBE because he solved a problem that had plagued mankind forever: visiting relatives. When asked how he did it, he said: 'It was simple. I just borrow money from the rich ones and loaned it to the poor ones. Then none of them come back.

Audience announcements

Another form of card humour, these announcements are used the same way as the news flashes. You can open or close with them or Just use them for a change of mood. Learn them well but appear to read them from the cards.

> Would the person who owns the Cadillac convertible with the cow-hide seat covers, please report to the parking lot, there's a bull attacking the back seat.

Lectures

Campbell McComas uses this technique brilliantly. Assume the role of authority on a certain subject, then begin to send up yourself, the subject and the situation. A financial lecturer could say something like: 'A lot of stock is bought on the greater fool theory. Once you buy the stock, you begin looking for a greater fool to take it off your hands. Of course, a lot of divorces are based on the same theory.'

Mock statistics

People don't like too many statistics; if you have to use them, throw in a mock one every so often.

> Statistics show that 15 per cent of men in this country are bachelors; five per cent of these men are afraid to get married; five per cent can't afford to get marrieds and the other five per cent of these men already have husbands.

Statistical humour can also be entertaining in written communication, either inhouse or for making proposals.

> A statistician is a person who, if you've got your feet in the oven and your head in the refrigerator, will tell you, on average, you're very comfortable.

Humorous Types

It is definitely an asset to be competent at using humour types to keep your personality fresh and presentation surprising. They will expand

and improve your possibilities and performances. Here we will discuss six Humour Types.

1. Quotations
2. Antidotes
3. Definitions
4. Good News, Bad News
5. Combination Crossed
6. Tongue Twisters

Humour Quotations

> People will pay more to be entertained than to be educated.
>
> Johnny Carson

When you're learning to use humour, the quotation is often the safest way to begin. It can be used as a buffer to deflect a cold response to your humour. Here's how to apply it.

You say: This is a quotation from America's funniest lady Phyllis Diller: "Everybody says I'm a beautiful person inside; leave it to me to be born inside out! If no laugh reaction is forthcoming, go on with: "Phyllis also said: "The meek may inherit the earth but not an audience s laughter."

A quotation:

- Provides you with authority
- Stimulates reflection
- Enhances credibility
- Gives you the power of freedom of expression because somebody else said it.

I yield to no one in my admiration for the office as a social centre, but it's no place to actually get any work done.

Katherine Whitehorn - Sunday Best.

Anecdotes

The most relatable form of humour from the audience's point of view is the self-anecdote. Your day-to-day life, seen through the eyes of humour, becomes a continuous anecdote. All we have to do is:

1. Pick an incident, a situation, an episode of our life.
2. Think and feel it through.
3. Add humour techniques and construction devices.
4. Fashion it for your audiences as a humorous piece of your life.

In the 60s, I was a Melbourne comedian. In those days, that was an oxymoron. I couldn't get work. I went everywhere to get work, but Melbourne was closed. If it were not for talent quests in pubs on the road, I would have starved. A blonde out-of-tune-singer, with big breasts and a low-cut dress, would always win. I'd always come in third, but only when there were three people in the talent quest. And third prize was always a free meal at the pub.

I was doing a spot one night in one of these places and just for a joke I said, Don't eat the food here, folks, the chef's a monkey'! The next second I hear a clanging in the kitchen; the door flew open and out charged the Hungarian chef brandishing a chopper over his head screaming, 'Dont call me a monkey! Thank God the audience thought it was part of the show; it was the biggest laugh I ever got!

Telling this sort of anecdote, of course, is done with facial expressions, body movement and voice modulation. A successful anecdote can build emotion, regain attention and help persuade the listeners to your point of view.

Definitions
Definition of a goldfish is a sardine that came into money.

Definitions are the first place to start when you have to add humour. They're not hard to write; they're short and precise and a valuable way to illustrate a point. Just pick the target subject or word to be defined, locate it carefully in a sentence, then mention the word again and highlight it with the definition.

> I went into a bank the other day. You know what the definition of a bank is, don't you? That's where you borrow money from - if you can prove that you don't need it.

A definition just restates the meanings of the key words in a laughable way. They can be used as topic jokes. When you finish a joke, select the key word then tell the definition.

> I took my wife to a humour conference. I had twice the expenses and about half the fun. You know what the definition of a conference is, don't you? That's where a group of men, who individually can do nothing, can meet and decide nothing can be done.

Good news and bad news
I have some good news for you and some bad news. The good news is, I'm going to tell you a joke; the bad news is, it's an old joke. A typical good news and bad news joke is:

> I have some good news for all the slaves on the galley: you are all going to get an extra ration of rum with the noon

meal. The bad news is: after dinner, the captain wants to go water-skiing.

Dr Virginia Tooper suggests you can use this humour tool in the following way. If your company is having a problem and you have a meeting to deal with the issue, you may be able to diffuse tension with a bad news good news starter.

> Bad news: you all know we had a flood at the warehouse this weekend. Good news: the water is being diverted into a new employees swimming pool.

This can work with any corporate crisis or disciplinary action.

Combination Crossed

> My heroes are Jack Nicklaus and Robin Williams and they have made a big impact on my life. I play golf as well as Robin Williams and I'm as funny as Jack Nicklaus.

Here I combine two people, two professions and two of my own interests and then put my self-putdown. The laugh is created by swapping the expected information in the final sentence.

About the same time as US President Reagan was using a lot of humour in his speeches, a trend in films was horror comedy. l combined these two facts to write this joke.

> The big trend in movies today is horror comedy. President Reagan has been approached to make his movie comeback by a director who wants to film his speeches.

You can make connections anything at all. in its simplest form, it's just a matter of crossing two species.

> I crossed a parakeet with a managing director. I don't know what I got, but when it shouts you sure as hell better listen.

> I'm puzzled: if you crossed LSD with IBM would you end up with the ultimate business trip.

Tongue Twisters

> The bull buys the bulldog, browses the big board, drops his bundle because of the bubble blow out becoming a big bang.

Tongue twisters are just a little higher on the humour register than the pun. However, they have their place because of some of their practical uses. They can be vocal exercises, training slogans, whiteboard headlines, mirth, and memos. They also add a little light listening relief in verbal communication.

In its most sophisticated form, it becomes the 'mind twister'.

> There once were two skunks named In and Out. By a strange coincidence, when In was out, Out was In and when Out was out, In would be in. One day Out was in and In was out and the mother skunk turned to her youngster and said: 'Out, I want you to go out and bring in In. This Out did and the mother skunk was so impressed she turned to Out and said, 'Out, how did you manage to find In so quickly, and Out answered: That's easy mother, instincts.'

As you uncover the secrets of humour, your ***Humour Attitude* will grow making it easier for you to put your *Humour Action* to work!**

Making Switches Multiplies Humour

Here's a switch on the oldest joke in the world. Who is that lady I saw you with last night. That was no lady, that was our new managing director.

Switching humour to your type, point of view or purpose is an enjoyable way to write humour. Eighty per cent of all humour comes from rearranging, re-patterning and reconstructing old humour. By doing it, you become a humour investigator learning about formulas, construction, rhythm, editing, subject, targets, set-up lines and punchlines - all valuable aspects for engineering smooth, sensitive and successful humour.

The simplest way to multiply humour is to take a subject of humour and change the situation, conditions and people involved. Let's use a traditional humour subject and formula. The subject: Is this man a salesman? The formula: exaggeration.

1. Is this man a salesman? During World War II he sold pension plans to kamikaze pilots.
2. Is this man a salesman? He could sell leaves to a home owner.
3. Is this man a salesman? He could sell nothing for something to customers who want something for nothing.

For highlighting or handling regular character traits, business frustrations, important key points and recurring problems, this remodeling humour method is tops. Another simple form of born-again humour is where you take a joke from one subject, re-work it and adapt it to the corporate scene. Example: To be a successful wife these days, a woman is expected to be a mother in the children's room, a cook in the kitchen, a cleaner in the laundry, a duster in the lounge room, and a seductress in the bedroom. The same joke switched to the corporate sector would read: to get ahead in business today, a woman is expected to look like a girl, behave like a lady, think like a man, and work like a dog.

We can all be funny by mistake, but to create humour that's effective for a specific purpose, you need skills. Even if you just master the skill of switching, you'll have ample humour for your professional needs.

We can understand born-again humour in more detail by dissecting this joke that was going around 20 years ago. We will transform the joke from being a personalised, corporate joke and localise it so it becomes an Australian joke. At the same time we will modernise it to: the businessman who wanted to become a hippy so he left home, gave up his job, spent $1000 beads and found out he was allergic to dirt.

The joke is based on the interrupted catalogue formula and comparisons between two people. Exaggeration is used to highlight the most vulnerable aspect of the target -in this case, the hippy. The joke is ideal for switching.

Pick two people, compare character traits and you have a new joke about the European who wanted to become an Australian. He gave up his job, spent $500 on thongs and found out he was allergic to beer. You could rewrite this joke continually, and if you used it sparingly, no one would be the wiser. The interrupted catalogue and comparisons formula can be used to switch almost anything. In the following exercise, which is a very basic example, we will change from one job to another. Fortunately, in this case, there will be no domestic backlash.

I went for a job at a contraceptive factory. The boss said: Have you got any dirty habits. I said: "Yes, I arrive late, drink, smoke and use condoms.

In altering the joke we will use the same set-up line and catalogue in the straight line. Then we will compare what the job is with its opposite; this means using the reversal formula.

I went for a job at a butter factory. The boss said: "Have you got any dirty habits. I said: "Yes, I arrive late, drink, smoke and use margarine.'

Following are some examples for you to do. Just add the punch line and complete the jokes.

1.   Petrol Station. I arrive late, drink, smoke and...
2.   Swimwear Company. I arrive late, drink, smoke and...
3.   Butcher Shop. I arrive late, drink, smoke and....

When you are tailoring old material into new joke jackets, you begin to identify the component parts, the ingredients you have to work with to write humour. Words, characters, situations, ideas, locations, conflicts, tensions, ambiguity paradox, possessions, contrast, simplicity, experiences, surprise, superiority, absurdity, honesty, contradictions, perspective, empathy, dialogue, plots, visual image, sub text, dynamics, energy and all the other ingredients from intellectual wit through to emotional humour, from absolute truth to absolute nonsense. Once you have completed a humour switch, run it through the remodeling checklist to see the humour is intact.

1.   That you haven't lost the point of the joke.
2.   That you haven't ruined the rhythm and rhyme.
3.   That you dont over-write the punchline.
4.   That you don't obscure key words and connections.

To close this aspect of the switching section, I would like to use the classical variation of this man a salesman. He once sold a milking machine to a farmer who only had one cow and he took the cow as a deposit.

Humour Ingredients List

Absurdity	Emotions	Relevancy
Affection	Energy	Repetition
Ambiguity	Expectations	Revelation
Appropriateness	Experiences	Rhyme
Association	Honesty	Rhythm
Action	Ideas	Results
Atmosphere	Identity	Similarities
Attitude	Identification	Simplicity
Authority	Image	Situations
Believable	Indirection	Stupidity
Blending	Interpretation	Style
Characters	Involvement	Subjects
Conflicts	Locations	Sub Text
Connections	Misdirections	Suddenness
Contrasts	Mood	Superiority
Contradictions	Paradox	Surprise
Clarity	Participation	Targets
Consciousness	Perception	Tension
Constructive	Persona	Timing
Deception	Plots	Transitions
Dialogue	Point of View	Trusting
Dying	Positive	Truth
Dynamics	Possession	Visual Image
Economy	Premise	Vulnerabilities
Effectiveness	Presence	Weaknesses
Effects	Punchline	
Effortlessness	Realism	
Empathy	Recognition	

Many Targets and Subject Humour

I saw it reported in the paper where Rodney Adler from HIH Insurance walked into Channel Nine's Melbourne studios and began gazing up at the pigeons sitting on the roof. He started shouting at them: 'Go right ahead don't just sit there; do it; everybody else does!

This joke could be used by any well-known businessperson who is know to be going through a financially hard time. Many targets and subject humour, it used cleverly can be used continually - specifically by sales persons, speakers, presenters, and trainers, because their listeners fluctuate. The following joke could have a hundred different punchlines. I really don't believe in the death sentence- with the positive exception of people who ask how's business with a smirk. The punchline for this joke could be, any little annoying habit, untimely action or negative behaviour. Any profession held in mild scorn by another profession can be the target of this joke.

The (name of the profession) was walking down the street and was suddenly knocked down by a car. A pedestrian came along, dug a hole and buried him. Just as he had finished, a policeman came up to him and said: "What did you do with the (name of the profession). He said: 'I buried him.' The policeman said: "Was he dead. 1he pedestrian said: He said he wasn't, but you know these (name of the profession), they're such bloody liars.

Start a collection of jokes similar to the ones following and when the occasion arises for you to add more humour you just fill in the blanks.

1. When I first started to work for (any name) 1 was a poor, struggling (any job title). He helped me get used to it.
2. He's been working at (any stressful job). He just won't accept that (any stressful jobs) was invented by a heart surgeon looking at drumming up new business.

3. (Any venue or location). This is an interesting spot in its way; it's quite beautiful, rather impressive. They must have poured at least $350 into this place.

Writing Your Own Humour Formulas

Now that you are familiar with formulas and understand some of the inner workings, the mechanics of humour, words and writing, you can create your Own humour formulas. All you need is a phrase that's flexible as the set-up line, and sometimes an imagination to make humour connections for the punchline. Here's a few examples.

1. What this country needs... are doctors who think more of the ill that they do of the bill.
2. What this country needs... are less bosses who always give advice and less workers who never take it.
3. Old bankers never die... they just lose interest in their remote disbursements.
4. Old accountants never die ... they just lose their balance when their fixed assets drop off.

The essence of humour is creativity: the ability to see and hear, to think and feel, things, ideas, values and beliefs, then present them in a new light.

The Eight Eyes of Humour

It takes time learning how to write, make connections and switch humour. The quality of the humour you do generate will improve enormously if you blend into the construction the eight eyes of humour.

- Persona-ising
- Economising

- Bulls Eyesing
- Personalising
- Localising
- Topicalising
- Modernising
- Humanising

Persona-ising

Research and writing humour is a learning experience in gaining knowledge and personal growth. An awareness of our sensory freeways – seeing, hearing, touching. tasting, teeling and smelling- provides us with the ability to interpret these sources of lite from our own original point of view. To personalise your frustrations, fears, joys, loves, wishes, dreams, values, beliefs, tone and delivery. The more you relate to your listeners, the more they get to know about you as aliving, breathing, caring human being. The best humour comes from sharing emotional insights, and when they're personalised they're felt and not forgotten. Now I am sure I am right about this. What's the difference; when I'm right no one remembers and when I am wrong no one forgets.

Economising

When you're writing humour, think of the economy; keep it brief, so you can get it finished before the price of pens goes up. I always wait a little while after I have written some humour, then re-read it, edit it and rewrite the piece again. At the same time I eliminate any words, ideas, characters or situations that aren't of maximum importance. This means the structure of the set-up and its connection to the climax of the pay-off always maintain a clarity of contrast for humour continuity. Economising your humour is the writing term meaning word management. This is just another form of time management and it can mean the difference between the failure or success of your humour.

Bulls Eyesing

The effectiveness of your humour relies to a large degree on the emotional energies released to the listeners. Humour spears us in our spirit so the targets for our humour arrows must be very clear to us and the bulls eyes become our objective. Care, caution and consideration must be practised when you're bulls eyesing a humour target. Some of the subjects that are guaranteed to get a big humour response are authority figures, relatives, sex roles, race, ethnicity, social class, religion and politics. There's the following joke about a chap I know who will never be unemployed. He walks up and down in front of Parliament House with a trumpet and he's paid to blow it when Australia becomes a republic. This joke will get a response, positive or negative. But is the after feeling of it what you really want to convey? Don't attack targets that people hold too dearly. They won't forgive you for it. If you use yourself and your life as the target, then most people will laugh with universal human conditions. Have targets such as pompous people, establishment figures, Madison Avenue, white-collar crime, feather-bedding competitors' products, the hand dryer in the men's toilet, and your parking place that's always full. The rule of fun when bulls eyesing is, try to hit the nail on the hand on the head as well as the nail on your thumb.

Personalising

We all need a swag full of Marco Polo humour: humour you can travel with across city-country borders, employer-employee barriers, class structures and the sexes, and that has cross-cultural appeal. Personalising your humour towards a known target, along with the other seven eyes of humour, can achieve this. The following joke could be used as a one-liner or throw-away line, but the laugh response would be far greater if it were personalized towards someone everyone knew and the occasion.

> 'As you know, the theme of this training session is The key to business success. We will be learning there Are three kinds of businesspeople: successful, Unsuccessful and those like our well-known trainer For the program, Jack Davidson, who gives lectures Telling the second group how the first group did it.'

You personalise whenever possible the name of the group, the purpose for the gathering, the profession, the points you will be making, your language in using jargon and technical talk, and some insight information you would have got if you did youor research. All this shows you are interested in them. Using humour for no specific target or situation can't compete with no personalized humour. Instead of telling a joke about nobody and nobody agrees with it, tailor it to the target, time, people and place.

Tom' management meeting are absolutely incredible to attend. Tom talks, nobody listens, then they all disagree.

Localising

Relocate your humour to your audience's emotional, physical surroundings. As humans, we have relationships with objects, places and things that either bring back memories, create a mood or cause us frustration, embarrassment or anxiety. You know the old expression:

Where do you complain about the complains department. Adapt the places, objects and locations of your humour into images with which your audience is familiar. Humour is more comfortable just as life is at home in your own TV chair, place at the dinner table and side of the bed. This makes your humour authentic and real. If you're speaking to a group of company salesmen in their office building, mention the nickname for the lunchroom and the pop art paintings on the walls. If there is no view from the boardroom, mention this. Say there is a wonderful view from the boardroom 10 miles straight up. If there is a big clock on the wall reter to it. That's an unusual clock; I bet your boss is the only one who watches it during the coffee breaks. Localising is rearranging your humour around your listeners environment. Refer to the conditions of the climate and important geographical locations such as hotels, racetracks and restaurants. By describing your experiences in their environment, similarities that make emotional connections are simple and you and your humour become genuine.

Topicalising

Time turns tragedy into humour and humour into tragedy.

Extremely sensitive topical items should be avoided at all costs. Even in standard humour, that part of your repertoire should be dropped in certain situations. Because of the frequent number of plane crashes, be careful when using jokes like the following: I always sit in the tail-end of the plane; whoever heard of a plane backing into a mountain? Topical humour that has lost its potency because of time should be updated as well. Topical humour directly deals with thoughts and feelings of common concern. At the same time, it highlights the fears and anxieties reflected in the values and beliefs of a society. These are what give it power and performance. To get maximum results because of the short life-span of topical humour, select targets that are continually topical, such as technology, travel, self-improvement, weather, and of course the economy. Jokes like this one can always be used. It's true the money is just not around any more. I heard one counterfeiter say to his mate: 'People are getting suspicious of cash; were going to switch to cars.'

The media, news and current affairs programs are usig more and more humour. People are saying they want to be informed with humour. The latest movies, books, TV shows, hobbies, interests, events, income statements, Chinese water torture tactics, managing directors' indiscretions, promotions, marriages, equipment breakdowns, and a host more can be classed as topical humour. Whatever you do, don't go over the top topicalising your humour. Use it the way a talented gossiper would to get attention and maintain it.

Modernising

Did you hear about the Wall Street genius who can earn money faster than his yuppie wife can spend it. I'm not saying they're rich, but their kid called Carly walked up to Santa Claus and said: "Santa, what do you need -anything This is post-yuppie humour. These jokes have been adapted from oil rich Texan jokes and modernised. Keep your humour contemporary; you don't want to put across your images or ideas to your listeners the same way as a movie made in the 1950s. Humour is a very trendy substance that must be new. Outdated subjects, topics and characters need to catch up. Keep your humour in a continual development cycle so its mood, flavour and references stay in verbal and visual image fashion. Modernise your language. Use the latest boardroom buzz words. Mention current themes, issues, subjects and targets. Show you have a vision of the future through your use of humour. Talk about subjects such as nano-tech and biotechnology, the new world order, and the knowledge nation. They're ail fascinating innovations and wide open for original humour. I went to a video conference the other day on the future of business. It's going to change. Rock the Wrestler was the humorist speaker. Stay up to date on electronic, technological and political trends. Use quotations from personalities from the present. Make mention of traditional and historical ideas, things and characters, but give your humour and your personality a state-of-the-art look, sound and feel. Be fresh and funny.

Humanising

'One day I found it hard to get any writing done. The kids were constantly after me for one thing or the other. Finally, I gave them what they wanted: the car and house. Gee, I hate that feeling you get when you are late for work. I said to myself, this is what I am going to do as soon as I am the manager. We can all identity in one way or the other with the previous lines. Why? Because we have all had those thoughts and feelings. We can relate to them. Humanising your humour is identifying with the emotional needs of your listeners. I used to get paid so little, that when I gave my pay cheque to the teller, he would ask how I'd want it, heads or tails. Although this joke aggerated, people can recognise the truth. We all feel we have a need for more money. Incorporate as many common human experiences and situations as possible into your messages, information and communication. Recognise that when you talk about yourself and your humanness, your listeners also need to be seen as human.

If you mention a town, ask if anyone has been there. If you mention a sport, ask if anyone plays it. It you talk about an achievement or failure, say we have all felt that at some time or other. Do human things: trip, forget, get angry. Feel human things: disappointment and loneliness. Say human things: I didn't think I could make it in the humour business. When I first started, things were tough, but I juSt gritted my teeth, pulled up my socks, rolled up my sleeves, spat on my hands and borrowed another few thousand dollars from Mum.

To summarise the eight eyes of humour:

> Persona-ise - Be you, About you
> Economise - Edit thoroughly
> Bulls Eyes - Target carefully
> Personalise - Just for them
> Localise - Make it their home
> Topicalise - Today's news
> Modernise - Bring it up to date
> Humanise - Identify with them.

Chapter Five Summary
The Secrets of Humour

1. To use humour well, we need to study the structure.
2. You need information and the desire to develop your *Humour Attitude*
3. Exaggeration works wonders during conflict.
4. The ability to think in reverse is vitally important in the quick and critical decision-making world of business.
5. The interrupted catalogue can also be a wonderful conversational humour device.
6. Mistaken Identity covers blunders brought about by incorrect or wrong identification of problems, emotions, actions, locations and objects.
7. The forms of humour set the mood and climate that influence the emotional reactions of the receivers.
8. A true satirist combines the painful realities of life with pleasurable experiences and can heighten our personal and social harmony.
9. Irony can be a forcetul communication tool.
10. You can use sarcasm to be assertive and protect yourself.
11. Wit is without doubt the most admired form of humour.
12. Parody is a good place to start when creating humour
13. Farce is an escape from reality.
14. If you're facing a seemingly insurmountable situation, you could eliminate some of the stress by seeing it in the surrealistic way.
15. A playful attitude helps you put problems, challenges and change into perspective.
16. Spend time preparing humour for using to the best of your ability.
17. Once the preparation stage is complete, practise the humour technique a number of times before you use it.

18. Don't give up; persist until you get it right.

19. Use the eight eyes of Humour - Persona-ising, Economising, Bulls Eyesing, Personalising, Localising, Topicalising, Modernising, Humanising

20. As you uncover the secrets of humour, you *Humour Attitude* will grow, making it easier for you to put your *Humour Action* to work.

CHAPTER 6

The Business of Delivering Your Humour

'To write a joke is much more difficult than to tell one. Just consider the arsenal of props available to you when you tell a story.

The Calculated Pause, The Ironic Inflection, The Ingenious Smile, The Warning Frown, The Accented Adjective, The Changes In Pace In Accelerated Rhythm, or The Decelerated Momentum.

All the devices serve to cue and control your listeners, gestures, nods, smiles, cunning chuckles, grunts or murmurs. The gasp of affected astonishment, the moan of pretended dismay.'

Leo Roster

Humour Delivery Considerations

The challenge of delivering your humour is exciting. It involves showcasing your skills, talents, and originality while conveying your vision and message to others. You can achieve success by using your spiritual, intellectual and emotional energies, and personal pre-performance rituals.

'Judge,' said Mrs Delaney, a witness in a murder trial. Give me a go, and let me tell my story my way.

I don't want any interruptions from that slick-looking shyster.'

'Madam, said the Judge, 'you are not allowed to call the Counsel for the Defence names like that."

'I'm sorry, I just want to say what I saw, without being interrupted by that… say what was that toffy name you gave that slick-looking shyster?'

Like the lady in this joke, you have to deliver your humour with feelings, sounds, silent expressions, visual images, actions, and reactions. Plus you must never forget that 90 per cent of our audience's brain power is connected to their emotions.

Pre-Humour Delivery Considerations

'His delivery of humour reminds me of the cross-eyed shotputter. He never won any medals, but he kept the crowd alert.'

There are certain fundamental rules that should be practised in the use of all humour. When these are understood and acted on, using humour becomes possible in nearly all situations and circumstances, both formal and informal. You need to consider the relationship between the users, listeners, surroundings, conditions, and targets involved in the humour use. This gives insight into the complexities and purpose that comprise the use of positive humour.

Preparing Your Attitude for Delivering Humour

How you get ready to deliver your humour is just as important as the actual delivery. It determines the mood that you present to the audience and this affects the way they respond to you. To do this, you can draw on elements of the emotional energies of humour-empathy, defence mechanisms and enjoyment - as well as the elements of humour-attitude, enthusiasm, courage and fun.

Pre-Performance Rituals

Part of your attitude preparation includes establishing what I like to call pre-performance rituals.

One ritual I have developed is a list of comedy cushions, which have been extremely useful.

Take time to reflect with work colleagues, friends and family, then start a laugh list of all the fun-filled, happy times you have had in your life.

Edit these down to the happiest, then write little essays highlighting the details, situations, and people involved. List your top 10, then read them on to a cassette tape to play whenever you need to.

This will help you recall these details before or during a performance.

I also call these cushions Attitude Savers. If your humour is not being well received, and your saving lines aren't working, you need to protect your attitude from being affected by the lack of audience response. Just conjure up a comedy cushion to mentally maintain a sense of fun. These can also be used on days when nothing is going right.

Like:

> You're on your way to work in the morning, and your born gets stuck, just as you pull in behind a band of Hell's Angels.

> At lunchtime you join the Anti-Inflation League. Five minutes later, you hear that on that morning, they raised their membership fee.

> You get to work and the *Sixty Minutes* team is waiting for you in your office.

When you have a day like this, you can fall back on a comedy cushion to help fight those frustrations and turn external failure into internal success.

Another pre-performance ritual is the humour distraction attraction.

One I use is a dossier of my favourite humorous speakers and comedians. It includes photos and collections of their best lines, so I can read through them before I get up to speak. we all have our own peculiarities.

Some prefer to be alone; others prefer to integrate with people. There are those who have to act out their feelings and others who like to meditate.

Find your pre-performance ritual, and turn your negative, nervous energy into positive, personal power.

Prepared Introductions

Ensure that you are presented to the audience in a way that sets up your humour identity and establishes your credentials, one of them being that you have the same sense of humour.

Write your own introduction on a small card and pass it to the compere, giving them enough time to read it thoroughly so they are confident with it.

Formal Introductions

An outstanding example of this technique that I like to call Introducement was delivered at The Melbourne Sales Congress in 1990, from one of Australian's leading speakers, Allan Pease.

Some of the humour lines included were:

> 'He has been a consultant to many of the world's largest corporations... a consultant being a man who knows 317 ways to make love, but doesn't know any women. (Allan's words, not mine)

> 'He lectured extensively in over 30 foreign countries, and Victoria.'

Leading to the climatic conclusion:

> Alan is a Fellow of the Australian Institute of Management, a Fellow of the Life Underwriters Association of Australia, and a Senator of the Jaycees. He received the CSP Accreditation from the National Speakers Association of America.

> In other words, he holds a FLUAA, an FAIM, the All CSP from the NSAA, and the SEN from the JCs.

> He is also a member of the RACQ, and he tells me he's a life member of the AA, and the Australian Farmers Association recently awarded him an EIEIO.

Informal Introductions

Of course, introductions don't have to be used only in formal moments.

When you are being introduced to someone for the first time, at an informal business situation, it's a great opportunity to use the self-image introducement.

> 'Hello, I'm Pete Crofts, self-made man. I take the blame; nobody else will.'

The colleague Introducement:

> 'Folks, let me introduce John, my workmate. I'm sure that they would replace him here, if they could figure out what he does.'

Once you have been introduced in a formal situation with humour, its professional to reciprocate with humour to the person who did the introduction.

These are sometimes called bounce-off lines - for example:

> Thank you for that well-written introduction, John. I don't know if you know this folks, but John and I write plays, and our wives help us. They burn them.'

Always use self-putdown when using bounce-offintroducement. A bounce off introducement line would be:

> 'Thanks, Terry. Terry's well adjusted. He can play golf as if it's a game.

Delivering humour is not just humour action, but also humour reaction.

Opening with Humour

A positive, humorous impression makes the best first impression. I like to apply audience participation and self-debasement in my opening. That way, I get them involved right up front. I demonstrate that I don't take myself too seriously and I get a few laughs in the first crucial seconds.

> 'Folks, put your hand up if you have a sense of humour. Now leave it up if you like to laugh. Again, leave it up if you laughed when you first saw me.'

Open with Humour That Suits Your Identity

The rules governing humour, are the ones that suit your humour identity. Some people are pressure humorists- using fast-paced humour immediately on opening. Others are nori-pressure humorists. They prefer to get the audience relaxed then comfortably move into their humour.

The social commentator humorist would be expected to react with satire on opening. The conversational humorist would comment thoroughly on the same news event with sincerity, casually making a humorous remark in passing.

The Psychological Gadgetry of Humour Openings Are:

1. ABILITY. EStablish this with any means you have - a strong introduction, a confident manner, a specific humour skill.
2. VISIBILITY. Be seen and be heard. Get attention and keep it by questioning, quoting, confronting, explaining and demonstrating through the use of visual aids.

3. VULNERABILITY. Be humble, genuine.

4. RELATABILITY. Talk about them, their industry and the occasion.

5. INVOLVABILITY. Have them feeling, thinking and physically participating.

6. KNOWLEDGE ABILITY. Know your audience. Will they understand your humour opening and find it acceptable and funny?

7. RESPONSIBILITY. Are you prepared to accept the fact that your humour opening could fail and affect the rest of your presentation.

As Geoffrey Howard says in his book Getting Through, the pace of communication has hotted up. Audiences have become more impatient and expect their attention to be grabbed right from the first frame. A lot of films don't open with credit titles; they begin with a slice of the action.

Techniques of Delivery

As the one-legged bicycle rider said: 'It's all in the way you put it Over.'

A week is a long time in politics. A second is a long time when you are delivering humour, because that's all it takes to lose an audience's attention, to confuse them, to upset them. There are techniques you can use to prevent this! I have chosen the ones I feel are paramount to the positive delivery of humour.

- Timing
- Pauseology

Timing

There was a new prisoner at the former Pentridge Prison and the warden cheerfully explained to him that he was running a model prison and making every effort to keep the prisoners happy. lo prove it, he gave him a joke hook to take to his cell. I he new bloke read the book and found all the jokes extremely funny. Later that night, he was amazed to hear the prisoners yelling at one another from their cells. One man would shout out 42', another bloke would scream out '67', and after each of these, the cons would laugh uncontrollably.

The new fellow was pretty confused, so in the morning he said to the warden: 'Why is it that when the fellow calls out those different joke numbers, everybody laughs?'

The warden said: 'That's easy! All those jokes in the book I gave you are numbered. When one bloke yells a number, the other blokes visualise the joke and laugh.

That night, the new bloke thought that he'd in join the fun. He yelled out 55, but nothing happened. He yelled out '87'. Dead silence again. In desperation, he called out the number of what he thought was the funniest joke. 99 he yelled. Nothing, not a sound. He was disappointed. The next day on the rock pile, he said to one of his mates:

'Listen old son, how come when those other fellows yell out the numbers they laugh and when I do there's dead silence. What's the matter?'

The other fellow said: 'You know how it is. Some fellows can tell them, and some can't.'

As Art Gliner says in his *Humour Workshop* tape: Timing is a skill that can be learnt. If you get up when the commercials come on TV, walk to the bathroom, put the cat out, get into the kitchen, grab a sandwich and get back in time for the show to start again, you've got timing already.

The Three Rules of Timing

1. Have a likeable physical and mental attitude
2. Concentrate on the mood of the moment
3. Feel it, don't force it.

Delivering humour is an emotional experience and encompasses all your sensory perceptions. Being able to feel your listeners energies, moods, motivations, reactions and needs is both a right-brain, emotional, intuitive activity and a left-brain, linear, logical activity. Bandler and Grinder, in their expansive book *Frogs Into Princes*, comment:

> 'You will always get answers to your questions in so tar as you have the sensory apparatus to notice the responses and rarely will the verbal or conscious part of the responses be relevant.'

Timing is feeling and being sensitive to the moment.

Ten Sensitivities of Timing

1. When to be silent, to talk, to be still, to move. When to stretch, to hold, to hesitate, to stop, to emphasise, to project, to punch, to throw-away, to build, to breathe.
2. Knowing what pace and pitch to speak.
3. When to appear serious or to appear flippant.

4. When to attack the listener and where to top them.

5. How long a time it takes to deliver the humour.

6. Knowing when to use the humour.

7. Gauging how long to pause for a laugh.

8. Once the humour is used, how soon do you use more humour:

9. Make sure the timing of the new humour is different to the timing of the preceding humour.

10. Consciously experiment with your style so your identity has its unique timing.

Improve Timing by Understanding Humour Construction

Your timing will improve if you make an effort to understand humour construction, energy and psychology. You will learn to express humour from your identity, choosing the right content for the right situation; fulfilling the right target; placing the right words in the right place; and executing the humour at the right variations of volume. This will ensure you have the right rhythm and rhyme and the punchline makes the right point for the right audience.

Audiences Pick Things Up Quickly

Audiences pick things up quickly. If they didn't know you liked onions, it wouldn't take them long to get wind of it! I've heard people say they would give their right arm to have good humour timing. They're the same people who would give their right arm to be ambidextrous. Humour timing comes from within, and is expressed in your pace, pitch, intonation, inflection, and projection. This is dictated by the emotions you are feeling and improved by the emotional reasons for using humour.

The Seven Secrets of Understanding Emotional Timing

1. Ask yourself, how do you want your audience to feel?
2. Zero in on the mood of the moment.
3. Synchronise your timing to the ever-changing temper of the audience's personality.
4. Put more of your own experiences into your humour content so when you speak, you feel.
5. Move from delivering with your left-brain logic to your right-brain intuition.
6. Trust your perception so that you can be honest.
7. Understand that 90 per cent of the audience have made up their minds about you in the first four minutes. If you can make them laugh honestly in that time, you can make them cry any time.

Sometime ago I started to question why I was so successful as a young comedian after having left school so early. I asked myself: Who am I trying to kid? As I was turfed out of school, it couldn't have been because of my word power. I communicated using no more than 2000 words, and after studying humour, I realised why. I had an enormous feeling and emotional vocabulary. However, I must've also known then, that feeling doesn't get results. Action makes results and I went out and did it.

The Man who Taught Lee Iacocca Timing

As Peter Wynden wrote in his book, *The Unknown Iacocca*, Lee acocca always had a plan when he was at Ford. On his bedside table he kept a chart of dates showing when he was due to reach a particular rung of the corporate ladder. When his vice-presidency came 18 months after his 36 birthday in 1935, the deadline he had prescribed for himself, he felt somewhat diminished.

He worked persistently on his shyness, feeling much liberated by a Dale Carnegie course in personal development and public speaking, to which the company sent him. In his autobiography, he included a generous and detailed commercial for the Dale Carnegie Institute and he spelt out the ways in which the coaches helped him relax.

Unmentioned was another guide, who according to the Iacoccalyte, did even more to unlimber Lee. The unsung teacher was Barry O'Daniels. He was an ex-vaudevillian and a living character of Boffo the clown, a comical figure with a bulbous nose and marvellously nimble feet, which could perform a great tap dance while Barry was sitting down. Like Dale Carnegie, Barry was hired by the company to polish the public image of executives. He was a likeable character who loved telling dirty jokes, but he knew a lot about projection, enunciation, and he taught tricks that produced a more sure-footed stage performance.

Wynden goes on to say in his book, that he taught Iacocca to slow his speech down, to reduce the pressure he put on himself and to be far less tense.

Don't Gut Your Company

It takes guts to grow and to use humour to express your feelings. The corporate world has been modelling one behavioral outcome of this through risk-taking. edge-cliffing and tree trade, but suppressing others such as self-expression, personal fulfilment, personality and individuality.

> A young executive discovered after being at the large corporation for six months, that all they served in the dinner room was fish. Fish for breakfast, fish for dinner and fish for tea. He soon got fed up with fish and being an innovator, he brought some sausages and took them to

the chef who said he didn't know how to cook them. He said: 'Its easy. You cook them the same way as you cook fish. You fry them.

The chef came back five minutes later and said: Are you sure that's the right way to cook sausages - the same as fish? The young executive said: "Yes, why do you ask? Well, said the chef, 'there's not much left after you gut them.'

Don't gut your company. Encourage humour use. We all know the difference between winning and losing is timing.

Pauseology

'I try to pay my taxes with a smile, but I couldn't ... they still insisted on money.'

The pause in the above one-liner is used to heighten tension to build Surprise, to give the listener some time to imagine the punchline, and just as it's on the edge of their consciousness, zap it!

Pauseology, the science of silence, is the key element in using humour professionally, as opposed to using it 'poorly. It suggests self-confidence. If you study successful speakers and humorists you will find that when they walk to the platform, they pause for a certain amount of time before they begin. This tells the audience they are in charge. This gives the impression of authority; that you're feeling the mood and weighing up what to says that there is no hurry because you know you can deliver the goods.

Your humour identity has a lot to do with your delivery, so the way you pause should foster your identity and be guided by it.

The 11 Points of Pauseology

1. I'm feeling great today. I got a five per cent loan yesterday - five per cent of what I wanted...'. When you write out your humour, write the pausing into it, adjusting it as you get the feedback from delivering it. You can do this by using dashes: one dash for the shortest pause, through to multiple dashes for the pause before or after the punchline. This will also depend on the material, situation, conditions and audience, and how you feel it should be played.

2. Practise breathing deeply, fast and slow during your pausing- preferably through your nose. This prevents your mouth from drying up by having air inhaled and exhaled through it. Oxygen in your lungs gives you a forceful voice. Oxygen in your brain allows you to think quickly and spontaneously.

3. Develop the pause of spontaneity. Pause by cutting into a line you're speaking without cause, then throw in a gag that is connected to the content of the humour you are using. This gives the impression to the listener that you're ad libbing it. The result will be stronger laughs.Audiences appreciate what appears to be comedy 'of the moment. Deliver every line as if you have never delivered it before. This is also a good technique when you are nervous and rushing, when you want to slow down, when you lose track of your routine, or you blank out. It gives you a way to recover

4. The ambiguity of delivering humour is apparent. You must memorise your humour thoroughly so there is no loss of memory causing annoying pauses and loss of rhythm and rhyme. Nothing kills humour more than pauses of uncertainty and hesitancy.

5. Pause to cue key words. A little pause before the word, a little pause after the word, can heighten the emphasis of the word.

6. Generally, it's effective to pause after the punchline but don't overdo it, or those laughing will suspect you are soliciting laughs.

7. Confidently pause atter the punchline, giving the listeners enough time to get the joke and to laugh. To use a correct humour term, don't step on the laughs or the listeners will get the feeling you're frightened of them, and they will be too embarrassed to laugh.

8. When you're stretching the post-punchline pause and the laugh is not forthcoming, don't jump straight into a saving line; try an audience encouragement line.

Example: 'Go ahead; figure it out; I can wait.'

If there is no response, do a saving line, then start the next line powerfully.

9. Find your onstage silence. It will become your humour identity strength. In time, you will build humour content that always evokes a big laugh. Then start spacing and stretching the pauses, touching their inquisitiveness; keep them guessing about the line. Have them hanging on the hook of the line, then flick the punchline

10. This is what a pause looks like.

11. In the case of the great Jack Benny, the pause itself was the punchline. In one of his shows, Benny was held up. The mugger said: Your money or your life. Benny paused and paused and paused, then the mugger said: Quit stalling, I said your money or your lite. And Benny said: 'I'm thinking it over. Benny's humour identity was so strong he got a 20-second laugh with that pause.

Pauseology During Conflict

Carry over the science of Pauseology into all aspects of your life. As well as being beneficial to your humour, it adds power to your humour attitude.

For example:

> When you're in a state of conflict, pause to get perspective, to find the right formula, humour-coping strategy or comedy cushion to help you in this situation. As Jean Westcott says: 'The object of using humour in a conflict is not necessarily to get others to laugh, but rather for us to be able to laugh at ourselves or find some other way of seeing the funny side of the situation.'

Identity Attitude Change Delivery

I believe also the attitude of the presenter should be attuned to the audience's attitude and the objectives of the occasion. I call this Identity Attitude Change Delivery.

Adapt it to:

- When you are presenting to a group of which you are a member
- A group made up of those from your industry who know of you
- A bunch of strangers that need convincing
- A two-hour workshop group that needs loosening up
- An after-dinner, loosened-up group that needs entertaining.

The attitude of your delivery needs to be as flexible as a headhunter for Telstra. You ned to have a range of presentation levels and attitudes that are attuned, intellectually, emotionally and physically, to all audiences personalities. Yes, audiences have personalities.!

Of course, we do this continually in our daily communication. We don't say the same things in the same way to our sales manager as we do to our teenage daughter.

Let's be honest; it doesn't matter what you say or how you say it to the teenage daughter, you won't win, and that's it! Along with a lot of other methods and ideas in this book which are worth researching and practicing there are methods of delivery.

A Couple of Methods of Delivery

1. Identity Attitude Change Delivery.
2. The Emotional Step-Out Delivery.

Funny Is How You Say It And Do It

> Evan Esar says in his book, *The Comic Encyclopedia*: 'Ed Wynn said a comedian is not a man who says funny things, but who says things funny. For instance, a comedian doesn't open a funny door. He opens a door in a funny way. This was Ed Wynn's way of explaining that it's not what you say or do that's funny, but how you say or do it.'

Methods of delivery are creative ways to make humour more effective and so more funny.

The Emotional Step-Out Delivery

When you are talking about something that involves the audience's feelings like changing jobs, relationships raising children - do the following: Before you go into your humour and while you are delivering the humour, Step out of what you are saying, and emotionally pull the audience in with lines like:

'Remember the first time that you did....'

'That really feels good, doesn't it?

'Has that ever happened to you?

'When was the last time you felt this way?'

'That's it, isn't it?'

'Remember the last time you....'

The lines act as emotional hooks that penetrate the barriers of formality pull the audience's feelings into your humour. The following diagram will give you an idea of how this works:

THE EMOTIONAL STEP-OUT DELIVERY CHART

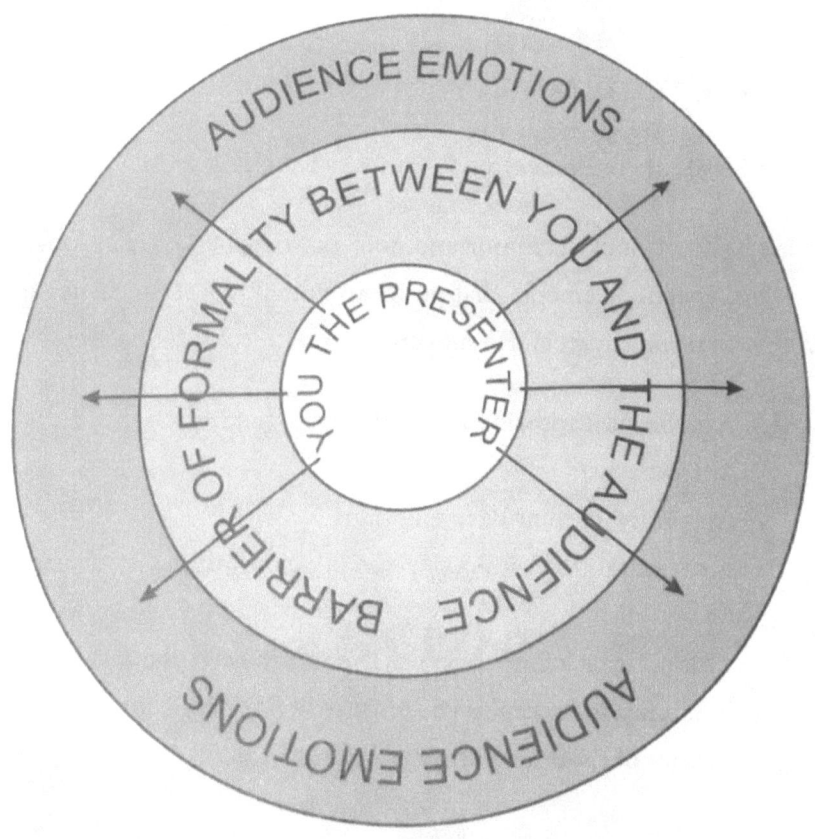

The Identity Step-Out Delivery

When you are presenting your humour, you may at any time, stop, then comment or react to anything you have said or done.

When Ben Elton, the English comedian, was performing in Australia, a strong part of his routine was a verbal and physical impersonation of a pubic hair. Halfway through it, he stepped out of the joke and said: 'I wonder if what I do in life is worthwhile. I fly 40,000 miles just to do an impression of a pubic hair! The audience could see the absurdity, and burst into laughter.

Another example is: "This next subject, I would rather not comment on; unfortunately, I have to; it's part of my presentation.

PREPARED SPONTANEITY

Seven Elements to Professional Comedy Excellence

In his brilliant book, Humour and Society, Marvin R. Koller looks at the ideal specific elements that go into the making of excellence in a professional comic career. He says criteria worth considering are:

1. A global or worldwide appeal that transcends social and cultural differences.
2. An ability to excite deep emotions.
3. A presentation that encourages people to think about human conditions.
4. The creation of a persona that demonstrates the resilience of humanity to meet the vicissitudes of life with courage, and to bounce back with determination and personal dignity.

5. Sustained performances that cover decades rather than brief time periods.
6. Versatility in terms of adaptation to changing media or new technologies.
7. Multi-dimensionality that symbolises the many-sided nature of human personality.

You could say the same criteria are necessary to be a successful manager these days too.

Koller goes on to say:

> 'The professional comic who most closely and admirably meets these criteria was Charles Spencer Chaplin.'

In a TV documentary I watched called *The Unknown Chaplin,* there are shots of his showing frustration about the now classic scene from *City Lights.* in which the blind flower girl sells the tramp a flower thinking he was a rich businessman. Believe it or not, Chaplin spent 62 days entirely on planning that scene, while his large crew lay around on full salaries, and when the comic idea did appear, he took 342 shots to get it right.

The point I am trying to make is, that successful comedy is about preparation.

Marco Polo Humour

Because of such a tremendous range of conditions and circumstances surrounding positive humour, I believe the term that sums up delivering humour best is, Prepared Spontaneity. We all need Marco Polo Humour. That's humour that can travel from one audience, one industry, one media, one town, and one country to another so that our presentations are successful. So prepared, tried, tested and true humour content is imperative.

The best way to see whether the humour you deliver gets laughs regularly is to have proven, roving pieces you can deliver flexibly within the modules of your serious content, at any time.

Roving Pieces

An understanding of transitions makes this possible as well, as a reservoir of proven, positive humour. For easy reference, let's call these Roving Pieces.

These could include:

Self-Disclosure Bits	Plot Jokes
Rule Threes	Character Players
Card Humour	Specific Humour Talents
Signature Pieces	Embarrassing Moments
Prop Bits	Audience Participation
Impersonations	Personalised Content

Prepared Spontaneity Transition Chart

Study the Prepared Spontaneity Transition Chart on the next page to see how it works, all the time, feeling the mood of the audience, inviting, encouraging, and exciting them to listen, laugh and participate. We will be discussing this in more detail later.

> We humour users live on laughter, that's why I'm so skinny. One thing is for sure, I would never become an obstetrician. Even now, after 30 years, my delivery is not

the best. I'm in a strange mood; I feel like the world is a tuxedo and I'm a pair of brown shoes.

Another aspect of prepared spontaneity is having lines ready for all audiences and all conditions you face.

Transitions

Let's move from discussing pausing to delivering transitions. The sentence itself is a transition because it moves from discussing one subject to another.

Mastering Transitions is Imperative

Transitions provide flexibility, improvisation, emotional energy, synergy, and dynamics.

They are to humour, speaking in public or any verbal or written communication, what roads are to suburbs and what driveways are to roads. They connect the towns and houses. They take us from one train of thought to another; from one joke to another; from instructing to encouraging; from asking to telling; from serious to humorous. Skilfully used, they should Integrate all your topics and techniques, all your audience's thoughts and feelings, just as a string in a necklace links together each bead.

Prepared Spontaneity Transition Chart

Once you have done your analysis of the audience and
conditions, you know what message module to start with.
(We will start with Time Management)

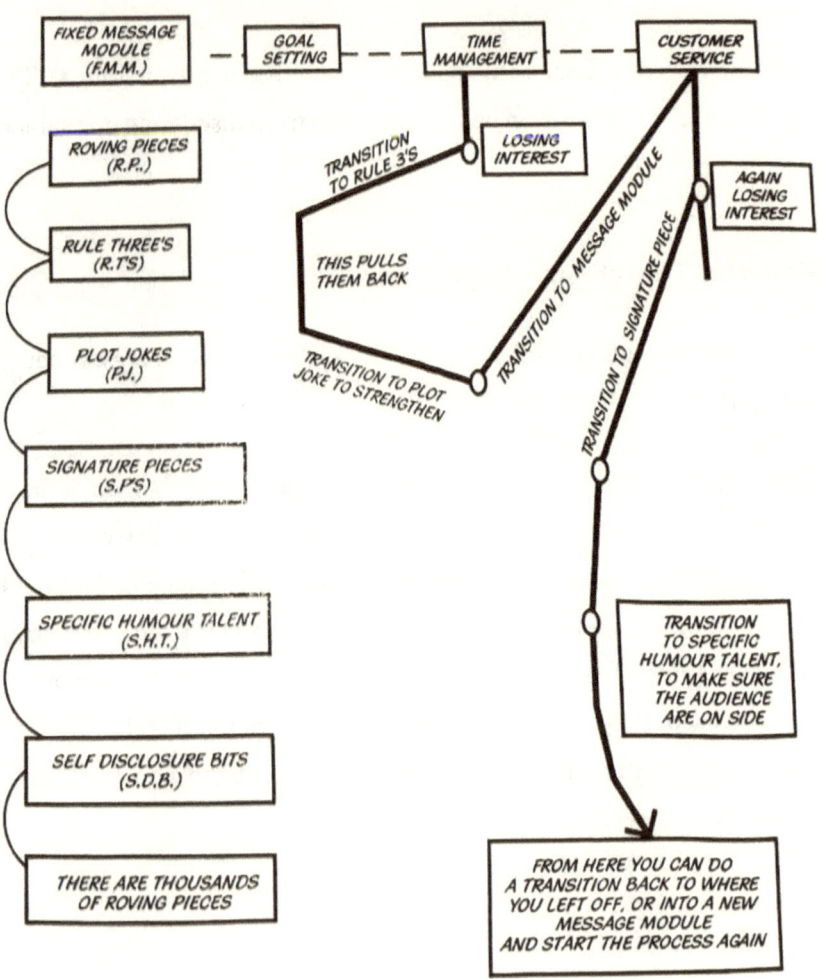

Now we know what a transition is, what's a recession? A period when you should tighten your belt. A depression is a time when you have no belt to tighten. And when you've got no trousers to hold up, well, that's panic.

The Playful Manner Transition

The transition into the above joke was not that strong, but if it's introduced in a playful manner and delivered with a throw-away air, the audience won't mind. Practise the playful manner transition.

It's a very positive way to add some light relief as well as pulling focus and getting attention when it's necessary.

A transition can be anything from producing a prop, playing music, physical comedy, a spin-off remark to the audience, a change of voice tone, a word, phrase, sentence or group of sentences that connect a preceding joke or idea, to a succeeding one.

The possibilities for transitions in humour are unlimited.

Seven Energy-Changing Transitions

These are the seven energy-changing transitions.

- Audience Participation
- The Privatised
- Abruptness
- The Geographical
- Narrating
- Brain-Storming
- Joking

1. Audience Participation transitions can be simple.

   'Hey, but what about working? Hands up all those here who like their jobs!'

The word 'hey' is without doubt, the most used transition in stand-up comedy.

2. Privatised

   'You know, life's great. I'll tell you what I enjoy most.'

From here you can go into any other personal self-disclosure truth humour.

3. Abruptness

   "Look, l am not going to waste any more of your time. Let's get to the heart of the problem.

Here you can follow on with whatever humour is relevant.

4. The Geographical

   'You know, I was in Canberra last week and if inflation gets any higher, it will be one of the many places in Australia where you won't be able to afford to live in the past.'

5. Narrating. When you finish with one topic, you say:

   'Well' (another great word of transition)

   "We all know it is not easy to cope with bankruptcy, but there are people who have to put up with worse things like...

6. Brain Storming

    'That's enough about that. What can we talk about now: Traffic, marketing, cash flow. That'll do. You know the way it is now. There are so many things you can bank on and my cash flow is one of them.'

7. Joking

    This is one of the most used forms of transition. You have a joke or line that you finish one topic with and it has a subject within it that you follow up with.

    'I know a large company that has developed a reputation for extra fast promotion for the young executives. One of my mates, who is an elder staff member, is a bit bitter because he has been overlooked for promotion for 15 years. He convinced the pub over the road to put up the following sign:

    'No vice presidents served at this hotel unless accompanied by their parents.'

    Speaking about signs, have you seen some of them these days...?

Transitions of Energy and Emotions

Think of transitions as transitions of humour ideas, energy and emotions. By inter-cutting, blending, binding, weaving creative transitions into a presentation, you have access to all the laugh-makers tools and techniques.

This could include:

Character Players	Props
Card Humour	Personal Experiences
Shock Value	Sight Gags
Audience Participation	Etc.

The Five Transition Performance Results

Mastering transitions can help you achieve the following five transition performance results.

1. You can increase your visual and verbal pace and appear to be performing spontaneously.
2. You can highlight the range of perspectives to not only a comedy piece but your whole presentation.
3. You can intensify the laughs whenever you want to, which means you have the power to prevent content from being static.
4. You have freedom to add individuality and originality to your identity and attitude.
5. Most important of all, the ways and means to turn what most performers would call a bad audience, into an appreciating, applauding audience.

In other words, become a laughing success.

Speaking Powerfully with Humour.

In business it's essential that you can speak powerfully and demonstrate you have leadership abilities; otherwise, you can be lost in a crowd and never reach your full leadership potential. I was invited to speak to the Victorian Chapter of Australian National Speakers some time ago. I was passionate about my message that too many speakers talk about facts and forget the audience's feelings. The essence of getting an audience feeling is through humour. I had become passionate about this point, because I had seen too many cold, boring and calculated over-serious speakers who made no impact on their audience.

When I was introduced, I moved quickly to the podium, made eye contact with the audience, and delivered a startling statement:

> 'Ladies and gentlemen! You are not public speakers today, in the age of telecommunications and computer super highways. Ladies and gentlemen: You need to be public feelers. Too many of you deliver facts, free of feelings. Forget your facts and deliver feelings through humour.'

This got their attention.

In America, there is the expression: 'If you want to be a professional speaker, you need to use humour successfully. This could also be applied to the corporate world. Despite the information super highway, we all have to be super communicators, so we can deliver a dynamic, inspirational, humorous speech. The book is full of ways of being entertaining and amusing. Making a powerful speech and using humour successfully demands a whole new set up of rules. To communicate your information with power, a speech must have a structure made up of a variety of message reinforcers:

- A creative involvement piece
- An earn the right piece
- A passion piece
- Three or four modules
- A variety of humorous signature pieces as roving pieces
- Some WIIFM'S (what's in it for me)

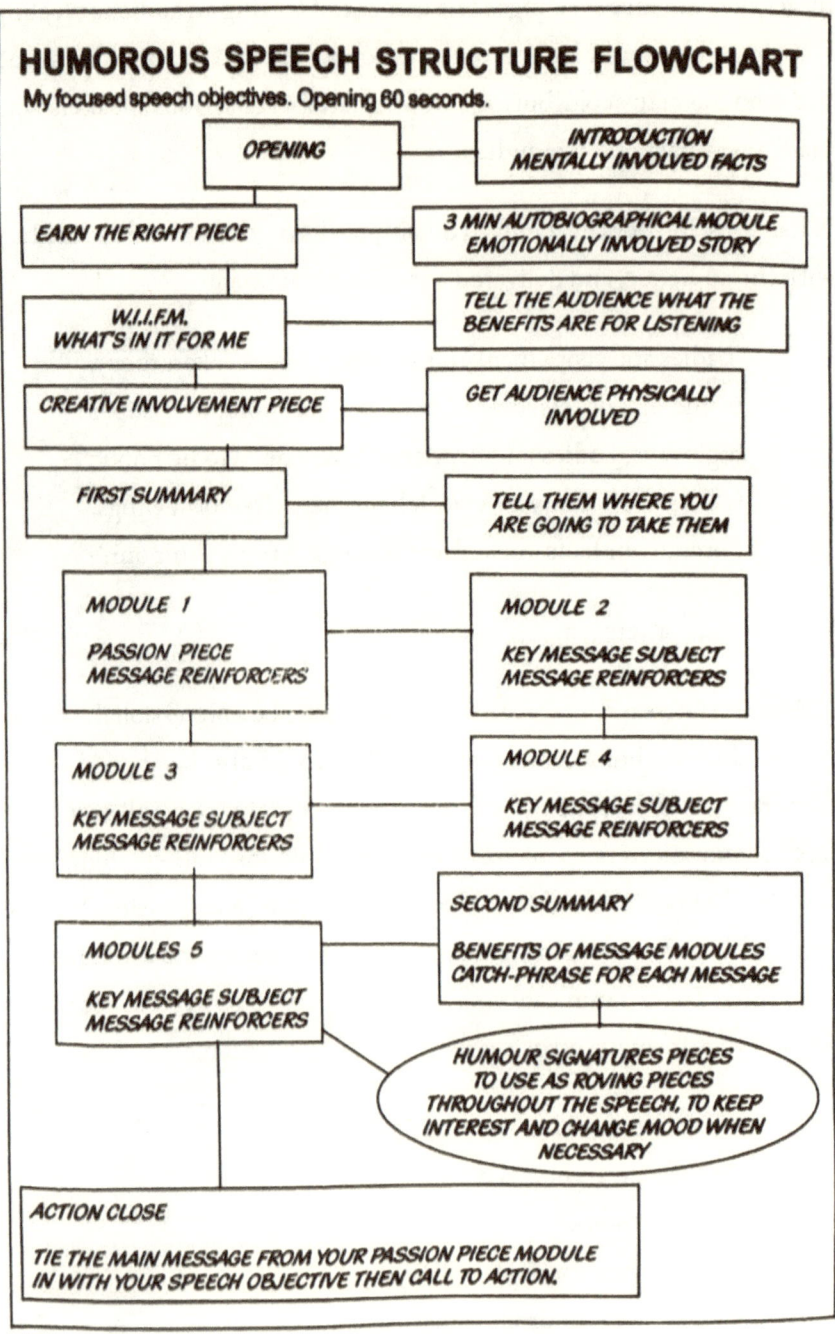

Message Reinforcers are any technique or device that you use to support your message. There is a kaleidoscope of them; use the ones that best suit our identity, or that suit the purpose of your talk.

- Role plays
- Repetition
- Book credibility
- Facts and statistics
- Testimonials
- Case studies
- Comparison and contrast
- Demonstration

The secret is to use the right message reinforcers to suit the different speech purposes. The basic speech purpose are to:

- Inform
- Persuade
- Showcase
- Motivate
- Entertain
- Inspire
- Amuse
- Impress
- Convince
- Express Appreciation

Examples of the right *message reinforcers*, for the right speech purpose, are:

- Say your speech purpose is to inform, then the message reinforcers would be used for explanation and clarification

- To persuade, the message reinforcers would be used to develop evidence to invite your audience to take the action you want them to do
- To motivate, the message reinforcers are used to demonstrate, to win over to influence your audience to believe in themselves more

Of course, humour can be used in all of the above. In my *Humour In Public Speaking Course* I need to motivate the students to put in the work necessary to use humour successfully. I used the following story to get them to think creatively on how to motivate themselves.

> A company director told his sale manager how he got his son motivated so he would not be late for school any more - he bought his son a car.
>
> The sales manager said: 'Well, how did that stop him from being late? The company director replied: 'Now he's to get to school early to find a parking place.'

Don't disregard any *message reinforcers* experiment, explore and continually re-evaluate the way you reinforce your message. Identify your key messages, then write them into modules. Include humour and then reinforce these key messages with techniques that suit your identity.

Move the audience to the response you desire. This, of course, depends on the purpose of your speech.

Case studies

Case studies are like games where each player must solve the puzzle using a clues sheet. I like to use verbal case studies because of the effect they have on an audience. The example of Woody Allen being helped by the comedy management team, Rollins and Joffe, has changed the lives of people to whom I have related it. One of the best places to find case studies is to read autobiographies of people.

Role plays

Role plays are ways of getting your audience involved in self-discovery. This can also be fun for the audience. They encourage natural spontaneity and creativity. Studies have shown that people learn more by doing something they enjoy than by any other way. A good role play shows your audience how to work their way through a situation and to realise their own result, rather than by being told. A well-scripted, quick-moving role play is nearly as good as the involvement in the experience itself.

Repetition

People learn by the repetition or reinstatement of what you say if you repackage your message through another technique. You are saying the same thing differently. Humour is perfect for this, because there are so many different types of humour in which to repackage your message.

Quotations	Definitions	Cartoons.
Light verse	Stereo characters	Funny slides
Comic props	Humorous announcements	Impersonations
Visual puns	Comic predictions	Physical comedy

One technique I like to use 1s what I call the re-echoing effect:

- Tell them what you are going to tell them
- Then tell them the same thing, in a verbal humorous way
- Then tell them the same thing in a physical comedy way
- Then get them involved in what you are telling them, in a creative participation way
- Then, using humour, tell them to take some action.

Comparison and Contrast

When you use comparison, you highlight sameness. When you use contrast, you highlight difference. Comparison and contrast put forward thoughts, ideas, concepts and facts that allow your audience to see things more clearly and to relate to them. Bob Bassindale, in his book *How Speakers Make People Laugh*, says:

> 'Comparison is so important to humour, that one Outstanding speaker, Dr Paul Nadler, of Rutgers University, believes nearly all humour is analogies in the final analysis.

Dr Nadler, an economist who is renowned for his ability to speak both seriously and humorously about economics, uses a gag like the one below, to point out that women can spend money faster than men can earn it:

> That's like the motorist getting a tank full of gasoline with the engine running. Finally the attendant says: 'Madame, would you mind shutting off the engine, You're gaining on me!'

Dr Nadler uses that gag and many others to draw clear comparisons between humorous situations and serious economic principles and problems. I use another comparison by telling a joke to do with the economy, where the target is a male and not a female.

> Economising is always a very delicate matter.

> Like the fella who does circumcisions, you have to be very caretul where you cut.

Writing this book, I have been working harder than an elephant dealer, during a two-for-one sale, but you can't stop me when I get going You might as well try to stop a rhinoceros by throwing a baked bean at it.

Like anyone running a business these days, I have a lot in common with playing snooker with eggs instead of balls. To win, you have to make an omelette without breaking the eggs.

Earn the Right

What right do you have to take up 30 minutes of your audience's time? If there are 200 people in the audience, that's a lot of time. To earn the right, you must explain why you have the right to speak. Tell the audience a mini-history of yourself: where you grew up; what happened to you; what lessons you learned; what you value and love. To bond with them and keep them interested, you must explore your humanity, disclose your weaknesses, open your heart, and pour out your past and future fears, frustrations and experiences.

Humour is ideally suited as an earn-the-right technique. In my earn-the-right speech, I tell my audience if it weren't for a talent quest in the pubs on the road, I would have starved. A blonde, out-of-tune female singer, with big breasts and a low-cut gown, would always win. would always come in third, but only when there were three people in the talent quest. Third prize would always be a free meal in the pub. It's what I called poetic justice, because my jokes went down like pub food anyway. Earn the right to speak by humorously telling the audience a mini-history of yourself.

WIIFM'S – What's in it for me?

What are the benefits to the audience of listening to you. You can state the benefits directly, or package them in humour. In one of my talks, "The Tickling, Titterlating Truth about Laughter, I package one of the WIIFMS in the following way by quoting Erma Brombeck, who said:

> 'You have asked me to share some of my personal experiences regarding the benefits of laughter. Not the least of them is a Mercedes in my garage, and three children with straight teeth.'

Creative involvement

This is a turning point in your speech because you have all the preliminaries out of the way. Its now time to take the speech to the physical-emotional involvement level to get the audience actively participating in your presentation. This takes courage, but its really worth doing to achieve presentation results. There are hundreds of creative ways of getting the audience physically involved; do this through the content of your speech.

In another of my talks, 'Selling with a Smile', at this point of the presentation I say.

> 'Selling and humour are very, very similar. One of the key skills to learn is observation. Would everybody please stand up, close one eye, and walk around until you have found a partner who has the same eye as you closed. I want you to choose who is to go first. Now stand face to face, and observe how your partner is dressed and looks. Look at every detail for two minutes. Now turn back to back and change three things about how you are dressed, or how you look. Take a minute to do this. Now I want you to turn around and take it in turns to see it you can pick the three changes that your partner has changed.'

There is a lot of humour in this creative involvement. It's linked to the central theme of my presentation: 'keep your eyes open and you will see the humour all around you, just as long as you are looking for it.

Passion piece

Passion is just another word for enthusiasm; it's the realisation that you have something to say that might be worth saying. The stronger the realization, the more responsibility you have to say what you feel passionate about. A passion piece takes time to surface, develop, and own. It's a risk saying things you have never heard other people say. You need a sense of humour, and confidence, to present a passion piece. The ideal spot in the structure of a speech is just after the first summary. The first piece should be your passion piece. A passion piece is an information piece that provides insight. It might be:

- A cause you want to support
- An issue you want to make people aware of
- A strong opinion you have on a subject
- A message you feel you need to share
- A lesson you have learned that you want to pass on.

When delivering a passion piece, be careful not to be too serious because then you can come across as self-righteous. Deliver a passion piece with power, but have a sense of humour to underline your point of view. You need to demonstrate a controlled and balanced identity to your audience.

First and second summnmary

The first summary tells the audience what you are to tell them quickly and clearly, in the main body of your speech, or modules. Each module has a key message, and this key message is then part of your first summary. For example, I have a presentation on 'How to Develop a Hdumour Skill that Works at Work'. My first module with the passion piece is Humour Building Relationships. After that I give the titles of the other modules I will be speaking about.

- Humour heals the body
- Humour handles stress
- Humour motivates people to action
- Humour forces us to focus on balance

This first summary makes the audience feel more comfortable because they know what's coming. The first summary is just the titles of the four or five modules to follow. Each module is between four and six minutes.

The second summary follows after the final module. With the second summary, you present the module titles, only this time you announce the benefits to the audience of each module.

For example: To sum up ladies and gentleman, humour builds a relationship and maintains that relationship. You can use humour here in the second summary if you want. For example: Humour can even solve the problems many visiting relatives. Like the businessman who borrowed money from his rich relations and loaned money to the poor ones; now none of from his rich them come back.

Do the same with the other module titles and benefits in quick succession.

Mention the module title, then the benefits of that module

Closing of: Call to action
Crab them by their hearts and motivate them to move on your message at the close.

When you open, state your purpose; when you close, accomplish your purpose.

The call to action states what action you want your audience to take.

- It must excite their feelings
- Challenge their behaviour
- Question their commitment
- Motivate their passion

All this can be done by using any one of lots of techniques

- Use a short, emotional story
- Paint a vivid word picture
- Demonstrate a practised skill
- Get the audience involved in an activity
- Recite a self-penned poem

This is my favourite *Call To Action Close.*

Dance to your Destiny

> When the night comes
> And the darkness shines
> Let your spirit free
>
> No thinking
> Just beings
>
> The shadows of your soul
> Dance in the light of the moon
>
> All for the purpose
> Of being in tune with your intuition
>
> To grow yourself silently
> In the quiet of the dark night
> Trust yourself to grow yourself
> You owe it to yourself to be yourself
> The selfish night provides the light

Lonely sounds and frightening fears
Hateful memories and devastating tears
Ghostly images and haunting refrains

The past is pushing
Your future self is calling
Your present self is grieving
Your old self is dying
Your new self is being born
Your true spirit is navigating

From what was you
To the new, true you

Self-transformation is the dance
Of your spirit, soul and shadow

And the rhythm is life
And the music iS meaning
And the melody is your soul's purpose
Dance to your destiny

A signature piece 1s something that you become recognised tor, for one many reasons:

- The entertaining way it's done
- The techniques that you use
- The point of view of the subject matter

Nearly everything can be turned into a signature piece, if you can see the long-term value in t. They can de used as roving pieces to bring into any aspect of your speech. Roving Pieces are freelance pieces of humour about 45 Seconds in length. They are brought into your presentation, if the material you are doing is not getting a response. You just make a transition from your speech, into the roving piece, then back out of the roving piece into your speech.

One humorist I know tells a lot of stories using Australian slang in his after-dinner talks where you need to use humour with more emotional impact than during the day.

> He tells the story of a 'greasy mop' who was patrolling lover's lane. He had a Captain Cook' in the first car and said to the 'charlie wheeler in the seat: 'What are you doing?" She said: 'Oh, officer! I'm doing the Mambo. Well, he 'pickled porked' over to the second car, he had a 'burcher's hook in the window, and said: 'What do you think you're doing?" And the 'horse and cart in the 'hammer and tack' said: 'Why constable, we're doing the foxtrot. He went to the third car, poked his head in the window, and said to the couple: Ah ha! I know what you are doing! You're doing the Bossanova. And the blonde in the back said: 'Oh no I'm not! I'm doing the boss a favour."

Jokes like this need to be told to the right audience at the right occasion and you never know when you might need them to boost the audience response. All successful humorous speakers have a stock of signature pieces, and in most cases, they either become a roving or a *Marco Polo piece*: one that you can travel with to any group, occasion, or medium.

Focused speech objective
Very Clear on what is the objective of your talk. What is it that you want audience to retain, to remember and to put into practice: When you are

writing, structuring and adding humour to your speech, keep asking yourself: Is this related to my objective?'

When it comes to using humour in public speaking, you don't have to use lots of types and styles. A little variation in techniques is a must. Surprising your audience adds power to your presentation. One way to develop more humour variety into your speech is to start a humour-using techniques chart modelled on the chart on the next page. Just tick the ones you are using, and tick the ones you would like to use. Grade yourself from one to 10 on how well you are using your current techniques.

The Humour-Using Techniques Chart

When it comes to using humour in public speaking, you don't have to use lots of types and styles. A little variation in techniques is a must. Surprising your audience adds power to your presentation. One way to develop more humour variety into your speech Is to start using a humour techniques chart modelled on the chart below. Just tick the ones you are using, and tick the ones you would like to use. Grade yourself from one to ten on how well you perform in the ones you are using.

HUMOUR	WHAT AM I USING	WHAT I WANT TO USE	POINTS OUT OF TEN
TRUTH			
PROPS			
JOKE ONE-LINERS			
JOKE TWO-LINERS			
JOKE THREE-LINERS			
JOKE FOUR-LINERS			
JOKE FIVE-LINERS			
JOKE TEN-LINERS			
PHYSICAL HUMOUR			
SIGNATURE PIECES			
CHARACTER PLAYERS			
SELF-PUT DOWN			
IMPERSONATIONS			
SIGHT HUMOUR			
EMBARRASSING MOMENT			
ROVING PIECES			
COMEDY THROW-AWAYS			
SPECIFIC HUMOUR TALENT			
CUSTOMIZED COMEDY			
HUMOUROUS INTRODUCTION			
AUDIENCE PARTICIPATION			
LIGHT VERSE			

Chapter Six Summary
The Business of Delivering Your Humour

1. The challenge of delivering your humour is exciting.

2. You have to deliver your humour with feelings, sounds, silent expressions, visual images, actions, and reactions.

3. You need to consider the relationship between the users, listeners, surroundings, conditions, and targets involved in the humour use.

4. How you get ready to deliver your humour is just as important as the actual delivery.

5. Performance Rituals can assist in delivering your humour.

6. Prepare an introduction - this can be formal or informal.

7. A positive humorous impression makes the best first impression.

8. Open with humour that suits your identity.

9. Timing and pauseology are great techniques for delivering humour.

10. The Three Rules of Timing are a likeable physical and mental attitude, concentrate on the mood of the moment, and feel it, don't force it.

11. Improve your timing by understanding humour construction.

12. Audiences pick things up quickly.

13. Humour timing 1s expressed in your pace, pitch, intonation, inflection, and projection.

14. It takes guts to grow, to use humour, to express your feelings.

15. Pauseology, the science of silence, is the key element in using humour professionally, not poorly.

16. Earn the right to speak

17. The attitude of the speaker should be attuned to the audience's attitude and the objectives of the occasion.

18. Funny is how you say it and do it!
19. When you are talking about something that involves the audience's feelings step out of what you are saying, and emotionally pull the audience in - grab them by their hearts and motivate them
20. Suprising your audience adds power to your speaking.

"FOR THE LIFE OF ME JENKINS, I CAN'T UNDERSTAND THIS BUSINESS SHOW"

CHAPTER 7

Business Show - Applying Humour Seriously

A Term to Title the New Age of Business

Humankind's intelligence, nature and needs have changed dramatically over the ages. However, we are beginning to analyse our antiquated, traditional ways of thinking, behaving and doing business, and can see our serious selves and laugh. From laughter comes swift change and the realisation that for the new age we need new attitudes and methods of action, not to mention a new terminology in which to wrap them. This is why I call this chapter 'Business Show', a term to title the new age of business.

Some people may be sceptical about the role that humour and laughter can play in business. T. G. Nelson sums up the scepticism well, in the opening of this book, *Comedy: The Theory of Comedy in Literature, Drama and Cinema*, when discussing the novel The Name of the Rose by Umberto Eco. He writes:

The setting was a medieval monastery... The protagonist seeks Aristotle's authority to uphold his views that laughter is desperately needed in a world dominated by seriousness, fanaticism, intolerance and fear.

The antagonist wants to suppress Aristotle's thesis, because he believes laughter embodies all that is demeaning and trivial; that it is a threat to religious faith and to the dignity of human life.

These contrasting views can be found not only in the fictional world of The Name of the Rose, but in the writing of philosophers, theologians, social reformers and imaginative writers, from classical times to the present.

Like the combatants in this novel, who each have contrasting views on the importance of humour to our existence, your own personal view will dictate your willingness to accept humour and laughter in business.

Comedy Challenges Tragedy

The 2000-year-old, ongoing argument between what is serious and humour is, in reality, a debate betweena philosophy of tragedy and a 'philosophy of comedy.'

Joseph W. Meeker, in his book, *The Comedy of Survival (Studies in Literary Ecology)*, argues that people throughout the ages have generally practiced a philosophy of tragedy. This has been passed down from the Greeks to the Jews, from the Jews to the Christians, to the rest of the Western World:

'The tragic view assumes that man exists in a state of conflict with powers that are greater than he is. Such forces as nature, the gods, moral law, passionate love, the greatness of ideas and knowledge all seem enormously above mankind, and in some way determine his welfare, or his suffering...

Tragic literature and philosophy demonstrate that man is equal, or superior to, his conflicts...'

But the search for personal identify and self-fulfillment, and the search to become superior to our conflicts, has minimised our sense of responsibility to our own and to the other species with whom we share the earth.

Humanistic individualism has encouraged Western society to ignore the multiple dependencies necessary to sustain all life. Meeker says:

'There is a tragic irony in the fact that man has achieved the long-sought mastery over nature, only to find that his very existence depends upon the natural balances, which were destroyed in the process.'

What has this to do with comedy: According to Meeker, comedy can teach us new skills for survival without destruction. He says:

'If the lesson of ecology is balance and equilibrium, the lesson of comedy is humility and endurance... Comedy illustrates that survival depends upon man's ability to change himself, rather than his environment, and upon his ability to accept limitations, rather than to curse fate for limiting him. It's a strategy for living....

To evolution, and to comedy, nothing is sacred, but life itself.'

The ability to change and to reject the tragic view of life may be necessary to end the long and disastrous warfare between mankind and the natural world. Freedom from the need for tragedy is an important precondition for the avoidance of ecological catastrophe, and for change.

The Rejection of the Tragic View of Life

> The solution therefore could lie in a wholesale change, and the adoption of the philosophy o Comedy. Take, for example, the situation of the old Italian whore-master in Joseph Heller's contemporary American novel, *Catch 22*, who claimed:

> 'I was a fascist when Mussolini was on top, and I am an anti-fascist now that he has been deposed. I was fanatically pro-German when the Germans were here to protect us against the Americans, and now that the Americans are here to protect us against the Germans, I am fanatically pro-American.'

When Nately, the naive, idealistic American soldier to whom he is talking, accuses him of being a shameful, unscrupulous opportunist, the old man reflects that at least that way he has lived to be 107 years old.

Young Nately, committed to the idealism of keeping the world safe for democracy, dies in combat before his 20th birthday.

THE PHILOSOPHY OF COMEDY IN BUSINESS

The corporate philosophy of 'Business Show' is created by the adoption of a philosophy of comedy in business. This chapter will set out to demonstrate that there is a 'marriage' between the show-business world and the serious world of business; it's up to the leaders of business to recognise this, and to capitalise on the 'honeymoon' ahead.

The Most Significant Behaviour of the Human Mind

Edward De Bono opens his book *I'm Right You're Wrong* with an introduction titled "The New Renaissance'. In it he claims that humour is the most significant behaviour of the human mind. This is because:

> 'Humour tells us more about how the brain works, as a mind, than does any other behaviour of the mind, including reason. It indicates that our traditional thinking methods and our thinking about these methods have been based on the wrong model of information system.
>
> It tells us something about perception, which we have traditionally neglected in favour of logic. It tells us directly about the possibilities of change in perception. It shows us that these can be followed by instant changes in emotion, something that can never be achieved by logic.'

In this way we can also use humour In business to discover possibilities that we have traditionally neglected by using logic and reason. Practically, humour can be applied to the following areas:

1. Corporate culture
2. Corporate identity and image
3. Marketing

By the end of this chapter you will be thinking creatively about 'Business Show' possibilities.

A woman, who really had a Business Show attitude, was the movie star who had four husbands to fulfil her lifetime plan. Her first husband was a banker. Her second husband was a movie producer. Her third husband was a beautician, and her fourth husband was a mortician.

You might ask: 'Where's the business plan in that?' One for the money, two for the show, three to get ready and four to go.

New Games, New Rules

After the invention of the one-day match, cricket was revitalised. This analogy is useful when talking about the effect of transforming your business environment into one that uses humour. In the *Australian Weekender*, Graham Lloyd wrote about Frederick G. Hilmer's book, *New Games, New Rules*:

> 'This country must do to business, what Kerry Packer (Australia's most successful television owner), did to cricket with his radical World Series proposal, that turned the conservative sporting institution on its head in the late 1970s. He used brightly coloured uniforms and one-day matches to enliven cricket, and broaden its community and commercial appeal."

The Appearance of Business Theatre

The roots of Business Show' can be traced back to the advent of television. When it first appeared in the US, television transformed American entertainment habits. It did the same after arriving in Australia in 1956, changing forever the public's concentration span, value judgments, and visual stimulation needs. Entertainment communication had arrived.

In the first text book on *Special Events*, Joseph Goldblatt writes:

> 'After World War II, television was the new sensation, and millions of Americans gathered around the little

boxes each night, watching the same kinds of comedy, variety and musical programs that had earlier drawn crowds at Vaudeville Palaces across the country.

The advent of radio and motion pictures had already precipitated the exodus of audiences from theatres. Television sealed the fate of live entertainment. Forums for live programs closed their doors, one by one, and by the 1950s, audiences were hard pressed to find theatres that offered the same kind of spontaneous live entertainment that the kings of vaudeville had presented.'

Around 20 years ago, terms like Industrial Theatre', Corporate Theatre and Business Theatre first appeared. Companies began following the American models, using entertainment to rejuvenate their conferences and to communicate their messages by creating spectacular and memorable events, and using all the techniques of vaudeville and theatrical productions.

The inspiration for many of these changes came from Jack Morton, who established his first New York office in the early 1950s, and sought to fill the live entertainment gap that the advent of television had created. As Goldblatt writes:

'Morton recognised the emergence of a new market. The convention and corporate market would, he predicted, take the place of vaudeville and burlesque, providing a new forum for live entertainment.'

Beyond "Business Theatre'

Today we have stepped far beyond Business Theatre. Television has created a global environment ere, in order to be informed, people also need to entertained. In his book *Amusing Ourselves to Death: Public Discourse in the Art of Show Business,* Neil Postman says:

> 'What I am claiming here is not that the television is entertainment, but that it has made entertainment itself the natural format for the representation of all experience. Our television set keeps us in constant communication with the world, but it does so with a face whose smiling countenance is unalterable. The problem is not that television presents us with entertaining subject matter, but that all subject matter is presented as entertainment, which is another issue altogether.'

'Infotainment' is the new buzz word of Business Show' and three of its main ingredients are humour, comedy and laughter.

Corporate Entertainment

There are many instances where entertainment 1s already used as a means of business communication. Andrew Crofts, in his book Corporate Entertainment as a Marketing Tool, says:

> 'Corporate entertainment is all around us, although half the time we don't even give it a second thought. Companies are pouring money into the restaurants that provide business lunches and dinners, and hotels that cater for conferences and travelling business people. The concept is ingrained so deeply into the world of selling, public relations, sales promotion and customer service, that it is virtually Impossible to distinguish it from everyday routine. If a Company is able to distinguish it,

however, and can learn to plan and control it in the same way as it plans and controls its purchasing of plant and raw material, or the requirements of its staff, it will be unleashing an enormous force. A company that analyses all its personal relationships, both inside and outside the company, and looks at the most effective way of developing them in order to increase loyalty and improve service, can't fail to improve its performance in virtually every sphere of activity.

The first step, therefore, is to recognise that corporate entertainment exists as a potential force, and then to harness it to the marketing cause."

Corporate entertainment is just another 'Business Show' tool. Once you recognise Business Show as a philosophy of business, you can then incorporate it into your company's mission statement and corporate culture.

The chart on the next page shows the rise of Business Show thinking.

Everything we do - our attitudes, our ways of thinking and of doing business and the form in which we present these- moves in two directions. We can apply a serious or humorous attitude, or we can embrace a lateral or linear way of thinking. The way we do business can be motivated by business or show business outcomes and we can present these in the form of comedy or tragedy. Traditionally, this split business and theatre. Television assisted the marriage of these two by providing infotainment as well as entertainment. We can merge these two in our business to create Business Show - the art of applying humour seriously. The result? More fun for our employees and our customers, a more positive work environment and increased productivity and profit.

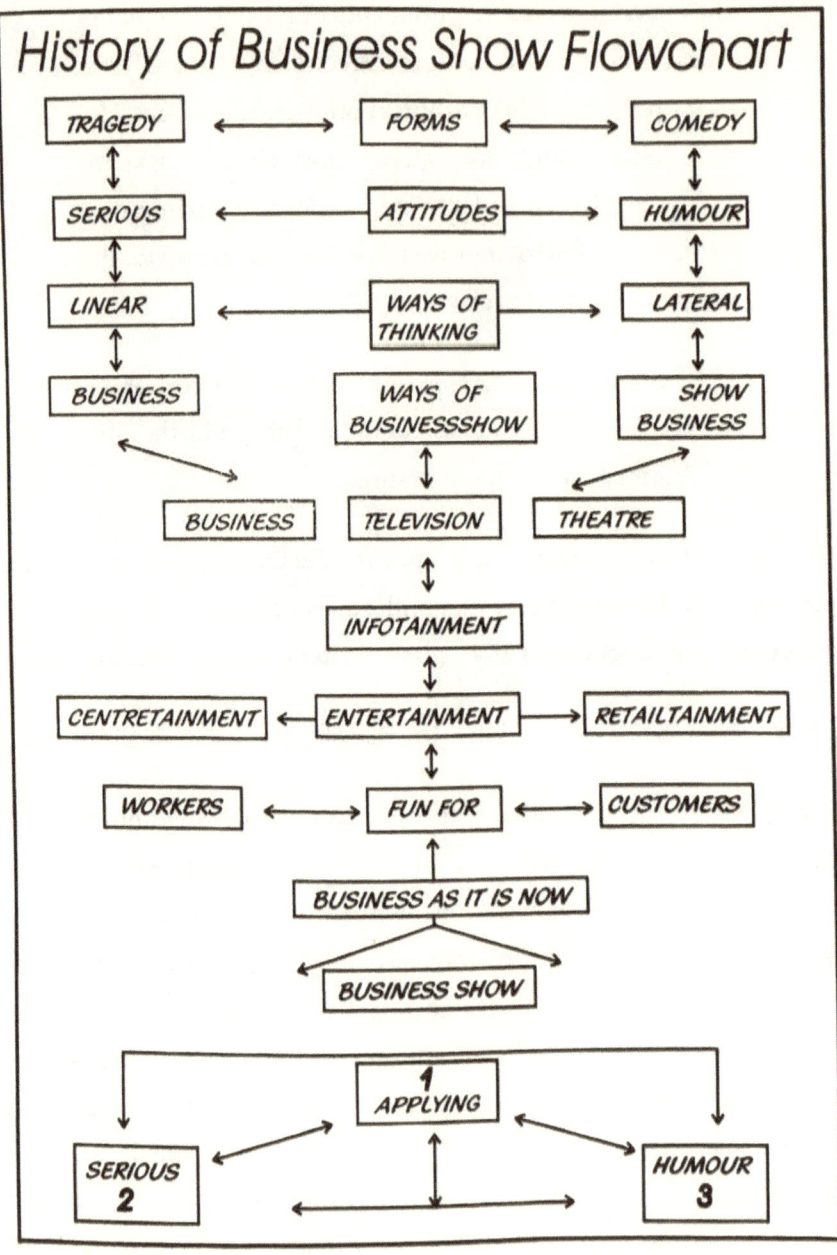

History of Business Show Flowchart

TRAGEDY ←→ FORMS ←→ COMEDY

SERIOUS ← ATTITUDES → HUMOUR

LINEAR ← WAYS OF THINKING → LATERAL

BUSINESS — WAYS OF BUSINESSSHOW — SHOW BUSINESS

BUSINESS — TELEVISION — THEATRE

INFOTAINMENT

CENTRETAINMENT ← ENTERTAINMENT → RETAILTAINMENT

WORKERS ←→ FUN FOR ←→ CUSTOMERS

BUSINESS AS IT IS NOW

BUSINESS SHOW

1 APPLYING

SERIOUS **2**

HUMOUR **3**

Humour in Training Videos

A phrase I coined some time ago was 'Entertainment'. People need to be entertained while they are being trained. In an article from the *Weekend Australian* entitled 'Humour, a necessity, not a luxury', Kylie Davis writes:

> 'Humour has become a powerful tool in the serious business of corporate training, and Australian comedians are licking the funny bones of some of our most senior executives.'

Some time ago, the chief executive of the Video Training Company, Mr Michael Earle, said:

> 'Being able to laugh at the mistakes of humorous characters allows the employees to see the behaviour without committing the errors themselves.
>
> Comedy plays a part in videos, which otherwise have serious messages about training. By laughing, you become more receptive to the message, and less threatened by its content. It makes it accessible.'

Humour Facilitates Learning

In the same way that humour can be applied to training, it can also be applied to many other areas of corporate life. In the same article, comedian John Cleese says:

> 'Humour should not be regarded as a frivolous way of passing time. We sometimes confuse being serious with being solemn. Solemnity is overrated; it induces feelings of rigidity and pomposity.

The correct use of humour facilitates learning Humour helps to change people's behaviour. It Creates an increase in creativity, and it helps people to feel less threatened by the prospect of change.'

Cleese also concludes that the real importance is in the correct use of humour. If, for example, you wish to produce a training video, the training message should be the basis of the humour; it's not just a case of simply inserting jokes into a training script.

WORKING WITH HUMOUR AND FUN

A New Breed of Manager

If, as Cleese says, the correct use of humour is all-important, then companies will require business managers who can best adapt to its use, and can see it through successfully. Let's revisit our cricket analogy, and Graham Lloyd's article in the Weekend Australian, in which he wrote:

> 'New rules also meant that all-rounders-multi-skilled players who could both bat and bowl well - were in high demand.'

Tom Peters, in his book *Thriving on Chaos*, takes it even further by saying:

> 'If the ability to deal with these paradoxes is the key to success, then we should promote, at all levels, those who show the greatest facility, in doing so. A new breed of manager is required and full-speed execution will not occur until the new breed is in place. It is imperative to dig into the ranks, or do whatever else is necessary, to get them in place, as rapidly as possible.'

What I believe Tom Peters is saying is that you should promote people with Business Show' attitudes and actions. Successful business people today are the people who have, or who are developing, those attitudes and actions, as well as Business Show skills and talents.

Make it Fun to Work

It is always important to remember that Business Show, and indeed business itself, should be 'fun. Employees and employers alike will get the maximum benefit from humour in their business environment.

Tom Peters describes this as a

> 'Sense of taking pleasure in accomplishment and interesting foul-up alike [which] will allow you to thrive amidst the ravages of change in a world turned upside down.

> ... The economic stakes have never been higher; therefore, it's never been more important, not to take yourself too seriously. We are in the midst of a great and crazy adventure, creating our brave new world, by error and trial, as we go along.'

In another Tom Peters book, *A Passion For Excellence*, David Ogilvy offers support for this 'fun' ethic, with his experience in relation to running his advertising firm:

> 'Make it fun to work in your agency. When people are not having fun, they don't produce good advertising. Encourage exuberance; get rid of the sad dogs who spread doom. What kind of paragons are the men and women who run successful agencies? My observation has been, that they are enthusiasts.'

Humour as a Tool to Maintain Morale

Humour and fun can lift morale within the corporate environment. As Malcolm Kushner, in his book The Light Touch, observed:

> 'Perhaps the most fascinating example of humour used to maintain morale during a critical period involves the merger between Allied Corporation and Bendix Corporation. Mergers always create a certain amount of fear and anxiety. People worry about lay-offs, they worry about changes in management styles, they worry about culture clashes and a sense of foreboding permeates the atmosphere.

> William C. Purple, the head of the Aerospace and Electronics Group, and a veteran Bendix executive, became one of five operating group vice presidents reporting to Allied chairman, Edward L. Hennessy.

> Purple tried to lighten the post-merger atmosphere by poking fun at sacred cows. For example, here's the way he introduced Hennessy at a Bendix Management meeting:

> "This is Ed Hennessy. He has had six jobs in 17 years. If his resume had come across my desk, I wouldn't have interviewed him."

> And his descriptions of Hennessy's background as a Catholic seminarian:

> "They gave him a collar on weekends, and told him to have a big time. Now you know what his idea of a big time is."

... Did Purple's antics have any effects?

The *Journal* reported that Allied Starchy Corporate Culture had been loosened up a bit by Bendix's "self-confident informality" and that intangibles, such as Purple's humour, were helping along what Mr Hennessy says is the smoothest of the roughly 20 mergers he had been through in his career.

According to the Journal, the humour was welcomed by Hennessy. He was quoted as saying that he wants his people to feel "comfortable about speaking up, and not to worry about retribution later on."

But Purple had the final word. He was quoted as saying that if Hennessy "couldn't take it, I wouldn't want to work for him".'

The Importance of the Office Clown

People like Purple, often referred to as office clowns, perform an important role in the maintenance of workplace morale, and in the general atmosphere of humour throughout the company. It was reported in the *Arizona Republic* newspaper:

'Humour is sorely needed in the workplace to lighten the mood and maintain morale in a world of increasing lay-offs, management upheavals and mergers. The office clown is an important figure among co-workers, functioning as a safety valve for employees who may be afraid to verbalise their frustrations.'

James Wilson, psychotherapist and business professor at the University of Pittsburgh, said:

> 'Clowns provide obvious relief from pain. Theres often a choice between anger or depression. The clown helps with the humour and acceptance, and builds a bridge to what we hope is the improved future. The office humorist is usually a highly creative and intuitive person, and is frequentlya lightning rod for feelings and turbulence around the workplace.'

Change and Humour

The office clown often uses humour to turn what could be a difficult or depressing situation, into one in which you can see the brighter side. As Dr Laurence J. Peters says in *The Laughter Prescription*:

> 'You can take almost any disagreement, any wrong, or injustice, any gripe, or any difficulty, and use humour to change things for the better.'

All results-oriented and vibrant corporate cultures thrive on change. Doesn't it make sense then to make humour one of the major ingredients of your corporate culture?

To have a sense of humour is to have the wisdom to accept the challenge of change. Humour eases the resistance to change.

Resistance Goes with Change

Very often, dramatic change within a workplace may be met with resistance. This is not necessarily a bad thing, according to Dr Joel

Goodman, author of Laughing Matters, and should be expected. The best way to deal with that resistance is to inject humour into the situation so people feel less defensive. Dr. Goodman writes:

> 'Humour allows a blending with the complainer, defusing the situation. One personnel manager at a large metropolitan hospital helped defuse the frustration of workers unable to find parking in the midst of the newest building project, by publishing a list of parking rules, in a highly unusual memo.

- Employees may participate in a demolition derby, that starts in employees lots, each morning promptly at 9 am
- When all the spaces are filled, employees who do not participate will automatically be declared losers
- Employees who park illegally one time will be warned
- After two times, they will be ticketed; after three times, they will be stripped and flogged in front of other violators.
- After four times, they will be forced to eat all their meals in the employee cafeteria.
- Employees who park sticking out in traffic lanes will have their rear ends painted red.
- If they continue to park this way, We will do the same thing to their cars.'

Hire a Humour Consultant

Low office morale can lead to reductions in productivity and creativity. A simple solution to some office morale problems could be to hire a humour consultant. The following was reported in Mode magazine:

'Picture it! A conference room of men and women in business suits. Some wear Groucho Marx glasses; some tell jokes to a video camera; others pull faces in funny mirrors; the rest are glued to Monty Python.

...Of course, there is a stress factor: an insidious, expensive problem, if you believe in statistics that claim stress costs the economy billions of dollars in absenteeisms and health problems.

So the guys at the top companies, such as IBM, Eastman Kodak and AT&CT (America's largest telephone company), have decided, and wisely too, that a big belly laugh with your colleagues just might be the answer.'

CREATING AND NURTURING A POSITIVE ENVIRONMENT

Successful and progressive companies create and nurture a positive environment, which encourages individuals to play an active, creative role in the running, growth and profitability of their organisation. A well-defined and executed corporate soul, using humour and its metaphors, can provide this.

Once you have identified your corporate soul's strengths and weaknesses, and once your Humour P'rogram is up and running, and getting results, review carefully both your business and marketing plans. Then look for ways of merging your humour philosophy and communication techniques into your corporate soul, by training your staff in them, and expanding them into your corporate identity and image.

A Totally Positive Environment

Generally speaking, humour in the workplace can be used to create a positive environment. This ideally gives your staff a competitive communication edge so that they can out-think, out-perform, and outlive their competition, and become a team that shares a unity of purpose to communicate to all the people who deal with the organisation. Do this by first asking three questions:

- What is our corporate soul?
- What are its strengths?
- What are its weaknesses?

Three Suggestions for a Positive Environment

To maximise humour's potential within the corporate culture, I suggest it would be beneficial to do the following:

1. Identify all your company's humorists, and bring in a humour consultant to train them in the positive business application of humour.
2. Hold a series of humour workshops for all staff members.
3. On their completion, put together a program to humorise your corporate culture. We will look at how to do this very soon.

Corporate Culture

Corporate culture is your company's beliefs, values and characteristics that have been shaped deliberately by training, or casually by experiencing your organisation's overall style and personality. This is what I call corporate soul. The understanding and strength of your corporate soul is important, but equally important is your cultures flexibility in meeting the needs of your customers, employees and shareholders, and its ability to initiate change when the need arises.

> 'A fun working environment is more productive than a routine environment. People who enjoy their work, will come up with more ideas. The fun is contagious.
>
> Roger Von Dech

What Makes a Poor Corporate Culture?

In an article in *Enterprise* magazine called "Quality Management, they claim that:

> 'Research points to the fact that 85 per cent of variations in quality are attributable to common causes such as poor training, poor design, poor equipment, poor work instructions, deficient lighting, failure to provide accurate information and poor communication.'

These points contribute to a poor physical and social corporate culture.

A Program to Humorise Your Corporate Culture

1. Start with two people who enjoy humour, so that the responsibilities are shared.
2. Research, discuss and finalise your aims. Write this into the 'Humour Program Mission Statement.
3. Work out your humour programs objectives. The following are some examples:

(a) Establish a Humour Room

Start with whatever space you have. Then as the humour program proves itself, look for the ideal location: somewhere colourful, with good views, plants, comfortable chairs, and a bungee cord for those who want to get of the building first the fun way.

(b) Design a Humour Bulletin Board Prototype

These, when developed, are located at strategic, over-serious spots in the corporation. They are visual ways of saying our corporate culture has a sense of humour. These could contain cartoons, personal bloopers, humour flow charts, comic strips or funny photos. You could have a graffiti, or a "bitch corner on the board as well. Also include quotes on humour by successful people to show that humour has credibility to 'agelasts' (people who don't laugh).

For example, this quote by former US President Dwight D. Eisenhower:

> 'A sense of humour is part of the art of leadership, of getting along with people, of getting things done.'

(c) Build and Operate a Laugh Mobile

Otherwise known as a Humour Wagon, or Comedy Cart. Make it lockable, with adjustable shelving, good strong rolling wheels, plastic glass doors for Viewing contents, and drawers for audio and video cassettes. Pack it with executive toys, cassettes, joke books, cartoon books, juggling balls, a few magic tricks, gag gifts and games. The idea is to move the Laugh Mobile around the company from the training room, to the boardroom, to the marketing department, to maximise its use. The content should be customised as much as possible to suit the group to which it is going.

(d) Start a Humour Team

Advertise in-house for people who want to be part of your humour team. Humour provides a common ground, the same as music or sport. It's also very democratic and egalitarian - so imagine a status clothes rack, and hang your status on it before you begin each meeting. Iry to get someone from every department, so there is direct access to all cultural arteries. You will find, initially, that people join because they have an interest in one comedian, or one style, or one aspect of humour.

(e) Name your Humour Team according to your Mission Statement

Give each member a nickname, based on some skill, talent or ability they might have, or their favourite comedian's first name spelt backwards.

(f) Draw up two Humour Inventory Sheets

One for any talent, skill or area of expertise your team needs (see next page), and one for equipment, props, supplies and furniture etc. that you need.

Humor Team Skills and Talent Inventory Sheet

NAME			DEPARTMENT		
LAUGHLINE			FAX		
Please tick as many areas of expertise and talent that you have					
DEPARTMENT			CREATIVE		
Committee			Humour Use		
Planning			Humour Writer		
Marketing			Stage Managing		
Research			Speaker		
Financial			Presenter		
Computer			Trainer		
Co-Ordinating			Performer		
Personnel			Musician		
Meeting Guests			Magic		
Meeting Assistant			Impersonations		
Catering			Cartoonist		
Technical			Audio Visual		
Organising			Designer		
Promotion			Director		
Secretarial			Compering		
Costume Props			Acting		
Management			Juggling		
Producing			Singing		
Others			Others		

(g) Create Special Interest Groups Within the Team

Make a list of all possible special interest groups that you feel would be appropriate. For example:

- Research and Development Group
- In-House Communication
- Creativity Group
- Newsletter Group
- Humour Training Group
- Humour Literature Group
- Staff Appreciation Group
- Humour Activities Group
- Industrial Relations Group

Then study the filled-out Humour Team Inventory Sheets, and find the right people for the group. This takes time, so make it a fun exercise.

(h) Arrange a Humour Team Meeting

From the first meeting, selecta committee and plan your first program. Start each meeting with a comedy quote whip-around so that everyone gets a chance to express their humour and share other people's styles.

Have a Dial-A-Joke Seat with the person sitting on it required to ring Dial-A-Joke, then relate it to the Humour Group.

Build a joking environment into your Humour Team Meetings. Develop Humour Rituals, humour symbols, and running jokes. Look for situations in the meetings where you can all laugh together: for example, when someone makes an outrageous or ridiculous remark like: 'I don't believe politicians could lie straight in bed. The team would all repeat this statement in unison, and at the same time give one another the 'thumbs-up sign. Build as much fun into the meeting as possible.

(i) Develop a Positive and Negative Humour-Use Assessment Tip Sheet

Pass it out to everyone at the first meeting. Ask them to read and study it as the future of the humour program depends on their understanding the difference between positive and negative humour.

(j) Identify the Goals of the Humour Team

1. Write a humorous history of your organisation. Research public relations clippings, newsletters, cafeteria chit chat, memos; interview board members etc.

2. Publish a company favourite joke book. Send to all members of your company, asking for their favourite joke. Compile them into categories, add a few cartoons, and photocopy as many as you need.

Publish the humour team's monthly newsletter, using all the skills and talents of your team.

3. Read through the chapters in this book for other ideas and insights you can incorporate into your humour program. These include:

- Humorous Signs
- Humour Bank and Humour Library
- The Laughter First Aid Kid, and The Humour Team Ad lib Album.

Everybody Wants to Have Fun

Once you have established a positive working environment, it should also flow on to other aspects of your business. Some of the practical elements that go into marketing Business Show were evident in an article in the *Wall Street Journal*, in which Joanne Kaufman writes:

> 'Everybody likes to have fun, said company president Stew (Stewie) Leonard Jr, 32, who, in a walk around the stores' one labyrinthine aisle, greeted customers, and more than a dozen of the 650 employees by name.
>
> Stew Leonard Jr aims for fun. Fun he gets. Just ask the little girl being twirled around the produce section by a guy in a bright yellow chicken suit.
>
> Just ask the people gazing above the frozen food locker at an eight-foot dog robot dressed in a confederate grey uniform, accompanying himself on the banjo to *Dixie* and *I'm a Yankee Doodle Dandy*. Stew Leonard's mission is to create happy customers. He does this by giving them cleanliness, quality and fun. His hero is Walt Disney.'

Marketing the Fun Experience

Fun is a three-letter word more powerful than any four-letter equivalent. The power of having fun is one of the qualities of having a humour attitude, as well as one of the key ingredients of 'Business Show.

In Max Boas and Steve Chain's book *Big Mac*, Carl Kay says:

> 'The whole McDonald's philosophy is that going to McDonald's is fun. The kind of place where you go to enjoy yourself.'

Fun, as in a humour attitude environment, can be used to enhance a corporate philosophy and identity. "Bumpa-T-Bumpa Auto Marts' reconstructed their outlets to not only sell accessories, but also to promote, through their staff, the fun of motoring.

They humanised all their business. They strived to sell people fun, and car accessories, not just for a price, but for an experience. This fun experience is also marketed in other companies, such as:

Disney	Focused On Fun
Swatch	Fun Time With Swatch
McDonalds	Food, Folk and Fun
South West Virgin Airlines	Fun To Fly
Fairstar	The Fun Ship

CORPORATE IDENTITY AND CORPORATE IMAGE

Corporate Identity & Image Discovery Diagram

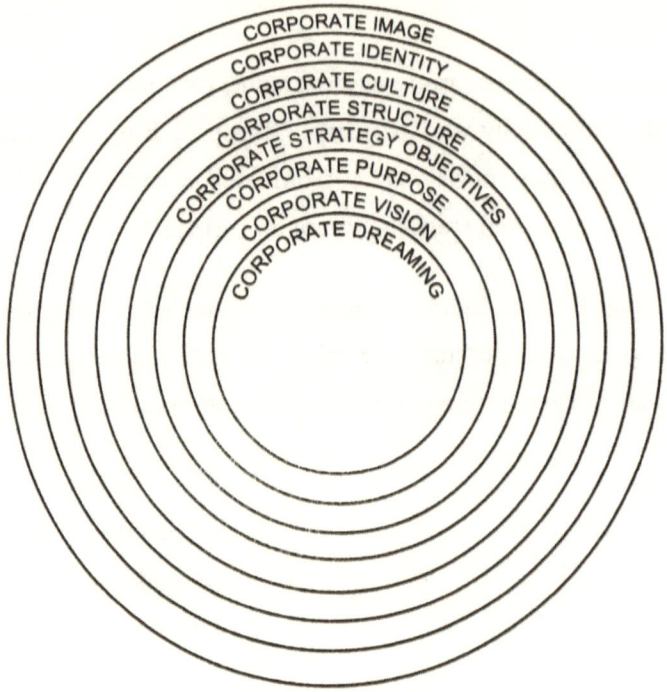

Researchers at the University of California School of Medicine in San Francisco reported that facial expressions associated with such emotions as happiness, sadness and anger may trigger some of the physical changes brought on by the actual emotions.

Your company's communicating face and the perception it generates could also work like this and have similar effects on your employees and customers.

Your corporate identity and your corporate image are your company's communicating face.

What is Corporate Identity and Image?

It is difficult to define corporate identity and corporate image, and there is some confusion between the two. Clarke Reschke sums it up best in *Marketing Magazine*:

> 'In the absence of any formal definition of corporate identity, I have defined it as the ongoing physical manifestation of an organisation's presentation to its various public, whereas corporate image is what people think of the organisation. Corporate identity Is an important component of corporate image, and1 contributes in a major way to corporate image. The two are intermeshed in many ways. Corporate identity is the basis of corporate image.'

In short, a corporate identity is a malleable element of the business, which can be continually reshaped and improved. Corporate image is how the public sees you, and in many ways, is out of the company's hands. The only way to change your corporate image and to be perceived differently by the public, is by changing your corporate identity.

Belonging and Purpose: The Two Faces of Identity

Wally Olins takes it further in his fascinating book Corporate Identity. He claims corporate identity can be controlled by formulating strategies to change your corporate structure and culture. Corporate culture, as explained earlier in this chapter, is your company's beliefs and values, and some of the strategies to control and change it have also been outlined. According to Olins:

'If the (corporate) identity is explicitly controlled, it can be the single most powerful influence on the corporate culture, and I believe visa versa.'

Olins also believes that to be effective, every organisation must make its sense of purpose clear to those within the organisation. It is this sense of purpose, coupled with a fostered sense of belonging, which are the two major facets of corporate identity.

Humour Instils a Sense of Belonging

One of the principal functions of humour is bringing people together and instilling in them a sense of belonging. This is done in many ways: from the comedy club comedian who unites strangers by talking about shared human experiences, to the heavy end of humour; the 'dirty' kind of humour.

Harry Levinson and Stuart Rosenthal wrote about such an experience in their book, *CEO: Corporate Leadership in Action*, in the chapter about Walter T. Writston, the man who transformed First National City Bank into the world's leading international banking institution. The section titled Barbed Wit begins:

> 'At policy committee off-shore meetings, after the business was over, there were always set dinners. An important part of the routine was telling jokes, and trading insults among the group... For some, that process did not come easily. It might take two or three years before they could muster the comfort to tell the necessary dirty jokes.
>
> In those sessions, members of the policy committee, who might be in conflict with one another, found

themselves sitting next to each other, or playing tennis as doubles partners, or playing golf together. There was a compelling cohesion, which echoed that of a military combat group. The same group met every Thursday morning; then the agenda was business, so the talk was about serious matters. But the joking and the same tone generally prevailed.'

TECHNIQUES FOR ESTABLISHING CORPORATE CULTURE, PURPOSE AND IDENTITY

Wide Awake Dreaming

Humour is about saying and doing deadly serious things in an enjoyable way. Let's try this by doing an exercise I call Wide Awake Dreaming.

Sigmund Freud in 1905 wrote a deadly serious book about humour, called *Wit and Its Relations to the Unconscious*. He wrote it shortly after *Interpretation of Dreams*, because he saw so many similarities between dreams and humour. These included:

- Frustrations becoming realisations
- Ideas going so far out, that they come back in again.
- Nonsense that suddenly makes sense

Using the cores of humour, such as brainstorming, spontaneity, improvisation and playfulness, creatively put yourself into a dream-like state and start to rant and rave into a cassette recorder about your dreams for your corporation.

It takes time to fashion this dream into a vision for your company, but this then becomes its purpose. From this comes your corporate objectives and strategy, your corporate structure and culture, followed by your corporate identity which creates your corporate image.

You might also include in the Wide Awake Dreaming exercises what John Naisbitt has to say about Roger Von Dech, in his book Reinventing the Corporation, under the heading 'Corporate Creativity'

A Whack on the Side of the Head

Roger Von Dech, the author of *Whack on the Side of the Head*, runs stimulating, idea-spawning sessions for companies such as Amdahl, Arco, Wells Fargo, IBM Cockheed and Xerox, in which he teaches employees to break out of their traditional modes of thinking and approach problems creatively. He says:

> 'It's really hard to see the ideas that are right on the side of you, or behind you. It's really hard to see fresh ideas, by looking twice as hard in one direction. Often what people need is a whack on the side of the head.'

How do you give yourself a whack on the side of the head? Von Dech suggests the following:

- Challenge the rules
- Inspect your own rules
- Fall out of love with your own rules and ideas
- Think frivolously, make jokes about the problems you are working on.

That last suggestion recalls the advice of the previously mentioned famous advertising man, David Ogilvy, who wrote a series of rules for creative thinking. His first rule was:

'The best ideas come as jokes; make your thinking as funny as possible.'

Have You Got a Mistaken Corporate Identity?

As we saw earlier in this book, mistaken identity is one of the most powerful humour forms. The following joke will remind you of it:

> A conservative, middle-aged factory owner was getting out of the taxi he had taken to work, when he said: Just look at that teenager over there going into my factory, with the ducktail haircut cigarette and blue jeans. I can't tell whether it's a boy or a girl!'
>
> The taxi driver said: 'It's a girl; she's my daughter.'
>
> The factory owner said: 'Please excuse me, sir. I didn't realise you were her father.
>
> The taxi driver snapped: 'I'm not! I'm her mother.'

As fashion has changed, values have changed. Have you got a mistaken corporate identity and image - one that looks, feels, behaves and talks in a contemporary way? Or does your corporate identity need to be changed, upgraded or improved?

Changing Values Means Changing Identity

To ensure you don't get a mistaken corporate identity, it's important to change with the times. It's easy to get out of touch as an article in the Weekend Australian showed. Christopher Forsyth looked at the changing values from the past to the present:

- Self-denial to self-improvement ethic
- Higher standards of living to better quality of life
- Traditional sex roles to a blurring of sex roles
- Accepted definition of success as a success-is-what-you-make it attitude
- Traditional family life to alternative families
- Faith in industry and institutions to self-reliance
- Live to work to work to live
- Hero worship to a love of ideas
- Patriotism to a less nationalistic view of life
- Unparalleled growth to a growing sense of need for limits
- Industrial growth to a growth in information and service
- Receptivity to technology to an awareness, but not subservience to technology

This article is now more than a decade old and aspects of this would have changed as well. Your corporate identity is changing continually, especially as we move out of 'economic rationalisation' to 'recognition economics.'

Only 'Human Face' Corporate Identities Will Survive

A lot of businesspeople have put corporate identity in the 'too-hard basket.' The incredible thing is, you won't find their golf clubs in the same basket.

When the going gets tough, the tough get laughing! Only those companies with strong, contemporary, flexible and human corporate identities will survive. That's because when all else is equal, you only have your corporate identity and image as a representative to communicate your purpose and benefits to attract and maintain loyal customers.

Anybody thinking of developing a corporate identity program would find Wally Olins book, *Corporate Identity: Making Business Strategy Visible Through Design*, a helpful companion.

Oh, What a Feeling!

Humour is the best tool to help add the human face to your Corporate Identity. For example, look at what Toyota has done with the international symbol of comedy: the chicken. They 'roast' it in both definitions of the term and, through personification, Tom Foolery and buffoonery, they create an identity for their cars by providing an experience for their customers.That is summed up in their catch phrase:

Oh, What a Feeling!

Corporate Identity as a Representative

Humour was also used as the essence of the Australian identity, when the Australian Tourist Commission carefully and cleverly chose Paul Hogan to represent Australia. The Americans took Hogan's mateship and happy-go-lucky attitude to heart, and even incorporated 'G'day, I'll slip an extra shrimp on the barbie for Ya', into their vernacular.

Hogan's warmth, innocence and strength were the attitudes the Tourist Commission wanted to sell as the quintessential Australian identity, which in effect can be called Australia's corporate identity. His humour which matured in the *Crocodile Dundee* films, and his Aussie identity showed Americans how they could be winners in the new way of comedy, and not in the way of tragedy. It showed them that they could be heroes without being macho, and how they could remain efficient and successful by being less serious and enjoying things a lot more.

In 1992, Ruth Da Cruz reported in Austrade's newsletter *Exporter:*

> 'Humour leads exports to Spain. If Crocodile Dundee could make such a hit in Spain, Australian exporters could do the same with their products there.'

Ms Ruth Da Cruz went on to say:

> 'Everyone I know claims that the most difficult export is a sense of humour. It is very difficult for Spaniards to laugh at the Australian sense of humour and, yet, they were captivated by Crocodile Dundee. The moral here is that if you can export humour, the most difficult product, you can export anything.'

If they can weave humour into an Australian identity, and sell it to the world, surely you can incorporate humour into your Company's Identity, thereby giving it that contemporary image and selling it to your public. Be careful, however, that you don't go about it like one particular CEO who called all his department heads into the boardroom and said:

> 'Ladies and Gentlemen, we need to change our corporate identity, create more of a contemporary image. From now on, we need to be seen as innovators, flexible leaders, that practise individuality. Now get back to your departments, and do exactly as I tell you.'

CORPORATE DESIGN

Corporate design has traditionally been accepted as the major force behind corporate identity. This is changing dramatically as consumers become far more selective and sophisticated. Consultants in corporate identity, organisational development and strategy, and public relations, advertising and marketing companies, are all joining the corporate designers to provide this very important element of company success - corporate identity.

Humorous Corporate Identity Tools

There are countless corporate identity tools available for you to add that humorous human face to your company. Here are some suggestions:

Graphic Trade Characters

Wally Olins says in *Corporate Identity*:

> 'M. Bibendum has been the prime symbol of Michelin since 1898. He is said to have been inspired by a pile of rubber tyres, and is unique among symbols for industrial companies, in being both memorable and friendly.'

Company Environment

The Ikea stores have a young children's playroom and older children's video room. Some stores have small bars and car washes. Their aim is to make Ikea stores friendly and entertaining

Cartoon Stereotypes

Thai-Royal Orchid Holidays have quarter page ads in newspapers, with the heading:

> Thailand seven days five nights, with all the trimmings.
>
> ($1160 and you're laughing).

Then they have a cartoon stereotype tourist with a camera around his neck, laughing his head off, and the caption at the bottom says:

No wonder they call Thailand the Land of Smiles

Attractive Smiling Faces

There is an old saying:

If you don't have a smiling face, don't open a business.

There have been many examples of companies which believe in that adage. One that grabbed my attention was Australian Airlines. The slogan at the top of their page was:

The Way We Do The Things We Do

This was handwritten across the hat of a beautiful, smiling air hostess, who was wriggling her nose for the extra effect. The message said:

To flight attendant, Cindy McKenzie, friendliness comes naturally, and to Australian Airlines, that's an asset worth its weight in gold.

A smile goes a long way with your customers. It also goes a long way with your employees.

Caring Cartoons

Manchester Unity Householder Insurance, which has sponsored The Melbourne Comedy Festival, placed a variety of Caring Cartoon newspaper ads. Written at the top of the cartoon:

My insurance company gave me a new for old on the stolen telly, but I grew old waiting for the cheque.

In the cartoon, an old man is sitting on a lounge chair with cobwebs draped down the back of it. He has a very sad looking cat at his feet, and they are both looking towards to the door, which has a slot marked 'mail. He's saying:

M.U. I think I need you.

On the side, there is a written message:

We've taken the hassles out of claiming on household insurance. It's the policy you'd expect from a company that spent 150 years caring for Victoria.

Establishing Likeability

Telstra's identity did a complete turnaround within a couple of years. They went out to develop a likable image, by using a variety of humour techniques and images. For example, they have a white-faced mime clown, who is laughing, to sell cordless phones. They took out full-page ads in most papers showing the giant laughing face of Melbourne's Luna Park, holding a telephone, with the caption across the top saying:

If you saved 60 per cent on Saturday calls, you'd be happy too.

Novelty Names

Mad Barry's Home Improvements Centres won the Franchisees Associations of Australasia Award For Excellence in Retail Franchising.

Through their novelty name, they created a specific identity which maded fun of themselves. In reality, if they were laughing at themselves, their success proved that their customers were laughing along with them.

Physical Fun

One of the masters of this technique is the Coca-Cola company. As Wally Olins writes in *Corporate Identity*:

> 'Through the most sophisticated techniques, supported by untold billions of dollars, Coca Cola has become synonymous, more or less throughout the world, with all the good things in life, with fun. That is why Coke commercials show young and physically perfect families of subtly differing shades of colour and ethnic origins, cavorting about the sea, or the mountains, displaying acres of pearly white teeth, clutching in their exquisitely, manicured hands, guess what? The Real Thing.'

BUSINESS SHOW: CONCLUSIONS

There may be some of you who are still sceptical about the power of humour in business, and indeed the whole concept of Business Show. It is a difficult transformation in attitude and action to make, but as we have seen, the rewards can be numerous. In conclusion, let me quote Melvin Helitzer, who has spent his life in advertising. He writes:

> 'The Humour Club membership includes many of the biggest names in advertising: Coca Cola, Polaroid, Xerox, General Mills, Bic Pen, Alka Seltzer, E. P. Hutton, Blue Nun Wines, Chiffon Margarine, Exxon, Time, Kelloggs,

Heinz, Huffy Bags, Stroh and Miller Beers and scores of
other Blue Chip Corporations.'

Helitzer says that a typical view of the value of humour is the rationale of
Timex executive, Paul Kuavis, who says:

'We have to take the consumer by the shirt, to say we've
got something different.'

But don't think that the ability to use 'Business Show' techniques is
limited to multinationals. It's also used successfully by some of the
smallest advertisers in the world:

Larry Robinson, a San Francisco chevy dealer in superman leotards, flew
from car to car extolling their virtues and price.

'Of course I feel silly sometimes,' he said, But Id rather be
silly, and sell cars, than look nice and go broke.'

Chapter Seven Summary
Business Show - Applying Humour Seriously

1. Business Show is the title of the new age of business

2. Your personal view on the role of humour will dictate your willingness to accept humour and laughter in business.

3. Comedy can teach us new skills for survival without destruction.

4. Freedom from the need for tragedy is an important precondition for the avoidance of ecological catastrophe, and for change.

5. The corporate philosophy of Business Show is created by the adoption of a philosophy of comedy in business.

6. Humour is the most significant behaviour of the human mind.

7. Use humour in business to discover possibilities traditionally neglected by using logic and reason.

8. The roots of Business Show can be traced back to the advent of television.

9. Entertainment communication had arrived!

10. Television has created a global environment where people also need to be entertained.

11. Infotainment' is the new buzz word of Business Show and three of its main ingredients are humour, comedy and laughter.

12. Once you recognise Business Show as a philosophy of business, you can then incorporate it into your company's mission statement and corporate culture.

13. People need to be entertained while they are being trained.

14. Successful businesspeople develop Business Show attitudes, actions, skills and talents.

15. Employees and employers get the maximum benefit from humour in their business environment.

16. Humour is an effective tool in maintaining morale.

17. To have a sense of humour is to have the wisdom to accept the challenge of change. Humour eases the resistance to change.

18. Look for ways of merging your humour philosophy and communication techniques into your corporate soul.

19. Develop a program to humorise your corporate culture.

20. Fun, as in a humour attitude environment, can be used to enhance a corporate philosophy and identity.

CHAPTER 8

The Branding of Australia

Our National Conscious Culture

In the globalised world of Business Show, Australia can lead the way. We are very fortunate in Australia because we have developed a basic subconscious philosophy of humour. Our National Conscious Culture of You've got to laugh, mate!" goes right back to the time when the white man first heard a Ha Ha Pigeon' - a kookaburra. Since that time, Ha Ha Skills' have been bred into Australians and this sets us apart from the way the rest of the Western World thinks.

With our sense of humour, we've been able to find success in failure, because seemingly there was no winning against the forces of our circumstances. We looked at life and said: You can't win; life's a game and if you survive, it's a draw, and yet we still laughed. Saying you can't win is not an acceptance of inferiority but rather an awareness of reality. History shows that nobody gets out of life alive! But in Australia at least, we're enjoying ourselves while surviving.

'Ha Ha Skills' give us a humorous way of thinking - one which I call paradoxical perception - that the best you can ever hope for in life is to be a 'successful failure.'

This comes alive in the story of the two Australian larrikins walking down the street. One suddenly bent over and picked up a pay packet and his mate said: 'Gee whizz, you are a lucky bugger! He had a look at the pay slip and replied: What do you mean lucky? Look at the flaming tax I pay!'

Being a successful failure means that there is no standing still: you either grow or rot. If you are successful, you have to keep risking. If you risk, eventually you are going to fail, and that's when you are really succeeding. That's why, as a country, we value imagination just as much as information; innovation just as much as tradition; play just as much as work. Being a battler is just as important as being the best; being an individual is just as important as being a member of a group; being a worker is just as important as being a boss. Were a fair, optimistic, creative, friendly, environmentally aware and good-humoured nation that can lead the world this century.

Slowly the rest of the world is beginning to come around to our way of thinking. They are coming to realise that in Australia there is a 'social experiment going on. Another attempt by mankind to find an answer to the age-old question: how should we order our affairs to get the best out of our brief life on this planet?' Ryszard Kapuscinski, the Polish author of Imperium, a History of the Rise and Fall of Soviet Communism told Australian author Phillip Knightley that as he travelled around the old Soviet Empire doing his research, person after person would say: 'Ryszard, we made the right decision to get rid of communism; it wasn't working, but my God, this capitalism is hard. I don't know if we can take it, and aren't we entitled to an alternative to the American model? You have been all over the world. Isn't there a country somewhere that has found a middle way, where market forces rule, but the government looks after the kids, the old, the sick and the poor? Somewhere where the bosses give the workers a reasonable deal? Somewhere where people help each other instead of just looking after themselves?' Kapuscinski told them: Yes, it's called Australia!'[1]

The Birth of the Australian Humour Attitude

Australian humour first began with a decision by the English court in 1787 to create a penal colony here. When the First Fleet arrived in 1788 from the Old World, it was mostly made up of the unwanted, emotionally wounded, desperately poor and chronically sick Irish, English and Scottish prisoners. As desperate and seemingly hopeless as their situation appeared, this convict cargo still managed to lay the foundations for our legendary sense of humour and give future Aussies the confidence to approach any situation with an attitude of No worries!'; 'No sweat!'; No problems!'; "She'll be apples!'; 'She'll be jake!'; She'll be right, Mate!'

The word most used to describe the Australian sense of humour is sardonic. It was categorised this way by Europeans in comparison to their way of thinking, their values, beliefs and judgments. But sardonic humour implies a laughter edged in bitterness, a cynical detachment and a mockery of self and others. Perhaps this would be true of the humour of the very first convicts and settlers, but comic awareness soon replaced cynical detachment, a sense of play replaced a sense of mockery and a sense of optimism replaced the bitterness. The Australian character became underpinned by a spirit of openness, make believe, light heartedness, a spirit of inventiveness, a willingness to experiment and a capacity to change and even the possibility of making for ourselves a fairer society'.[2]

This optimistic humour perspective always allowed them to rise to the occasion and to take a rise' of their situation. They never recognised defeat or aspired to victory, but rather would ride the pendulum between both, on the cushion of the spirit and tradition of Having a go!; 'Giving it a burl!'; 'Ripping into it.'

The "she'll be right, mate!" attitude, which is the essence of our ethos, gave us the tolerance, courage and flexibility that we needed to change, adjust and adapt. Australians began to realise that they could use their creative innovation and inventiveness to come up with an answer to all the challenges and dangers of day-to-day existence. This made those challenges and dangers exciting, and to the Aussie, 'exciting' is just another word for 'fun?'.

Paradoxical Perception as a Result of the Anniversary of Federation

Peter Coleman quoted in The Weekend Australian from John Hirst's book, The Sentimental Nation: 'Many thought Federation would only create another parliament of windbags and another cast of bureaucrats. What made the difference was sentiment. We, or enough of us, felt we were a nation, a separate people, a passionate majority. The Nationalists wanted a new nation with a new constitution to express this new identity; we are, in other words, not a people forged in blood, revolution or war, but a sentimental nation.

Our spirit of humour gave us the courage to believe in ourselves as a nation in rimes of conflict and change. We began to realise that when you can laugh together, you can grow together. It was harnessed nationally and helped us bring our great nation together as one people in peace, unlike other countries that were brought together through war.

People say that the creation of the Australian nation is boring because we lack the murderous drama of the European model. We lack the deceit, the intrigue, the conflict, the cunning, the anger, the suspicion, the fear, the hatred. This is not true; we've had boatloads of that. We lack the bloodshed because our national humorous attitude released the tension of the dramas before they could build the slaughter.

Before we could slaughter one another, we could laugh at ourselves and each other. We had developed an interest in incongruity; a tolerance for ambiguity; we could see the justice in juxtaposition of nature, and through these we had developed paradoxical perception. Over the years we had watered down the racism, bigotry, animosity, religious dogma, class distinction, political fixations and other attitudes from the old pessimistic world. We had developed a grudging affection, a cheerful criticism, a joking relationship with one another.

Our adventurous nation was not founded in the place of war or a battlefield, but a place of peace, a park. We were the first nation to be voted into existence by its people with a fair dinkum form of democracy somewhat different to others and based on a fair go for all. As Edward Barton, Australia's first Prime Minister said, for the first time in history, we have a nation for a continent and a continent for a nation'.

Geraldine Doogue said, in opening the Federation Ceremony in Centenary Park: 'Australia is a place of many stories, of triumph, struggle and humour.'

Rob Sitch, from the Working Dog team that gave us *The Castle* and *The Dish*, said in *The Bulletin*: I think sometimes we make a mistake in drama, I mean, humour is such an important part of life. I think to take humour out of drama is to distort life. I think one of the Australian characteristics, if there is one, is that blokes particularly, try to make a joke in the most difficult circumstances. Humour and drama go together in this country possibly more than anywhere else.

What it means to be Australian

> You don't have to play sport to be an Australian. You
> don't have to own your own home to be an Australian.
> You don't have to sleep with a member of the opposite sex
> to be an Australian. You don't have to like a cold beer to
> be an Australian. You don't have to believe in God to be
> an Australian. You do have to have a sense of humour to
> be an Australian.
> Pete Crofts.

Collin MacInnes says in Craig MacGreggor's book Profile of Australia:

> 'Phenomenally brave, open-handed, shrewd, humorous,
> adventurous, fanatically independent, and most blessed
> of all, contemptuous of fuss. There is undoubtedly
> a greatness about the Australian people, a bigness, a
> wideness, an inborn capacity for the large - the heroic
> gesture. If people are born serfs or princes, as they are,
> the Aussies are a kingly race.'

This folklore image of the pioneering, laughing Australian was created in stories about such incredible characters as the Wild Colonial Boy, the Bastard from the Bush, the Sentimental Bloke and the Man from Snowy River. The sense of adventure, and humour were our innovative ancestors only choice in learning to live in harmony with the harshness of their environment, the unrelenting climate, the isolation of the continent, the size and emptiness of the country. To the women, the shattering loneliness; to the men, the devastating vastness.

When the Australian met with triumph or disaster, they treated both imposters the same - with a laconic, understated, deadpan punchline. To those unaccustomed to the Australian genius for deadpan understatement, the humour is seldom recognised, as it is hidden in cultural characteristics, only identified by other Aussies. The raising of an eyebrow, the wink of an eye, the turned-up corner of a mouth - these could all be classed as a belly laugh to a lot of ustralians.

A spirit of adventure and a philosophy of laughing, along with the ironic character of Australian humour, have been passed down through the years along the bush paths, the drovers' tracks, the riverboat waterways, and through the mouths of our enthusiastic storytellers. They are represented in the conversation between the old bush Aussie giving advice to the young city Aussie. The young Aussie is whingeing. He is saying: I can't go anywhere; I've done my licence; my girlfriend has gone back to Greece with her parents; I've been out of work for six months; the doctor reckons I will have to give up smoking. As well as that, I've been banned from the race track and I can't afford a beer.' The old Aussie's advice: Laugh it off, mate!'

This is our heritage, our legacy, our culture and national identity, our brand of philosophy.

There is a classic Australian cartoon, drawn by Stan Cross, which illustrates this well. The scene is set during the Depression in 1933 and shows two Australian construction workers who have slipped off a skyscraper – one hanging from his fingers, the other hanging from the bloke's ankle- causing his mates pants to be pulled down to his feet. They are both laughing hysterically. The top bloke who was hanging on to the rafter by his fingers is saying: 'For gawd's sakes, stop laughing; this is serious!' This cartoon portrays the way Australians felt during the Depression. The message: 'All you can do is hang on and keep laughing; if you don't, you die.'

Spinning a Yarn - Australia's Story Telling Tradition

Our story-telling tradition really began with the end of the transportation of convicts around 1868. This was the beginning of the golden age of Australian yarn spinning. This next yarn could be classed as uniquely Australian. It's about two old swaggies living it up in town, which consisted of a pub and one tiny general store.

> The swaggies are sitting on the step of the pub as a man comes down the street on his horse. 'Oh well,' said one swaggy to the other, 'I'll be on my way as soon as this traffic dies down.'

'Storytelling is one of the healthiest activities of the comic wave. As long as our species has possessed language, we have used it to tell our stories to one another.[3] When other 'new countries were settled, including America, it was done differently to Australia. They settled in groups, re-establishing the patterns of the villages from their old country. The Australian tradition of one man going off with his swag and his dog, spending his life non-stop tramping around this vast island, very seldom happened in the early days of American history. It was these travelling, story-telling humorists, the Jolly 'brand' swagmen, who helped educate the different cultural groups about the of the new land.

Stories help to bond families together and help create bodies of shared experiences. It is through storytelling that wisdom and knowledge are passed on from older to younger generations. Stories have always helped people understand the dynamics of their natural environments, to find benefits and to avoid dangers. Human relations with animals are motivated by stories, and through stories, animals become symbolic creatures, bearing cosmic and metaphysical meanings. What we have learnt about good and bad behaviour, manners and morale, customs and habits, gets transmitted through the stories we tell. Stories help heal our wounds as we tell how we were wounded, just as they heal those who listen. Stories are essential to the comic purpose of affirming and perpetuating the normal conditions of life.

We need to be aware of our individuality and live it. It is our real story and from where our future income will come - as a person, as a business and as a nation. Ralph Jensen, director of the Copenhagen Institute of Future Studies, says in his book, The Dream Community - How the Coming Shift from Information to Imagination Will Transform Your Business: Businesses need to imagine their futures, the way good novelists imagine their stories. What's the future of business after the information age? It won't be the latest technology or newest product, but the story behind the product that will provide the competitive edge. The company with the best story wins. Consumers will pay for the story that sparks the imagination, that reflects how we see ourselves and how we want others to see us. What are the most important raw materials of the 215 century? Stories that will translate information for consumers into accessible emotional terms. As cookie clutter products inundate the market, companies of the future will have to stand out by creating stories about themselves, who they are and what they stand for - stories that appeal to the heart of the consumer. Some of the world's most successful organisations, such as Disney, Nike and Rolex, have long recognised society's appetite for a good story. They have demonstrated the ability to satisfy that need by entertaining the consumer as well as providing information, and will reap the financial reward well into the next century. These cutting-edge companies are ushering in the dream society, the age of storytellers.

My Own Yarn Spinning Tradition

Telling stories and yarn spinning is part of the Australian brand. This is something I was stamped with from the moment of my birth - coming from a Catholic, Protestant, Communist, capitalistic family background! My mum, Iris Crofts, said my first words were: You never never know. ' She said I would repeat these words dozens of times a day. I grew up in the only milk bar for miles around in the small Gippsland town of Morwell in the 1940s and '50s - the period of the pubs closing at six o'clock. My grandfather was the first secretary of the ACTU; my Dad, a labour politician. I was surrounded by union bosses, local politicians, community leaders and Catholic priests - all enjoying a quiet glass of beer in the milk bar, well into the night. All of them, even without a beer, were great storytellers. All of them had hope in their hearts for their new land and dogmatic points of view about politics, economics and religion. They were all convinced that they were right and that their brothers, sisters, friends and enemies were wrong. Mum told me that whenever one of the movers and shakers of the small community was telling and selling a story, whether it be about communism, capitalism or Catholicism, I would pop up at the most inappropriate time with, You never never know. Many of them would burst out laughing and agree with me .

These men and women, these ancestors, were from an old pessimistic world. In their new land, they were optimists. They loved to enjoy themselves; they loved a good healthy belly laugh as much as any political or religious point of view.

Australia's Diversity and the Australian Humour Tradition

Australians have always had their own agenda. They are individuals but in the true spirit of paradoxical perception, they are also magnificent team players, as the successes of our sporting teams testify. All Australians, no matter what their background, can be built into a team of individuals, like the old bumper sticker, Individuals of the world, unite!

We should not underestimate humour's ability to unite us. For 50,000 years, the rightful owners of our land, the indigenous Aboriginal people, treated and protected the Kookaburra as a sacred bird. They woke up every morning to the sound of laughter. The Kookaburra became known as the great laughing spirit. He reminds all Australians, black and white, to have a joking relationship with the environment and a sense of humility with the size and distance of our land. The Kookaburra provided Australia with a jolly and cheery bush alarm clock. Today, the Kookaburra's laughter, larrikin attitude and courage is at the heart of our national identity. His laughter is the symbol of the mateship of our multicultural nation. The Kookaburra will forever remind us that we can't take our politics or religion too seriously; that it's better to be optimistic than pessimistic; that you've got to laugh, mate!

The Softening of Ethnic Traditions

As we swiftly surf from the past to the future we must bring with us our cultural tradition, our legendary Australian sense of humour. Being a nation of some 200 ethnic traditions, Australia's future depends on future generations' sense of perspective. All their choices will depend on how they see things. If their cultural beliefs, family traditions and ethnic values are seen through the lens of humour, then there is a softening that provides hope, and that gracefully opens one's feelings to the uniqueness of each of us. This leads to a sense of individuality, independence and a sense of personal freedom, which is the key to creativity and innovation in the face of constant change.

Through the lens of humour we may more easily tackle many of the enduring conflicts that face us: our ethnic diversity; Aboriginal reconciliation (a sense of humour means you are vulnerable enough to say you are sorry); the democratic versus the aristocratic; the bush versus the city; the larrikin versus the wowser; the republican versus the royalist; the nationalist versus the globalist; the intolerant versus the tolerant; the pessimist versus the optimist: individualism versus community-ism; the fear seeker versus the fun secker; the dogmatic perceptionist versus the paradoxical perceptionist;, the important issues of youth suicide, ageism, and women's equality.

Phillip Adams, broadcaster, humorist and one of Australias leading advocates of laugher says: In the final analysis, the ultimate war on this planet will not be waged between East and West, black or white, communist of capitalist, atheist or agnostic, but between those of us who laugh and those of us who don't. Another way of saying this is, between those of us who are locked into a tragic way of thinking and chose of us who have developed paradoxical perception and can, when necessary, move over to the human comedy side of the street.'

Women in the Australian Humor Tradition

> I heard a woman say the other day: 'A woman who tries
> to be equal to a man today, lacks ambition.'

In the Australian chapter of *National Styles of Humour,* which I co-wrote with the late Hyram Davies, and, which to this day, Phillip Adams calls the 'only serious academic attempt to analyse Australian humour', we say: The essential nature of Australian humour is male dominance and this was shaped to some degree by English attitudes towards the roles of women. Male dominance of the social, bureaucratic and political structures was firmly established in the predominantly male convict society of the late 18th and 19th centuries. In this strong, sexually deprived, male environment, men found their attitudes towards women.

'Indeed, the institutions had been formed by males and remained firmly in male hands and still do to a large extent today. Isolation also reinforced the subservient role of women, as men worked planting crops, shearing sheep, droving cattle and prospecting for gold. Women looked after children, often by themselves, on isolated properties. With the urbanisation of Australian in the late 1860s until the 1900s, the isolation of men from women began to change, and with it, their attitudes towards females.

'Through all the titillating tales and shameless sagas, wanton fables, boastful reports and questionable anecdotes, Australian sexual humour reveals profound anxiety towards women and their relationship to men. The bravado, the jaunting arrogance of the larrikin, are merely attempts to cover up the social awkwardness, and man's fear of sensitivity in the company of women.

'Early in the '50s, the male dominant publication, *Smiths Weekly*, ceased to be and gave way to a variety of womens magazines,. Women finally had a voice. This means they couldn't be stopped from joking; they could now express themselves openly. This energy led to the birth of legendary Australian comedians such as Dawn Lake, Mary Hardy and Ruth Cracknell, and more contemporary Denise Drysdale, Gretel Killeen, Kaz Cook, Wendy Harmer, and so on. Women have been, and still are, a big part of our humorous folklore. For every drover who sat around a campfire cracking jokes with his mates, there was the drovers' wife, doing the same around the kitchen table.'

Like the lady who said: 'The only reason I have nine children by him is that I'm hoping to lose him in the crowd! You know, we've been married for better and worse; he couldn't have done better and I couldn't have done Worse!'

Transforming Tradition

The 2000 Sydney Olympic Games lifted Australia's image of itself: from insufficient national pride; a shyness to blow its own trumpet; fear of the tall poppy syndrome; shame of our convict origins; cringing from its culture; a lack of confidence in itself to be itself - to a country confident in its heritage and culture; proud of its people and their achievements; and thankful of its easygoing likable nature.

We were pleasantly surprised at our Business Show skills in producing the most inspiring, educational, culturally healing and globally appreciated sporting event of the last century. As four billion people around the planet watched in anticipation, the announcer explained our history and character. He said: The figures inspired by the famous Ned Kelly series of paintings by the late Sir Sidney Nolan, the trials and tribulations of early European settlement, helped to forge the unique Australian characters of pioneering spirit, energy, ingenuity, humour and larrikinism. At last we had broken free from the shackles of the British jail sentence of some 200 years earlier. We were now unique, culturally proud people, who were proud of our past, enjoying the present and optimistic of our future.

When Cathy Freeman lit the Flame For All Time, she joined the dreamtime of black and white Australians as one nation. It felt great to be an Aussie, free from the stereotypical image imposed by our ex-patriots, our media and the British press. Editor-in-chief of the *Bulletin Magazine*, Max Walsh said:

'The Olympics gave us the opportunity to not only look at the way we really are, but also to define ourselves on a world stage. The very fact we could stage the Olympics with professional efficiency, without compromising the laidback charm of Sydney and its people, captured, for me at least, the essential quality of Australia at the opening of the new century.

While Sydney is not the totality of Australia, it embodies most of what this nation has become: a self-confident, economically successful, technologically skilled, multicultural, tolerant society that has developed, thanks to its rich ethnic diversity, its own style, its own culture and its own sense of humour. The Games provided a rare opportunity for the nation to take stock of itself; to showcase itself to the rest of the world. In doing so, I believe it discovered a great deal about itself that it may have doubted.

Australian Branding: the Future Reflects the Past.

With Australia hosting the 2000 Olympic Games, many companies were branding their products as Australian, thereby branding Australia according to their interpretation. Melbourne Age writer Caroline Overington interviewed Chris Dibley, account director for the advertising agency MJW, about the I believe Fosters Beer Campaign, and he had this to say about the claim that 'stereotypical' Aussie sentiments and images (blokes in bush hats, cattle dogs, that kind of thing) are dated: 'Some things about Australia will always be true. One of the lines we use is "this is the best address on earth", and that is probably more true now than it ever was. Research groups show that young Australians, while more worldly than their parents, and certainly more travelled, nevertheless believe that mateship, larrikinism, and good times, are essential to the

Australian character. They believe the same things that their parents believed about, what it means to be an Australian.

The Fosters campaign was accompanied by a website that opened with the word 'G'day'. Contributions on what it means to be an Australian were welcomed. They included: 'Only in Australia would we leave our cars worth hundreds of thousands of dollars in the driveway and store our junk in the garage.

Australians: the Future Thinkers!

While our nature and needs have changed in this new, globalised century, our thinking and behaviour haven't. The tragic ways of thinking in previous centuries needs to be replaced with new attitudes and actions, new beliefs and new values, in order to 'keep up with changing technological times. Let's face it, tragic thinking in technological times is like jumping out of a plane with a bullet-proof vest instead of a parachute!

It's my belief that Australia has made a great start on the road to this new world view. Humour Action and Humour Attitude (Ha Ha) skills were developed by our heroic pioneers to cope with the sacrifices, overcome the obstacles, find the opportunities and adapt to the biological, geographical and cultural circumstances of our new home. The Australian characteristics of optimism, friendliness, irreverence, a fair go, playfulness, flexibility, tolerance, courage, creativity, individuality and lack of respect for authority, are all Ha Ha Skills.

These inherited gifts of our ancestors are our culture's intellectual capital. We Australians are naturally creative and clever thinkers and we should be able to harness this intellectual capital to take advantage of boundless Aussie business opportunities. And if necessity is the mother of invention, then improvisation is almost certainly the father! We can all do it - even I have connected my creative and clever thinking to come up with a business-joke formula to generate some practical business opportunities.

Think of a product that costs 10 cents, sells for a dollar and is habit-forming. Invent a breakfast food that will drain the energy from kids! Invent a quick-drying cement that sets before a dog can walk on it! It's time for us to become the future thinkers. It's time to use our inherent Ha Ha Skills for fun and profit!

Intellectual Capital and the Knowledge Economy

In the business world, a company's intellectual capital is even more important than its physical capital. It can be measured by looking at the gap between a company's balance sheet and its market valuation. This gap comprises the company's indirect assets - intangibles such as product innovation, customer loyalty, employee morale, patents and trade marks and these are what makes the difference between prosperity and insolvency.[4]

In fact, so bankable have these intangibles become that they have developed their own sub-economy known as the 'knowledge economy'.

One anecdote that helps explain the conundrum between valuing time (your labour) and valuing knowledge (your know-how) comes from a most unlikely source, Picasso. In the 1950s, Picasso is said to have been approached by a young woman in Paris who wanted him to do a sketch for her. He agreed. When Picasso handed the sketch to the young woman, he charged her 50,000 francs. The woman objected, saying it had taken him only 10 minutes. Picasso replied that it had, in fact, taken him 30 years. He had charged the young woman for his knowledge, not his labour.

In today's 'knowledge economy', those with regular, renewed and updated skill sets; diverse work experience in sectors that matter; and ability to think creatively, solve problems and work in teams, will be the gold-collar workers. Such people are the ones best placed to offload their 'intellectual property at a premium price and they should be aware of their own value. Given the rise of entrepreneurship and the trend to work for yourself, it is not a bad idea to think of yourself as a gold mine with potential raw materials. Anybody who wants the benefit of your knowledge needs to strike a claim in your resources.[5]

Commercialising our Intellectual Capital

Australians are intelligent but make out they are not. As we recognise and prize our sporting heroes, and take pride in our innovative talents, we need now to take the next step and publicly appreciate our intellectual community.

This is starting to happen. On September 4 last year, sports champions, scientists, Prime Minister John Howard and other prominent Australians, gathered with special guest Nelson Mandela, in Sydney for an Olympics of the mind, called, What Makes a Champion'. In lending his support to this exclusive and expensive forum, Howard said that it would reinforce Australia's reputation for innovation, intellectual achievement, creativity and understanding.

If science as a national sport is to move beyond these words, action is required to deal with the deficits and problems. When Australia returned empty handed from the Montreal Olympic Games, a concerted and successful effort was made to improve the quality of sport and training. In contrast, the Australian University Teachers Awards, funded by the Federal Government shrunk to six in 2000, from eight in 1999 and 11 in their first year, 1997. Is this how we would treat our sports coaches?

It is easy to measure the effectiveness of sports investments, by championships won and medals collected. There is much less certainty about how to measure the success of investment in science, with a tendency to think in monetary terms, rather than national pride and international standing.

Beverley Head, in Business Review Weekly, said: 'If Australia is to stand any chance of shedding its cargo-cult mentality regarding science, engineering and technology, it must find the catalyst needed to revitalise industrial R&D budgets. She follows this by saying: 'R&D tax breaks are therefore not enough to fix the problem. What is of greater benefit to entrepreneurs is a culture that supports science, engineering and technology, and an environment that promotes and nurtures ideas. Money is also critical, be it from government in the form of more attractive company tax regimes or seed capital, or investment by industry and venture capitalists that can nurture an idea through to commercialisation. Once we have the idea to a commercial stage, we are now faced with Australia's biggest hurdle: being a leader in the new knowledge- based globalised economy'.

Cultivating Egalitarian Tall Poppies

This requires paradoxical perception of the highest order. We need to become a population of egalitarian Tall Poppies. It's a matter of extending the value of achievement we have for sporting and entertainment personnel to science and business personnel - successful Australians in all fields who are encouraged to stand up and speak up for the good of all of us.

The Tall Poppy Syndrome was termed in the 1930s by the working class to define themselves from the arrogant aristocracy, who were about putting down the battler. This is something that belongs to all nations, only in different forms. In the United States, it's known as the 'Crab Pot Syndrome'.

Each crab's frenzied effort pulls the leader back to the panicking pack, no escape.

We now live in a country where we all have a chance to be Tall Poppies ourselves. For the past 25 years or so, I have been training comedians, speakers and business executives in Business Show speaking and humour skills. I often refer to myself as a 'Tall Poppy gardener', someone who grows Tall Poppies.

Ian Stephens, one of my clients, says in his newsletter, Tall Poppy Tips: No matter how you label it, the corporate world is not immune. Industry leaders face the Tall Poppy Syndrome daily, fighting to maintain market position, while smaller companies with lower overheads try to cut them down to size. Typically, the view of Tall Poppy corporations is negative. My message is: it's time to make a mind shift. No longer can we afford to cut our Tall Poppies down to size; the future of our nation, our children and our successes in the world economy depend on a move away from putting our Tall Poppies down. We must start to learn from them.'

Historically, we have always loved the larrikin, as long as he never became too much of a show-off. Let's celebrate the positive qualities of the larrikin, the way C J Dennis did in the Sentimental Bloke. George Reed says in the introduction to the story of the Sentimental Bloke, who, in spite of hardship and adversity, preserved a great good humour, a lightness of touch in all his work and an abiding love of trees and birds of the Australian countryside: 'The egalitarian Tall Poppy needs to have the good humour, lightness of touch and love of the environment, and at the same time be a business show-off: meaning, being able to stand up, speak up and hold up to the spotlight, our country, so it can be seen and heard in an Australian way in the kaleidoscope of the selling sounds and images of the globalised market-place.'

The Australian Cultural and Business Brain Drain?

In 1984, Robert Orben, the famous American comedy writer, came to my comedy and laughter bookshop in Sandringham and was amazed at the comedy books and services we provided, He said that if I had opened up the business in the United States, it would have been a smash hit. For 25 years, my family and friends have been saying that I should have taken my ideas in business offshore to the US. Because of my love of Australians humour and their spirit, I could not do that.

Humour and Australians go together like Phar Lap and winning, Bradman and runs, a digger and his mates. I couldn't leave my mates; I wanted to play a part, no matter how small, in Australia, recognising one of its most natural resources, its humour. For years there have been evacuations of creative talent from Australia to the world: producers, writers, actors, directors and the cream of our county's theatre personnel. Ex-patriot journalist Philip Knightley was quoted in an article in *The Australian* newspaper by Nicholas Rothwell, about whether he made the right decision in choosing to leave his home. 'I realised that I swapped a sunny, happy, optimistic country with an eye on the future for a dull, pessimistic nation heavy with melancholy. It has taken me until now to see that I might have made a mistake, but back in 1954, I unwittingly gave up a chance to play some small part in the making of modern Australia, one of the most exciting social experiments going on in the world today.'

Alan Deans, in an article in *The Bulletin*, says: Sydney will become to the world what Adelaide has become to Australia: a nice place to live, but largely irrelevant.'

It is a sobering thought, coming not that long after we dazzled everyone with how progressive, attractive and successful we have become by staging the Olympics. However, the dynamos of our economy are being drawn elsewhere. It seems inevitable that those corporations, which employ hundreds of thousands of Australians and are the focus for our savings, will one day be American, European or Asian.

Those under threat are our highest achievers, the ones who cut the mustard' with the world's best and are prospering. They are using their strong Australian foundations as a springboard for their success. We no longer offer enough opportunity to keep them. They are adolescents looking to leave the nest.

It would be a shame if these companies become globalised before they become Australianised, because they would be wonderful ambassadors for our Australian new way of chinking. Not only that, if these companies look inward to the intellectual capital, then inward further to their Australian cultural capital, they might catch the tidal wave that will have them sailing the new seas of business success, the globalised, cultural capitalism storm.

Australian Branding - the Role of Business Show

Australians have to reinvent certain aspects of ourselves. In a world dominated by Business Show, corporate storytelling, political spin doctors, marketing gurus, celebrity executives, and image makers, our planet is a 'high-visibility' intensive society, rocketing into the age of pleasure, where a feel-good' lifestyle and a healthy life span are desired. Recognition economics has arrived. Being seen and not being seen is the difference between being successful and being a failure, whether for an employee, a small businessperson, professionals, corporations or countries.

Australia is perfectly branded and positioned. We have the

- Intellectual capital
- Friendly national identity
- A new world way of thinking
- Adventurous spirit
- Innovative nature
- Courage of greatness.
- Natural story-telling abilities
- Belief in fairness
- Tolerance for difference
- Optimistic outlook
- Flexibility for fun and play
- Environmental awareness
- Economic soundness
- Social multiculturalism
- Government of mateship
- Well-developed Ha Ha Skills
- Desire for global peace

All we need is the confidence and community encouragement to develop our Business Show skills.

Alexandria Harris, in an article in the *Australian Financial Review*, said: 'Corporate image, branding, professional sales pitches, comprehensive public relations campaigns are all essential ingredients of success in the globalised marketplace. Sadly, it's as if Australians are embarrassed to talk about our great products, our services, ourselves. We don't like to brag, to sell, so imagine being an Australian trying to sell any kind of product or service to an American. Perhaps that explains why so many Australian inventions remain unfunded, unbuilt, unsolved. Perhaps it's why we have difficulty being taken seriously, and why so many Australian businesses fail in their attempts to capture that mythical one per cent of the US market. If we are to do business with the Americans, we simply have to do business better. We have to learn to sell, in the American sense - call it marketing, call it PR, call it business development, its all sales. That doesn't mean we have to lose the essence of being Australian - our humour, our innovation, our friendship - but it does mean we need to adjust our manner and image. And most importantly, we have to influence other people's opinions of us, or we will continue to luck out in export and investment attraction efforts. Perception is all there is. We have to tell our story and understand that they are expecting it.'

The most prized people in this millennium are Business Show people with well-developed Ha Ha Skills. A Business Show person uses the right side of the brain more than the left. A Business Show person has paradoxical perception. A Business Show person communicates and sells from the heart, as well as from the head. A Business Show person has fun and makes profit. A Business Show person tickles your spirit as well as tickling your bottomline. A Business Show person can spin an emotional and imaginative story, while they are showing, telling and selling.

Fortunately, we have a whole crop of Business Show people emerging in Australia currently - Steve Vizard, Max Markson, Eddie McGuire, Kevin McKuay (Big Kev) to name a few.

Using Humour directly in the Knowledge Economy

The development of a sense of humour is no laughing matter! It's intellectual capital that can be harvested in many, many ways. The most obvious way, of course, is through the use of corporate comedians - like Elliot Goblet, known as the 'safe corporate humorist', who tailors his presentations to suit his audience.

'Corporate comedy is designed to integrate, not to tear apart, to bring together people and the organisations they serve and to harmonise those organisations with the society of which they form a part. 'It is a self-deprecating form of humour, which pricks the bubble of pretentiousness among professional elites and reminds us all that professional status is a responsibility to be taken seriously, not a right to take ourselves too seriously.

The work of people like Campbell McComas, an acknowledged pioneer of corporate comedy, has created a strong tradition of Australian humour in business, which has implications for the mainstream of Australia's economic life. In doing so, he elevates comedy in the workplace to a high form of art. His efforts have pioneered the way for other professional comedians, creating an appreciation among Australia's business and professional leaders of the positive values of comedy and its potential to enhance organizational effectiveness and harmonise the workplace.[7]

As we have seen throughout this book, the intellectual capital capacity of Ha Ha Skills are endless. This applies to everything from personal health, selling, marketing, leadership and advertising, to corporate culture, and national identity.

The Bakers Delight retail bakery chain, has a set of golden rules to remember when working with customers: In building a rapport with your customers, always remember a sense of humour and a sincere smile; it's the first thing a customer notices. They go further - right into the realms of Business Show by suggesting a virtual theatre of delightful behaviour, conversation, noise, and oven beepers be provided to complement the aroma of fresh bread. This sense of activity and ambience is very important in living the chain's promise of real bread baked fresh daily. With bakers bringing out bread and the staff and customers having fun together, more people were attracted to the bakery and more people were leaving with smiles on their faces.

In the year 2000, Richard Branson decided to bring Virgin Airlines to Australia. Virgin is seen as a highly successful business and Ha Ha Skills and Business Show have been used well to create the Virgin Group brand. *In Strategy and Business Magazine* in 1998, the radical Mr Branson explained that his only business role model was a person who had failed. Entrepreneur Freddie Laker had attempted to take on British Airlines with a low-cost Trans-Atlantic airline a few years earlier and had been driven out of business by the competition. Nevertheless, Mr. Branson, sensing a kindred spirit, sought Mr Laker's counsel in the early 1980s. Mr Laker advised him that to succeed, the airline had to concentrate not only on low cost but also on offering quality and value for money. It had to be innovative, but most of all fun. The airline's employees were the real asset, not the planes. It was Mr Laker who brought out the Barnum and Bailey in Mr Branson by suggesting that if Mr Branson were going to take on Pan Am, TWA and British Airways, he had to use himself as a promotional tool, dressing up in a captain's outfit, to launch the airline. 'That way, you will get on the front page, he told Branson. "If you turn up in ordinary business clothes, you'll be lucky to get a mention. Remember, the photographers have a job to do. They'll turn up to one of your events and give you one chance. If you give them a photograph that won't get them on the front page, they won't turn up to your next event.

Matt Weinstein says in his book *Managing to Have Fun*: 'am always amazed when people proudly proclaim, "I never mix business with pleasure". I reply: "What is wrong with you?" If you want to build a successful team at work, your management philosophy should be exactly the opposite. You should always mix business with pleasure; you should be constantly finding ways to bring pleasure into business, to yourself, your employees and your customers. To many companies, building a team means creating a high-powered, smoothly functioning organisation that has plenty of muscle but not much heart. It is the actions of the human side of business that depletes employee morale and contributes to job dissatisfaction and burn-out. By adding an element of fun and celebration to a team-building program, you can take an important step towards humanising your workplace and creating a sense of heart and soul in your organisation.'

As part of the international speaking circuit, I joined Mark Victor Hanson, Daniel Goleman and Amanda Gore on a tour of Asia in 1998. My main message was, and still is, that as a leader; if you do take yourself too seriously, you are missing the biggest joke of all, yourself The leader who can laugh at themselves and be laughed at, has taken another step towards the perfect sanity, which brings peace on earth and goodwill to all people. The statement that attracted the most media coverage was my quote: The only thing you can take seriously is humour; if you take seriousness seriously, you are insane."

Having Fun at Work

Humour thrives on self-deception. Humour lies in the spaces between win and loss, war and peace, work and leisure, pain and pleasure, right and wrong. Paradoxical perception gets to the heart of humour attitude by allowing us to be successful failures, to have competitive cooperation, calculated creativity, prepared spontaneity, organised dreaming, intentional intuition, confident vulnerability, and detached involvement.

On a personal level, the idea that humour resides in a gap between an individual's outer persona and his or her real self is long established. In Twelfth Night, Shakespeare derides comedy from the vain and pompous Malvolio who deludes himself into thinking he is the object of a young woman's desire. And in L'Avare, the author pokes fun at Harpagon who thinks he is projecting an image of generosity when his every word and deed betray his miserliness. Contemporary examples include Basil Fawlty (Fawlty Towers), who sees himself as the only sane, rational person, when in truth he is the originator of all the chaos. Or Jim Hacker (Yes Minister) who believes he is rather adept at getting his own way when it is he who is the guileless victim of manipulation.

To a lesser extent the same problem confronts people in organisations. They too have to put on an act, one which befits their organisational role. At senior levels, the aim is to project oneself; to be seen as a person who looks, sounds and behaves in such a deeply, even heavily serious way, that everyone is convinced that he or she is a person of great depth, honour and sustenance, and one who will deliver. On occasions, that mask of professionalism slips and base, non-corporate motives surface: managers saying one thing and meaning another; managers leading each other into impossible situations; managers pretending to be what they are not. And when managers somehow give themselves away, humour, both mocking and defensive, is never far behind.[8]

I think we are moving into a time where people won't leave home to go to work and will not have to leave their individual self, their real self, at home with their families. We are demanding to be who we are, wherever we are.

David Firth, in his book *How to Make Work Fun* said: We spend 41 per cent of waking hours at work. Since we are asleep for a further 35 per cent, it seems crazy to consign life, and with it, any hope of fun to the remaining 24 per cent. Why do we leave our personalities behind when we set off for work in the morning? Why do we envy people who tell us that their work is fun, yet somehow feel laughter is somehow out of place at the office? How can we deliver excellent service, or be better than our competitors, if we'd rather not be working at all?'

Psychologist Abraham Maslow spoke of finding a purpose beyond one's self. He alludes to the fact that in work, this purpose is to have fun, and goes on to say that pay is generally highest in fun jobs and whatever you think is fun, you tend to become good at. However, the salary is really only just the trophy awarded to the really passionate corporate participant.'

This is a new way of thinking and should we follow it, it will allow us a new way of feeling, a new way of working, and a new way of being - our real individual selves. No longer will we have to work hard or work smart, but work heart. Find your purpose and pursue it with passion!

My Purpose and How I've Pursued It

Our lives are our stories. We need to tell our story by the way we live it. People don't listen to leaders; they observe them. The mantra for the new millennium is: 'All is One, Everything I am and Everything I do is One, I am my product and soul. Every thought and every feeling I have, has been given to me to learn from and to earn from. I see my IC (Intellectual Capital).

I have lived the above mantra and in the process developed The Humourversity. My Dad told me, I was conceived in a pub - being Australian, I guess I can't claim to be Robinson Crusoe there - not far from an army barracks. Dad told me he was on leave. I guess that's why they call it leave; he left something of himself with mum that became me. I was born on November 14, 1943, five minutes before 12 o'clock. I was holding back to be born exactly at midnight. That way, I could have two birthdays. It was right smack bang and just a lite before the big bang of the global slaughter that took the lives of 70 million people. It was a tragic time for humanity and for one mother and her newborn son. My mother told me that on those lonely nights, laying awake with the world at war and with me kicking inside her, she wondered what would become of us, her husband, family and country. During this time, she would sing me songs, hour after hour, song after song. And when I was born, for the first 10 months of my life, Mum would do the same thing with me on her shoulder. Song after song, night after night. We were pretty close, Mum and me. When Dad came back from the wat, I was pissed off to the back bedroom, with my elder brother, Michael. Dad quickly went to work to create my younger sister, Margaret. I have spent most of my life fighting a fear of abandonment and 'fighting funny' to get some attention again. So, as a young baby boomer, I began studying the thinking and behaviour concepts of comedy that later became my Ha Ha Skills. I wanted to adopt a way of thinking that opposed tragedy so that my children and your children wouldn't die in a world war, much more devastating than the one I was born into. Well, that's my story and I'm sticking to it!

After years of research and study, at times working four jobs and battling to survive with a wife and young family, I went on to be the first person to represent Australia at an International humour conference in 1987 at Arizona State University. I was the keynote speaker, headlining with the top humour academics in the world. My paper was entitled Laughter or Slaughter? I pointed out that these two words are identical once you take the 's' off slaughter and if you make that 'S stand for 'sense of humour Then you have world peace, not world war. One of the aims was to establish humour as a legitimate political ideology called 'Comedyism'. The policy of this ideology would not be based on morality, nationalisation, hierarchy structuring, economic imbalance, adolescent mentality, racial or sexual discrimination, but the survivor of the species - the human being with a sense of humour. Comedyism's philosophy is in line with Marx - not Karl, but Groucho Marx! Our campaign funds consisted of more than 400,000 jokes. Our Minister for Defence was a coward, and our Minister for Education was calling for a sense of humour to be studied in schools. We would all learn a sense of humour the way we learn a sense of religion or a sense of politics. We are not born voting Labor or Liberal! Then we would all have a common sense. To be fair dinkum', we would need to place more emphasis on Australian humour and its many manifestations - both traditional and contemporary - in our art, music, literature and performing arts, our physical and behavioral sciences, and in our everyday life. That is so the true blue dinky-di essence of the Aussie ethos, which is essentially one of comedy, can be experienced!

Active Optimism

In this hundred years of Federation of National Unity, when we reflect on our history in people, our values and beliefs, our leaders and heroes, our myths and miracles, we need to liberate ourselves from some traditional values and myths. We must empower ourselves to maximise the true social capital of our people, our imagination and optimism.

Paul Wilson says in his book Calm for Life: Most optimists succeed; all pessimists fail.' One of the earliest discoveries we make in life, is that it's easier to complain about problems than it is to offer solutions. As a result, we see large parts of our society obsessed with what is wrong. This applies not only to protest movements but also to members of the clergy, teachers of politics, and most particularly, the media. It requires very little insight, effort or character to be able to highlight the wrongs of life. The real challenge is to present constructive possibilities.

Once you make a habit of seeing life from a positive perspective, this becomes easy. It is now fairly widely established, that having a positive mental attitude not only enhances your immune system and circulation but also significantly reduces your risk of encountering an accident or bad luck. If you ask the more progressive immunologists for the best prescription against cancer, most will volunteer diet and/or optimism as a predictor of longevity. A positive, optimistic attitude is so important that many believe it has more bearing than any of the risk factors conventionally cited, including smoking, sedentary lifestyle, diet and genetics. However, it is important that optimism is seen not just as an expectation of certain outcomes, but as a real commitment to positive behaviour and attitude. In other words, optimism is active not passive.

'Beware the man that laughs and his belly does not jingle'. Buddha.

Martin Seligman PhD, who wrote, *Learned Optimism* and has been called the Freud of the next century, says in the magazine *Psychology Today*: The overall goal of positive psychology is to enhance our experiences of love, work and play. This is a revelation for a group that has traditionally focused on dysfunction, illness, healing and coping strategies. It is no surprise that in the psychological literature over the past 30 years, there have been 54,040 abstracts containing the key word "depression", 41,416 naming "anxiety", but only 415 mentioning "joy".

Furthermore, Seligman believes that only a small number of the 18 million people diagnosed with depression actually suffer from biologically based depression, which he says means our conception of depression is all wrong. 'It is not something created by rejection, or childhood traumas that make us feel bad, or saying negative things, he says, 'it's much less complex than that. Maybe, what looks like a symptom of depression, negative thinking, is itself the disease. Using Seligman's logic, maybe the problems of the Western world aren't capitalism or communism; they are merely the symptoms of the tragic thinking training of the Western world.

A National Humour Day - a Day for the Spirit of Play.

David Malouf, who is acknowledged as one of the world's leading novelists, in the 1998 Boyer lectures, titled 'A Spirit of Play, The Making of Australian Consciousness', explored the spirit of play. 'A spirit of openness; make believe; light-heartedness; a spirit of inventiveness; a willingness to experiment and a capacity to change and even the possibility of making for ourselves a fairer society. This is the spirit that underpins the Australian character. Never before was this more evident than when, as a nation, we experienced the shared meaning of the power of play and of being an Australian during the Olympic Games.

Jeremy Rifkin goes on to say in *The Age of Access*: Now that we are moving from industrial to cultural capitalism, the work ethos is slowly giving way to the play ethos. Play is what people do when they create culture. It is the letting free of the human imagination, to create shared meanings. Play is a fundamental category of human behaviour without which civilisation could not exist.

Dr Joseph Meeker picks up the purpose of the spirit of play by saying: 'Play rather grows from our sense of freedom; it produces strength and skill for the players;, stimulates the imagination and encourages agility and self-confidence. As the puritans articulated the work ethic, so now it is our privilege to give voice to a new ethic of play. If we were to have a play bill of rights, it may include the following:

- All players are equal, or can be made so
- Boundaries are well observed by crossing them
- Novelty is more fun than repetition
- Rules are negotiable from moment to moment
- Risk in pursuit of play is worth it
- The best play is beautiful and elegant
- The purpose of playing is to play, nothing else

Although serious people may think comedy is silly, I believe it holds truths that speak to the deepest parts of human nature. Comedy also moderates healthy relationships among people and between people and the earth's natural processes. It connects us with other species through shared evolutionary history and through pleasant play that crosses species lines. Comedy is a contributor to survival and a habit that promotes health.

In an article titled, The Competitive Advantage of Nations', in the *Harvard Business Review*, Ian Porter says: National prosperity is created, not inherited.'

It is now time for Australia to take its inherited humour ethos a little more seriously. This process has begun, but it needs community awareness. So I am proposing a National Australian Humour Day, a play day, where we celebrate, educate and communicate to ourselves and the world our brand of humor and its many facets.

Defining the Branding Of Australia

On a personal level, we need to have a harmony between our mind, body and soul. Corporately and culturally, we need to have harmony between our brand, mission and strategy.

Our Australian brand is

- Australia, the fairest and friendliest experience on earth
- Australias mission, to be the world's leading imagination, innovation
- Australia's strategy, to economically support and publicly encourage all Australians in Business Show Ha Ha Skills

As our merging Australian identity humorously fights for its political and cultural independence from the transplanted British culture, and adjusts to radical, social, cultural and economical upheaval, our humour encourages and motivates us to identify just how important it is to a young and free, creative and clever, bold and brave, confident country.

We need to believe in magnificent goals; to fulfil the dreams and visions that our folklore heralded. As we begin the new millennium, our sense of humour is one of our culture's biggest assets. It will help us succeed as a nation through the attitudes it portrays; the action it takes; the values it represents; the fears it alleviates; the hopes it creates; the profit it makes; and the dreams it visions. Our humour attitude is one of individual freedom, and of global peace.

Let's not leave this national identity treasure, You've got to laugh, mate!' attitude, to chance. As we swiftly become a multicultural community of 50 million people in the volatile Asian Pacific region, yet remain a small part of a growing globalised community, there is one thing we need and the world needs. It is the optimism, friendliness, flexibility, innovation, courage, tolerance, playfulness and humility that the legendary Australian sense of humor demonstrates.

In this communication and creative technology, Australia leads the world. Our pioneering ancestor's tradition of Humour Attitude and Action are Australia's international competitive advantage and our unique selling point... And remember: 'You've just got to laugh, mate!'

Chapter Eight Summary
The Branding of Australia

1.   In Australia, we have developed a basic subconscious philosophy of humour

2.   You can't win; life's a game and if you survive, it's a draw'

3.   The 'She'll be right, mate!' attitude, which is the essence of our ethos, gave us the tolerance, courage and flexibility we needed to change, adjust and adapt

4.   Over the years, by adapting to the landscape and compromising to the climate, Australians developed a paradoxical perception

5.   You do need a sense of humour to be an Australian

6.   Telling stories and yarn spinning is part of the Australian brand

7.   Laugh it off, mate!' is our heritage, our legacy, our culture and national identity, our brand of philosophy

8.   Some things about Australia will always be true. One of the lines we use is, this is the best address on earth

9.   If necessity is the mother of invention, then improvisation is almost certainly a father!

10. People with the ability to think creatively; solve problems; and work in teams, will be Australia's gold-collar workers

11. Let's celebrate the positive qualities of the larrikin

12. For years there have been evacuations of creative talent from Australia to the world

13. Recognition economics has arrived; being seen and not being seen is the difference between being successful and being a failure

14. All our nation needs is the confidence and community encouragement to develop our Business Show skills

15. We now live in a country where we all have a chance to be Egalitarian Tall Poppies.

16. Corporate image, branding, professional sales pitches, comprehensive public relations campaigns are all essential ingredients of success in the globalised marketplace

17. The most prized people in this millennium are Business Show people, with well-developed Ha Ha Skills

18. Humour lies in the spaces between win and loss, war and peace, work and leisure, pain and pleasure, right and wrong

19. We must empower ourselves to maximise the true social capital of our people, our imagination and optimism

20. The Branding of Australia is: Australia - the fairest and friendliest experience on earth

BIBLIOGRAPHY - Chapter 8

1. Philip Knightley, in his book, *Australia, a Biography of a Nation* says: 'The 20th century will be remembered for the failure of a great social experiment, communism. Its collapse, in 1989, was such a triumph for the West that some claim it heralded the end of history. From now on, there was no path for people to follow other than that leading to the democratic free market. But while communism was floundering in the Northern hemisphere, in the South there was a different social experiment going on. Another attempt by mankind to find an answer to the age-old question: How should we order our affairs so as to get the best out of our brief life on this planet?' In Australia, the world's new country, an eclectic mix of people from the Old World was trying to create a different society - one described by Ryszard Kapuscinski, the Polish author of *Imperium, a History of the Rise and Fall of Soviet Communism*. Kapuscinski told me that as he travelled around the old Soviet empire doing his research for *Imperium*, person after person would say something along these lines: Ryszard, we made the right decision to get rid of communism; it wasn't working, but my God, this capitalism is hard. I don't know if we can take it, and aren't we entitled to an alternative to the American model? You have been all over the world. Isn't there a country somewhere that has found a middle way, where market forces rule, but the government looks after the kids, the old, the sick and the poor? Somewhere where the bosses give the workers a reasonable deal? Somewhere where people help each other instead of just looking after themselves?' Kapuscinski told them, Yes, it's called Australia!, only to see them look bewildered. He said he was amazed so few Europeans knew anything at all about Australia or had any idea that, despite problems, the experiment of the middle way was still going on. Some thought Australia was just an extension of Britain in the South Pacific. Others thought it was a little United States.

Those who had sought enlightenment from British friends often ran into British prejudices, like the sentiments expressed by journalist, Jeremy Clarkson. With the South of France, God can say, I did okay there. But we must never let Him forget Australia, a vast and useless desert full of spiders that kill you and men in shorts.' Kapuscinski, who had been to Australia, did his best to advise them correctly, saying: No, Australia was not another United States, and never would be. The Pilgrim Fathers were people of strong religious beliefs, who were convinced they were following divine will in founding America for God's edict. Australia, on the other hand, was founded by criminals and their jailers. The pilgrims stepped gracefully ashore at Boston on to a seaside rock still revered to this day. The First British settlers landed in Sydney Cove where the criminals persuaded the jailers to dole out some rum and Australia was born in an orgy of drunkenness, violence, and sexual debauchery! The paths these two nations have taken have been different ever since!'

2. David Malouf, who is acknowledged as one of the world's leading novelists, in the 1998 Byer lectures, titled 'A Spirit of Play, The Making of Australian Consciousness, explores the spirit of play. 'A spirit of openness; make believe; light-heartedness; a spirit of inventiveness; a willingness to experiment; and a capacity to change and even the possibility of making for ourselves a fairer society. This is the spirit that underpins the Australian character.'

3. Dr Joseph W Meeker, in his breakthrough book *Comedy of Survival*, says: "Storytelling is one of the healthiest activities of the comic wave. As long as our species has possessed language, we have used it to tell our stories to one another.

4. Leif Eduinsson and Michael Smalone, in their book *Intellectual Capital* said: The proven way to establish your company's real value is by measuring its hidden brain power.'

5. Fiona Stewart, from the *Sunday Age,* had this to say: Getting your head around the "knowledge economy" is no easy task. For most of us, at its base level, the "knowledge economy" is about selling knowledge, know-how, intellectual property, IP, call it what you will.'

6. Lesley Russell reports in the September issue of *Business Review Weekly.* Regarding science as a sport might be akin to heresy although there are some people who would not think so."

7. Jessica Miller Davis had this to say of Campbell McComas: Corporate comedy is designed to integrate, not to tear apart; to bring together people and the organisations they serve; and to harmonise those organisations with the society of which they form a part.'

8. Jean Lovis Barsoux says in his book, Funny Business, Humour Management and Business *Culture.* Thus, the contrast between the expectations that organisations have of people and what those people are really like, leads to a constant mismatch which is charged with comic tension.

BIBLIOGRAPHY

Chapter 1
How Humour Improves Your Business Communication

Wescott, Jean M.		Humour and The Effective Work Group Shrift, G. (1981 Summer) Laughter and Confidence Squibbline Page 2-4
Consalvo, Carmine. M.	1989	Humour in Management No Laughing Matter Humour International Journal of Humour Volume 2 Number 3 Research 2966
Adair, John	1989	Effective Leadership Pan Books Page 55
Orben, Robert	1980	Orben's Current Comedy Edited by Robert Orben Issue Number 624 Volume 32 Number 5
Adair, John	1983	Effective Leadership Pan Books Page 199
Krotte Jr. James	1987	Take My Boss- Please Across the Board Magazine February 1987 Page 33
Juan, Stephen	1988	Laughing All The Way To The Top Sydney Morning Herald 22.9.1988
Kushner, Malcolm	1988	Humour As A Management Tool. Magazine Article IABC Communication World Volume 5 Page 32/33

Motley, M. T.	1987	What I Mean To Say Psychology Today 21 24 to 28
Esar, Evan	1978	The Comic Encyclopedia New York Doubleday Company Page 52
Peter, Dr. Laurence J.	1982	The Laughter Prescription New York Ballantine Books Random House Inc
Kent, Robert W.	1985	Money Talks New York NY Pocket Book A Division of Simon& Schuster inc. New York Page 34
Al Schock	1976	Jokes for All Occasions USA Hal Leighton Printing Company
Krotte, Jr. James	1987	Take My Boss - Please Across the Board Magazine February 1987 Page 32
True, Dr. Herb	1990	Funny Bone USA American Humour Guild Page 89
Blumenfeld, Esther and	1986	The Smile Connection U.S.A. Alperm, Lynne Prentice Hall Inc New Jersey

Chapter 2-

How Humour Can Work for You in Business and Life

Koller, Marvin R.	1988	Humour and Society Houston Cap and Gown Press, Inc. Page 26
Tooper, Dr. Virginia	1988	Laugh Lovers News Pleasanton, California
Evans, Bergen	1978	Dictionary of Quotations NY Avenge Books Page 211
O'Connell, Dr Walter E.	1987	Handbook of Humour and Psychotherapy. Saratoga FL Professional Resource Exchange Inc. Page 55

Mason, Jackie	1987	The World According To Me New York NY Simon& Schuster Inc Page 23
Robinson, Dr. Vera M	1977	Humour and the Health Professions USA Slack Incorporated Page 2
Cousins, Dr Norman	1979	Anatomy of an lness USA W.W. Norton & Company Inc
Peters, Dr. Lawrence	1982	The Laughter Prescription New York Ballantine Books
Fry, Dr. William F.	1968	Sweet Madness USA First Pacific Books
Bandler, Richard		The One Minute Sales Person The source of this line is unknown.
Hopkins, Tom	1993	How to Master The Art of Selling UK Granada Publishing Page 123
Heller, Steven and Anderson, Gail	1991	Graphic Wit New York NY Watson -Guptill Publications Page 5
Blumenfeld, Esther and Alpern, Lynne	1986	The Smile Connection New Jersey Prentice Hall Inc. Page 68
Leonards, Stew.	1982	Growing A Business USA Video produced by KQED TV San Francisco Ambrose Video
Metcalf, C. W. and Felible, Roma	1999	Lighten Up New York NY Addison Wesley Publication Company Inc. Page 168
Bassindale, Bob.	1976	How Speakers Make People Laugh, New York, Parker Publishing Company Inc. Page 141
Klein, Allen	1991	Quotations To Cheer You Up New York Sterling Publishing Co Inc Page 105

Chapter 3 -
Developing Your Humour Attitude

Mindess, Harvey	1971	Laughter and Liberation USA Nash Publishing Los Angeles
Klein, Allen	1989	The Healing Power of Humour Los Angeles Jeremy P. Tarcaer Inc. Page 48
Cousins, Norman	1979	Anatomy of an lness NY W.W. Norton and Company Inc.
Mindess, Harvey	1971	Laughter and Liberation USA Nash Publishing Los Angeles Page 35
Goodman, Dr. Joel	1982	Laughing Matters USA The Humour Project Saratoga Springs
Lefcourt, Herbert M. and	1986	Martin, Rod.A. Humour and Life Stress New York Springer-Verlag Pages 19-21
Peters, Dr Laurence	1982	The Laughter Prescription New York Ballantine Books

Chapter 4 -
The Nature of Humour

Jobson, Sandra	1986	Paul Hogan The Real Life Crocodile Dundee London W.H. Allan Page 53
Evan Esar	1978	The Dictionary of Humour Quotations New York Avenel Books Page 166
Fry, William F. and Waleed, A. Salamett	1987	Handbook of Humour Psychotherapy USA Professional Resource Exchange Inc. Saratoga FL
Bono, Edward De P O Australia	1972	Penguin Books Page 80

Paulson, Terry L.	1989	Making Humour Work California Crisp Publications Inc. Page 16
Eastman, Max	1937	Enjoyment of Laughter Great Britain Hamish Hamilton
Dundes, Alan	1987	When You're Up to Your Ass in Alligators USA Wayne State University Press Page 95
Hornadge, Bill	1980	The Australian Slang Slanguage Cassell Australia Limited Page 184
Goodheart, Dr Annette	1982	Laugh Your Way to Heath Audio Tapes Santa Barbara California
Dundes, Alan	1987	When You're Up To Your Ass in Alligators USA Wayne State University Press
Peter, Dr. Laurence J.	1982	The Laughter Prescription New York Ballantine Books
Esar, Evan	1954	The Humour of Humour Great Britain Phoenix House Ltd Page 2

Chapter 5 -

The Secrets of Humour

Chapman, Anthony J and Foot, Hugh C.	1977	If's A Funny Thing Humour England Pergamon Press Ltd Page 403
Goodman, Dr Joel	1982	Laughing Matters New York The Humour Project Publication Volume 3 Page 13
Whiting, Percy, H.	1959	How to Speak and Write With Humour New York McGraw-Hill Book Company Inc. Page 84.
Bruce, Lenny	1967	The Essential Lenny Bruce New York Ballantine Books Page 7

Wannan, Bill onl eno	1982	The Great Australian Book of Humorous Quotes Melbourne Currey O'Neil Page 4
Wright, Stephen		The source of this line is unknown
Delvey, John		The source of this line is unknown
Eastman, Max	1937	Enjoyment Of Laughter Great Britain Hamish Hamilton
Carson, Johnny		The source of this line is unknown
Whitehorn, Katherine		The source of this line is unknown
Tooper, Dr Virginia	1986	Sarcastics Anonymous California Pleasanton USA Volume V11 Number 1

Chapter 6-

The Business of Delivering Your Humour

Gurney, John	1984	A Guide to Employer Speak Melbourme Australian Society
Ziv. Avner	1988	National Styles of Humour USA Greenwood Press Page 26
Van Costine James	1989	The Business Special Englewood Cliffs Prentice -Inc. Page 133
Gordon. Harvey C.	1983	The Art of Punning NY NY Warner Books Inc
Rostens. Leo	1984	Book of Laughter Elm Tree Books Uncorrected Book Proof Page 2
Howard. Geoffrey	1989	Getting Through Reed Back Pty Ltd. Aust. Page 42
Bandler. Richard & Grinder John	1979	Frogs Into Princes Real People Press Page 7

Wynden, Peter	1984	The Unknown Iacocca Sidgwick & Jackson United Great Britain Page 57
Westcott, Jean	1988	Humour and Laughter as Stress Moderators 1032 Dayview Ave. Oakland CA USA
Esar, Evan	1978	The Comic Encyclopedia Doubleday & Company Inc New York Page 307
Koller, R. Marvin	1988	Humour and Society Cap &Gown Press Inc. Houston Texas USA Page 319

Chapter 7

Business Show Applying Humour Seriously

Nelson, T.G.A.	1990	Comedy. The Theory of Comedy in Literature Drama & Cinema Oxford University Press NY Page 1
Meeker, Dr Joseph W		The Comedy of Survival Pub Charles Scribner s Sons NY USA
Holland, N. Norman	1982	Laughing A Psychology of Humour Cornell University Press London Page 17
De Bono, Edward	1990	I Am Right You Are Wrong Viking Penguin Vic Aust Page 1
Lloyd, Graham	1990	Players Must Lift Game Australian Weekend Dec 9-10 Page 40
Goldblatt, Joe Jeff	1990	Special Events Pub Van-Nostrand Reinhold NY USA Page 149
Postman, Neil	1985	Amusing Ourselves To Death Elisabeth Sifton Books NY USA Page 85
Crofts, Andrew	1982	Corporate Entertaining Mercury Books London Page 168

Davis, Kylie	1992	Humour A Necessity Not a Luxury Weekend Australian April 18-19 Page 40
Peters, Tom	1989	Thriving On Chaos Pan Books Great Britain Page 396
Peters, Tom	1985	A Passion for Excellence Random House USA Page 264
Kushner, Malcolm	1990	The Light Touch Fireside Pub NY USA Page 136/137
United Press International	1987	Humour Eases Work, Therapist Says Arizona Republic September 14
Wilson, James		Professor at University of Pitsburgh The source of this line is unknown.
Peters, Dr Laurence	1982	The Laughter Prescription Ballantine Books NY USA
Goodman, Dr Joel	1985	Laughing Matters The Humour Project NY USA Vol. 3 Num. 3 Page 93
Clark, Lucy	1992	Hire A Humour Consultant Mode Magazine April Page 104 Pub ACP Pty Ltd
Naisbitt, John	1986	Re-Inventing The Corporation Futura Books MacDonald Ltd. Pub London Page 137/138
Crosline, Ron	1984	Quality Management Enterprise Mag. Vol. 3 No. 2 Page 83
Kaufman, Joanne	1987	In the Moo Shopping at Stew Leonards The Wall St. Journal Thurs Sept 17 Page 28
Boas, Max & Chain, Steve	1977	The Unauthorised Story of McDonald's Mentor Books NY USA
Peddley James	1990	Laughter Works New Letter Vol. 2 No. 1 Winter Sacramento C.A. U.S.A.

Reschke, Clark	1990	Image vs Identity Marketing Mag. June Page 114/115
Olins, Wally	1989	Corporate Industry Themes and Hudson Page 33
Levinson, Harry & Rosenthal Stuart	1984	CEO Corporate Leadership in Action Basic Books Inc. NY USA Page 57 and
Oech Von Roger	1983	A Wack on the Side of the Head Angus&Robertson Pub. UK
Forsyth, Christopher	1989	The Inner You Weekend Australia Feb 18 & 19 Page 16
Da Cruz, Ruth Humour Leads Exports to Spain	1992	Australian Trade Commission Exporters June Vol Number 2
Helitzer, Melvin	1986	Company Writing Secrets Writers Digest books Ohio USA

Chapter 8
Branding of Australia

De Bono, Edward	1999	Why I Want To Be King of Australia Penguin Books Australia Ltd Page 19
Twain, Mark	1973	Mark Twain in Australia and New Zealand Melbourne Penguin Facsimile of Following the Equator 1897
Knightley, Phillip	2000	Australia a Biography of Nation Pub Jonathan Cape Great Britain Page 30/31
William, Henry	1971	Australia, What Is It? The source of this line is unknown.
Malouf, David	1998	A Spirit of Play The Making of Australian Consciousness Audio Tapes Boyer Lectures ABC Audio Enterprises Sydney Australia

Bokun, Bronko   1986   Humour Therapy
Vita Books London Page 133

Adams, P   1982   Uncensored Adams, Melbourne
Thomas Nelson

McPhee, Margaret   1993   The Dictionary of Australian Inventions and
Discoveries Melbourne
Allen& Unwin Pty Ltd Page 2

Eduinsson, Leif   1997   Malone&S Michael Intellectual Capital
Great Britain Harper Collins Pub Inc Back
Cover

Stewart, Fiona   2000   Why Your Knowledge Is Worth More Than
Hours
The Sunday Age Oct 1 Page 14

Ruthven Phil   1999   Talk is Anything But Cheap
The Australian Financial Review
September 30

Davis, Jessica Milner   1997   Campbell McComas and Australian Corporate
Comedy
Special Issue of Australian Journal of Comedy
Volume 3 Number 1 Page 155

McComas, Campbell   1997   Reflections on Lies, Damned Lies and My
Entire Career
Special Issue of Australian Journal of Comedy
Volume 3 Number 1 Page 157

Rifkin, Glenn   1998   How Richard Branson Works Magic
Strategy& Business Fourth Quarter Issue 13
Page 48/49

Mulkay, Michael   1988   On Humour UK
Polity Press

Goleman, Daniel   1997   Vital Lies Simple Truths
London Bloomsbury Pub Page 11

Barsoux, Jean-Louis   1993   Funny Business
London Cassell Page 22/23

Gates, Bill	1999	Business @ The Speed of Thought Australia Viking Penguin Book Ltd Cover Flap
Jensen, Rolf	1999	The Dream Society NYNY McGraw-Hill Page 145
Kiyosaki, Robert T	1992	If You Want To Be Rich and Happy, Don't Go To School Calif USA The Excellerated Learning Pub Co Page 243
Weinstein, Matt	1996	Managing To Have Fun Australia Viking Penguin Books Page 26
Luck, Peter	1979	The Fabulous Century Melbourne Circus Books Page 161
Firth, David	1995	How to Make Work Fun England Gower Publishing Limited Front Cover
McGregor, Craig	1996	Profile of Australia London Hodder and Stoughton Page 18
Meeker, Joseph W.	1997	Comedy of Survival USA. Arizona Press Page 114/115
Wellner, Alison Stein&	2000	Happy Days David Adox Psychology Today May/June 2000 Page 32/36
Giles, Niel	2000	Australia The Shape of Things to Come Melbourne Now Magazine July/August Page 13/14
Walsh, Max	2000	Take a Bow, Australia The Bulletin ACP Pub. Sydney Oct 10 Page8
Overington, Caroline	2000	Aussie Aussie Aussie, by Jingo Age Newspaper Saturday September 9 Page 5
Ziv, Avner	1988	National Styles of Humour USA Greenwood Press Inc Page 24

Roddick, Anita	2000	Business As Unusual Harper& Collins Australia Back Cover
Rothwell, Nicolas	2000	Distant Voices The Australian Review of Books Sept. vol 5 Issue 8 Page 27
Deans, Alan	2000	The Bulletin Oct 17 ACP Pub Sydney
Rifkin, Jeremy	2000	The Age of Access Penguin Books Vic Australia Page 7
Russell, Lesley	2000	From Weird to Sport Science BRW September 8 Page 40
Head, Beverley	2000	Dump-Down Time for R&D BRW September 8 Page 38
Stephens, Ian	2000	The Leaders vs the Bleeders all Poppy Tips Vol 1 Issue 1 Nov 2000 Page 1
Jameson, Julietta	2000	The Beagle Has Landed The Bulletin ACP Pub Sydney Oct 10 Page 97
Hurrell, Bronwyn	2001	Stand Up and Enjoy Being Silly Melbourne Herald Sun Tues Jan 2 Page 4
Wilson, Paul	2000	Calm for Life Penguin Books Aust Ltd Page 265/256
Harris, Alexandra	2000	They Don't Call them Septics for Nothing The Australian Financial Review Page 25
Rifkin, Jeremy	2000	The Age of Access Penguin Books Aust Ltd Page 260/261
Meeker, Dr Joseph W.	1997	Comedy of Survival The University of Arizona Press Page 10
Porter, M.E.	1990	The Competitive Advantage Harvard Business Review 68 Page 73 to 93

HUMOUR POWER – CORPORATE TRAINING PROGRAMS

A sense of humour is part of the art of leadership, of
getting along with people, of getting things done.

Dwight Eisenhower

A 1980 survey of 480 executive officers (Shrift 1981) clearly indicated
that the majority of the corporate leaders felt that a sense of humour
was essential to their work. There is a growing belief among the top
management people in the world that business can be more enjoyable and
productive when humour is part of daily functioning.

The humour power corporate programs are: -

- Leadership through *Humourship*
- Selling with a sense of humour
- Managing to have fun and make profits
- Customer Service with a smile
- Powerful business show presentations
- Creative and outrageous thinking
- Humour in TV and radio advertising
- Australian *humour attitude* and *action* training
- Teamwork through humour play
- Setting up a humour room in your company

The humour power programs are designed to meet the needs of all levels within an organisation, whether to enhance leadership skills for CEOs and senior executives, or sales and customer service techniques for your frontline people. The humour power programs can be conducted on their own or as modules within your staff training programs. The humour power series ranges from half-day, to full-day, to five-day programs. Support one-on-one training is also available, as well as a corporate residency humour consultancy service.

Please call us for a complete Corporate Humour Power Training Kit.

PETE WILL PERSONALISE AND CUSTOMISE THE HUMOUR POWER TRAINING TO YOUR COMPANY'S NEEDS AND WANTS.

GENERAL PUBLIC PROGRAMS AND WORKSHOPS

For nearly 30 years now, we have been leading the way in the world when it comes to educational workshops and programs to do with humour comedy and laughter at the Pete Crofts Humourversity. Some of our most successful programs are:

- Public speaking with humour
- Stand-up comedy principles
- Humour laughter in health and healing
- Comedy writing
- The humour of business, the business of humour
- The laughter lifestyle program
- How to use humour in teaching and training
- Discover the clown in you
- Separation with a sense of humour
- Acting for comedy performers
- Performers lifestyle game plan program
- Business show marketing for small businesses that want to get bigger
- How to tell jokes that really work all the time
- Comedy improvisational training
- Profitable business show presentations

- The history of Australian humour
- Comedy, the philosophy of thriving and surviving
- The business showcase advantage for small businesses

In groups of six to 10 people, the programs run from seven to 12 months, one two-hour session a week, either in the morning or in the evenings, with one-on-one sessions for each participant between the group sessions. Please call us for a copy of our General Public Programs and Workshops catalogue.

TOURING AUSTRALIA WORKSHOPS

- The workshops we tour include:
- Public speaking with humour
- Stand-up comedy principles
- Humour laughter in health and healing
- The business show case advantage
- Comedy writing
- The laughter lifestyle workshop

Bookings for any of the above two-day weekend workshops can be made at any time throughout the year from any city. The Pete Crofts Humourversity also provides regional touring Australia with any of the above workshops. Please call us for a copy of our Touring Australia Workshops date schedules.

PETE CROFTS HUMOURVERSITY LAUGHLETTER

Humour All-Ways - Ha Ha Skills to lighten up your personal and professional life for fun and profit. To order your six editions per year, please contact Pete Crofts Humourversity.

AUSTRALIA'S CORPORATE HUMOR SPEAKER

Pete Crofts is a humour power speaker who changes thinking, excites emotions, transforms beliefs, empowers people, motivates actions, and tells jokes that make people laugh. Because of his many years as a comedian, entertainer and speaker/trainer, Pete can be used as:

A conference *kick-off, ice-breaker* speaker; an *after-lunch, keep-them-motivated* speaker

A *conference-closing* keynote speaker; an *after-dinner humor* speaker

Pete Croft Talk Titles:

- The Business of Humour, the Humour of Business
- Business Show, Applying Humour Seriously
- How to Change Life from a Rat-race to a Fun-run
- Leadership through Humourship
- Profit from Running a Funny Business
- Laughter is the Best Medicine
- The Seven Humour Habits of Happiness
- How to Live Single when Married
- Putting Fun into Your Relationships
- Selling with a Sense of Humour
- Humour and Laughter in Health and Healing
- Makings Sense of Humour

- A Great Australian Sense of Humour (You've Got to Laugh Mate)
- The Chemistry of Comedy (The Comedy of Survival)
- Coping with Comedy by Fighting Funny (Pete's adventurous life as Australia's humor pioneer)
- The branding of Australia (Australia, the future thinkers)

For sure-fire speaking results Pete will personalise, tailorise, customise, humanise and localise his talk to fit and suit your requirements and your audience's needs. Please call us for a complete copy of the Pete Crofts Humour Talk Portfolio

AUSTRALIAN HUMOUR / COMEDY
TRANSLATOR AND COACH

Pete Crofts acts as the touring speaker, business executive and comedian translator and coach to climatise, customise, localise, topicalise and humanise your identity, material, delivery and language to the Australian sense of humour and psyche.

HIT'S - HUMOURVERSITY IT SERVICES
. -LEARNING PROGRAMS

Website: www.humourversity.com

These are the most exciting times ever to be involved in learning as well as helping individuals and organisations to grow their Intellectual Capital. Learning is a vital component of success in our knowledge economy. For organisations to survive and individuals to thrive, learning must outpace change. New technologies enable us to do things, which were never before possible. The Pete Crofts Humourversity believes we must not allow technology to dominate our strategies. We must begin with performance and learning, then build our strategies and use technology to appropriately implement those strategies. Only then can we realise our potential. For online learning with punchline results, use HIT'S at www.humourversity.com

PETE CROFTS HUMOURVERSITY
SERVICES & PRODUCT INFORMATION SHEET

PLEASE TICK WHAT YOU WOULD LIKE MORE INFORMATION ON:

- ☐ Business Show training.
- ☐ Australian humour business training.
- ☐ Australian humour in advertising workshop.
- ☐ Pete Crofts Humourversity corporate humour consultant
- ☐ The Elliot Goblet corporate comedy residency.
- ☐ Hire a humourologist as your media consultant.
- ☐ How to use humour in teaching and training.
- ☐ Humour Power: 12-day boot camp for business leaders.
- ☐ How To Make Marketing Fun And Profitable Programme.
- ☐ The Many Ways Of Making Money From Your Meaning Workshop.
- ☐ Selling With a Sense Of Humour: 8-day boot camp.

HUMOUR COMEDY & LAUGHTER PRODUCTS

- ☐ How To Use Humour In Business & Life (the book)
     (5 copies or more for 20% discount)
- ☐ Humour Power pack (6 cassettes tapes).
- ☐ How To Tell Jokes That Really Work All The Time, cassette tapes (6 cassettes).
- ☐ How To Tell Jokes That Really Work All The Time, video tape (73 minutes).
- ☐ The great Australian Sense Of Humour, cassette tapes (6 cassettes).

PLEASE ENQUIRE ABOUT OUR PRODUCT RANGE OF:

- ☐ Humour, comedy & laughter tip sheets.
- ☐ Humour, comedy & laughter joke sheets and monologues.
- ☐ Novelty executive gifts.

IN WHICH OF THE FOLLOWING AREAS WITHIN YOUR OWN BUSINESS ARE YOU INTERESTED IN HAVING HUMOUR EMPLOYED?

- ☐ Improved motivation
- ☐ Reduced stress
- ☐ Empower leadership
- ☐ Increased sales
- ☐ Delighting customers
- ☐ Creative thinking

- ☐ Enhance corporate image
- ☐ Team building
- ☐ Effective communication
- ☐ Enjoyable workplace
- ☐ Other

- ☐ Why not surprise someone by having a copy of "How To Use Humour In Business & Life" sent to them as a gift?

For information on any of the above contact the Pete Crofts Humourversity

PETE CROFTS HUMOURVERSITY
Ph: 61-3-9596 0411 Fax: 61-3-9596 0422 Mob: 0414 443 589
12 Montclair Ave, North Brighton, Victoria 3186 Australia
e-mail: croftsp@humourversity.com web: www.humourversity.com
Telephone: 1 800 00 18 11

- ☐• If you would like a free fact sheet, "How To Use Positive Humour For Positive Results" please fax the Pete Crofts Humourversity on 61-3-9596 0422

THE LAST LAUGH

The attitude of having the last laugh comes from expecting the unexpected things in life - disappointment, rejection, divorce, betrayal, loneliness, unemployment, sickness, death, bankruptcy, accidents, theft, being sacked, sudden changes etc. When we play the game of life with the Ha Ha Skills, we are better equipped to cope when the unexpected happens. We can learn to expect the unexpected with a smile (a cosmic chuckle) to deflect negative energies and emotions that could grow to become constant fears. As a society, we have become addicted to the chemical of fear. Ha Ha Skills fight fears and encourage us to take more risks. There's no safe path to happiness and success. The only way to live life 'right is to live it wrong a few times! And if your life's not fun, you're not living it right anyway. Find the funny to fight fear; laugh at yourself as you grow to be yourself and to have the last laugh!

I would very much like to hear from anyone who reads this book and applies *humour attitudes* and *humour actions* **to any situation in their life or work when they've had the last laugh. Please drop me a line. I could use it in my next book.**

Lots of fun and profits in all you do; laugh mates!

Pete Crofts,

INDEX